THE BELLEEK POTTERY

Errata

The correct caption for photograph on page 105, at lower right, is:

D120-5, Henshall Basket, large size, painted. D121-5, Henshall Twig Basket, small size, painted. (Richard & Margaret Degenhardt Collection. Dale Monaghen photo.)

Adjustments to the value guide are as follows:

D1-I	Figure of Erin	L	7,000
D263-II	Cardium on Shell, size 4	C	175
D1235-II	Water Lily Vase on Rocks	D	3,000

BELLEEK
The Complete Collector's Guide and Illustrated Reference

VALUE GUIDE

Richard K. Degenhardt

Wallace-Homestead Book Company
Radnor, Pennsylvania

INTRODUCTION

The appraisals contained in this Value Guide are based on items in *mint condition:* perfect in every aspect. True firing cracks, which seldom occurred, do *not* remove an item from the mint condition classification. Additional criteria considered in the appraisal of each piece are *age, rarity* and *decoration.*

Values are given in 1993 U.S. dollars and reflect the author's opinion of the realistic purchase value of each listed piece. These values do not relate directly to specific items in particular collections.

Handwoven baskets from the early three-strand periods, i.e., prior to 1921, and flowered work from the first (I) and second (II) periods of the pottery's history, have become increasingly difficult to find in mint condition. A petal chip or missing leaf part removes the piece from the mint condition designation. In the opinion of the author, a new designation of "superior condition" may become necessary in the future because of the fragile and delicate nature of these items. This designation would be employed only when the term "mint condition" is not appropriate, and when *minor* damage has occurred to the hand-applied flower and leaf parts.

Periods of Crafting (Excluding Baskets)

I   1863–1890
II   1891–1926
III   1926–1946
IV   1946–1955
V   1955–1965
VI   1965–March 31, 1980
VII   April 1, 1980–December 22, 1992
VIII   January 4, 1993–present

Periods of Crafting (Baskets)

1   1865–1890, BELLEEK (three strand)
2   1865–1890, BELLEEK CO. FERMANAGH (three strand)
3   1891–1920, BELLEEK CO. FERMANAGH IRELAND (three strand)
4   1921–1954, BELLEEK CO. FERMANAGH IRELAND (four strand)
5   1955–1979, BELLEEK ® CO. FERMANAGH IRELAND (four strand)
6   1980–1985, BELLEEK ® IRELAND (four strand)
7   1985–1989, BELLEEK ® IRELAND "ID NUMBER" (four strand)
8–12   1990–present (Refer to *Belleek,* Chapter 5)

Decorating Codes

A	Plain (glazed only)	H	Painted Shamrocks and Gilted
B	Cob Lustre	J	Mother of Pearl
C	Tinted	K	Painted and Gilted
D	Painted	L	Bisque and Plain
E	Painted Shamrocks	M	Decalcomania
F	Gilted	N	Special Hand-Painted Decoration
G	Tinted and Gilted	T	Transfer Design

Note: All decorations, with the exception of "M" (Decalcomania) and "T" (Transfer Design) are hand painted.

Designations

t	tea cup
s	tea saucer
cr	cream
su	sugar
cc	coffee cup
cs	coffee saucer
mu	mustard
os	open salt

Note: NM = "no pottery mark." On rare occasions, a piece known by the author to be genuine Belleek has been given an appraisal. This has occurred only when the piece is exceptional. The "NM" designation follows the Degenhardt number of the piece, replacing the period of crafting number.

FIGURES, ETC.

Degenhardt No.	Item	Code	Value ($)
D1–I	Figure of Erin	L	8,000
D2–IV	International Centre	L	17,000
D3–I	Prince of Wales Ice Pail	F	7,500
D4–II	Minstrel Comport	L	9,500
D5–I	Minstrel Centre	F	11,000
D6–I	Bittern Comport	F	6,000
D7–I	Figure of Bather	A	2,500
D8–I	Boy and Fish Spill	F	1,900
D9–I	Singl Boy and Shell, middle size	A	1,600
D10–I	Minstrel Paper Weight (cymbals)	A	2,300
D11–II	Double Boy and Shell	D	2,800
D14–I	Bust of Clytie	L	3,200
D14–II	Bust of Clytie	L	2,800
D15–I	Belgium Hawker (female)	D	2,400
D16–I	Crouching Venus	F	8,500
D17–I	Girl Basket Bearer	D	1,800
D18–I	Prisoner of Love	L	18,000
D19–III	Boy Basket Bearer	A	750
D20–I	Figure of Meditation	D	3,500
D21–I	Belgium Hawker (male)	D	2,400
D22–II	Figure of Cavalier	L	2,900
D23–II	Jack-at-Sea Trinket Box	L	2,800
D24–III	Jack-on-Shore Trinket Box	D	2,800

DESSERT WARE

Degenhardt No.	Item	Code	Value ($)
D25–II	Belleek Fruit Basket	J	10,000
D26–I	Shell Dessert Plate	A	200
D27–I	Shell Comport	A	475
D28–II	Greek Comport	K	1,250
D29–I	Greek Dessert Plate	K	475
D30–I	Basket Comport	A	850
D31–I	Basket Dessert Plate	D	425
D33–I	Boy and Swan Comport	F	5,200
D34–I	Prince of Wales Centre	A	5,500
D35–I	Thorn Plate, 9	K	450
D36–II	Thorn Comport	K	1,200
D37–I	Trihorse Comport	L	3,000
D38–I	Vine Comport Pierced	K	1,900
D39–I	Vine Dessert Plate	D	900

FLOWER POTS

Degenhardt No.	Item	Code	Value ($)
D40–II	Finner Flower Pot	J	1,900
D41–II	Belleek Flower Pot	A	1,800
D42–II	Thorn Flower Pot	A	1,800
D43–II	Rathmore Flower Pot	A	1,800
D44–IV	Flowered Spill, small size	D	85
D45–II	Flowered Spill, large size	J	375
D46–II	Oak Flower Pot, Footed	J	2,400
D47–II	Belleek Flower Pot, Flowered, small size	A	225
D48–II	Belleek Flower Pot, Flowered, middle size	J	300
D48–IV	Belleek Flower Pot, Flowered, middle size	J	120
D49–VI	Pierced Spill, Flowered, large size	D	125
D50–II	Panel Flower Pot, Footed	A	2,200
D51–II	Belleek Flower Pot, Footed	J	2,400
D52–II	Rathmore Flower Pot, Footed	J	2,400
D53–IV	Lipton Flower Pot, Footed	D	1,000

VASES, ETC.

Degenhardt No.	Item	Code	Value ($)
D54–II	Bird Vase, Flowered	J	1,200
D55–II	Aberdeen Vase, Flowered, large size	J	900
D56–IV	Table Centre	D	1,400
D57–II	Bird Nest Stump	J	2,400
D58–II	Aberdeen Vase, Flowered, middle size	J	750
D58–IV	Aberdeen Vase, Flowered, middle size	D	300
D59–II	Aberdeen Vase, Flowered, small size	J	600
D60–VI	Princess Vase, Flowered	D	500
D61–II	Single Henshall's Spill, Flowered	J	300
D61–V	Single Henshall's Spill, Flowered	D	125
D63–II	Flowered Frame, large size	J	4,800
D65–I	Shell Frame, medium size, 10½x8½ in.	C	2,500
D66–I	Double Photo Frame	A	5,800
D68–I	Diana Vase, Pierced	F	1,400
D70–II	Aberdeen Vase, large size	G	650
D73–II	Prince Arthur Vase	J	750
D77–VI	Irish Harp, small size	E	130
D78–VI	Irish Harp, large size	E	175
D79–II	Straw Basket	J	500
D80–II	Erne Basket	C	450
D82–II	Tulip Vase	C	675
D83–II	Erne Vase	C	550
D84–II	Nile Vase, large size	A	500
D85–IV	Nile Vase, middle size	B	95
D86–VI	Nile Vase, small size	B	60
D87–VI	Moore Vase	B	60
D88–II	Island Vase	C	425
D88–VI	Island Vase	E	90
D92–I	Triple Tulip	C	1,250
D93–I	Tulip Vase, large size	J	3,200
D94–I	Typha Jug Spill	B	300
D95–I	Marine Vase, large size	J	2,200
D96–II	Imperial Centre	C	4,200
D97–II	Hippiritus Centre	C	2,800
D99–I	Naiads Flower Pot, tall	L	3,400
D100–II	Naiads Flower Pot, low	L	1,900
D101–II	Fern Flower Pot, large size	A	1,000
D105–II	Pierced Spill, small size	B	300

HAND WOVEN CARD OR FRUIT BASKETS, ETC.

Degenhardt No.	Item	Code	Value ($)
D106–5	Sydenham Twig, small size	D	1,200
D108–2	Sydenham Twig, large size	J	3,500
D108–6	Sydenham Twig, large size	D	1,500
D109–2	Shamrock Basket, small size	A	850
D110–5	Shamrock Basket, large size	D	475
D111–II	Forget-Me-Not Box	A	650
D112–III	Shamrock Trinket Box	A	425
D113–3	Oval Covered Basket, large size	J	6,500

Degenhardt No.	Item	Code	Value ($)
D113–6	Oval Covered Basket, large size	D	4,000
D114–2	Oval Covered Basket, small size	J	5,000
D114–6	Oval Covered Basket, small size	D	2,800
D115–6	Round Basket, No. 8	D	2,400
D116–III	Flowered Salad Bowl	J	650
D117–3	Rathmore Oval Basket	J	9,500
D117–7	Rathmore Oval Basket	D	7,000
D118–6	Oval Basket, large size	D	1,600
D119–6	Oval Basket, small size	D	1,250
D120–3	Henshall's Twig, large size	A	5,000
D121–2	Henshall's Twig, small size	A	2,800
D121–10	Henshall's Twig, small size	A	1,100
D122–7	Round Convolvulus Basket	D	1,700
D123–2	Bird's Nest Basket	J	950
D124–3	Round Covered Basket, small size	J	5,000

FLOWER HOLDERS, ETC.

Degenhardt No.	Item	Code	Value ($)
D128–VI	Victoria Shell	B	350
D129–I	Seahorse and Shell	A	1,000
D130–I	Seahorse Flower Holder	A	750
D131–I	Nautilus on Coral	C	1,000
D132–II	Covered Vase	A	1,200
D134–II	Marine Jug Vase	C	800
D135–V	Marine Vase	B	575
D136–II	Victoria Vase	C	1,400
D138–II	Imperial Shell	C	1,250
D139–VI	Fermanagh Vase	G	70
D140–I	Clam Shell and Griffin	A	1,000
D141–I	Clam Shell	A	850
D142–I	Honeysuckle Vase	N	850

SPILLS, VASES, ETC.

Degenhardt No.	Item	Code	Value ($)
D146–II	Single Hippiritus	C	800
D147–I	Ivy Stump Spill	D	375
D148–I	Amphora Vase, large size	K	1,850
D149–I	Amphora Vase, middle size	A	1,100
D150–I	Amphora Vase, small size	F	625
D151–II	Single Root Spill	D	425
D152–I	Quiver Vase	K	2,400
D153–I	Ivy Trunk Stump Spill	D	275
D154–VI	Feather Vase, large size	B	50
D155–III	Feather Vase, small size	B	75
D155–V	Feather Vase, small size	B	40
D157–I	Onion Spill, small size	D	450
D158–VI	Panel Vase, large size	B	80
D159–II	Panel Vase, small size	N	250
D160–II	Hand and Shell Vase	C	900
D161–VI	Rock Spill, small size	B	40
D162–II	Rock Spill, middle size	C	275
D163–II	Rock Spill, large size	A	350
D166–I	Cane Spill, middle size	D	725
D167–I	Cane Spill, small size	F	650
D168–I	Flying Fish Spill	C	675
D172–II	Triple Flower Holder	B	550
D174–I	Lily Basket	D	1,850
D176–II	Tobacco Brewer	B	2,900
D178–V	Daisy Spill	E	50
D180–VI	Harebell Vase	K	70

Degenhardt No.	Item	Code	Value ($)
D181–II	Frog Vase, large size	D	1,000
D182–II	Frog Vase, small size	D	850
D184–I	Fish Spill	C	850
D188–II	Sunflower Vase	A	250
D189–II	Dolphin Spill	C	375
D190–I	Indian Corn Spill	A	300
D191–II	Shamrock Spill, green	E	165
D191–IV	Shamrock Spill	E	55
D193–VI	Cleary Spill, large size	A	35
D196–III	Thistle Top	J	275
D200–II	Typha Spill	D	95
D203–III	Lily Spill, large size	B	150
D203–IV	Lily Spill, large size	B	45

FLOWER POTS, ETC.

Degenhardt No.	Item	Code	Value ($)
D204–II	Irish Pot, size 5	A	225
D206–II	Irish Pot, size 3	B	155
D207–II	Irish Pot, size 2	A	125
D208–III	Irish Pot, size 1	B	65
D209–II	Nickel Flower Pot	A	225
D209–VI	Nickel Flower Pot	B	70
D211–III	Tiny Belleek Flower Pot, Flowered	D	175
D213–III	Irish Pot, Shamrocks	E	125
D214–III	Grass Mug	D	125
D214–V	Grass Mug	B	75
D215–II	Rope Handle Mug	B	175
D216–II	Shamrock Mug	E	100
D217–VI	Thorn Mug	B	48
D218–III	Cleary Mug	B	60
D219–VI	Octagon Flower Pot, middle size	B	48
D220–II	Octagon Flower Pot, small size	B	185
D221–II	Belleek Flower Pot, middle size	A	170
D223–VI	Cone Flower Pot, middle size	B	40
D225–IV	Diamond Flower Pot	K	150
D226–II	Double Shell Flower Pot	C	425
D227–III	Individual Sugar	B	250
D228–II	Crinkled Flower Pot	B	185
D229–IV	Boat Ash Tray	B	38
D230–IV	Pig, small size	B	55
D231–I	Pig, large size	B	225
D231–III	Pig, large size	B	145

SUGARS AND CREAMS

Degenhardt No.	Item	Code	Value ($)
D232–III	Irish Pot and Cream, size 2	A	145
D233–II	Irish Pot and Cream, size 1	B	195
D234–III	Toy Shamrock Sugar and Cream	E	145
D234–IV	Toy Shamrock Sugar and Cream	E	98
D235–I	Lily Sugar and Cream	A	250
D235–II	Lily Sugar and Cream	A	180
D236–III	Rathmore Cream	B	80
D237–II	Ivy Sugar, large size	B	130
D238–I	Ivy Cream, large size	D	200
D239–I	Ivy Sugar, middle size	A	150
D240–I	Ivy Cream, middle size	A	170
D240–III	Ivy Cream, middle size	B	85
D241–II	Ivy Sugar and Cream, small size	B	190

Degenhardt No.	Item	Code	Value ($)
D241–III	Ivy Sugar and Cream, small size	B	120
D242–II	Scroll Sugar and Cream	B	185
D243–IV	Ribbon Sugar and Cream	B	78
D244–II	Lotus Cream	C	95
D244–III	Lotus Cream	A	50
D245–III	Lotus Sugar	A	45
D246–VI	Boat Sugar, small size	B	25
D247–VI	Boat Cream, small size	B	30
D248–II	Fan Sugar and Cream, painted	D	250
D249–I(cr)	Cleary Cream	C	150
D249–IV(cr)	Cleary Cream	B	55
D250–V	Toy Shell Sugar and Cream	B	60
D254–I	Swan, large size	A	325
D255–VI	Swan, small size	K	65

MISCELLANEOUS

Degenhardt No.	Item	Code	Value ($)
D256–II	Cardium on Coral, size 4	G	700
D260–II	Cardium on Shell, size 1	G	85
D262–I	Cardium on Shell, size 3	B	200
D263–II	Cardium on Shell, size 4	C	95
D267–I	Triple Cardium, size 4	A	1,500
D268–III	Flowered Crate	J	375
D269–I	Appleleaf Inkstand	B	2,100
D270–VII	Appleleaf Candlestick	D	75
D273–II	Shamrock Salt	C	75
D275–II	Flowered Menu Holder	A	500
D279–I	Nautilus Cream	C	375
D279–II	Nautilus Cream	A	250
D281–II	Round Tumbler, size 2	T	150
D282–I	Round Tumbler, size 3	B&F	200
D283–II	Round Tumbler, size 4	B	100
D288–VII	Double Shell Cream	B	65
D289–I	Tub Salt, large size	B	125
D290–III	Tub Salt, small size	B	55
D291–II	Hexagon Salt	A	60
D293–III	Diamond Salt	B	40
D295–III	Cleary Salt	B	40
D296–NM	Spoons, Coral and Spade	B	95
D298–II(os)	Shamrock Open Salt	E	45
D300–II	Emerson Mug	B	150
D301–I	Lifford Cream	B	225
D301–VI	Lifford Cream	B	45
D305–III	Undine Cream	B	80
D305–VI	Undine Cream	C	45
D306–III	Scale Cream	B	30

TRINKET SETS, ETC.

Degenhardt No.	Item	Code	Value ($)
D335–I	Scent Bottle, Thorn	K	375
D336–II	Ring Peg, Thorn	D	350
D341–I	Cherub Candelabra	L	5,500
D342–I	Single Boy and Shell	L	1,250
D343–VI	Dolphin Candlestick	K	400
D344–VI	Thorn Candlestick	D	75
D345–I	Boy and Vine Candlestick	K	1,100
D346–I	Night Light Holder—Light House	A	2,000

ECHINUS EGG SHELL TEA WARE

Degenhardt No.	Item	Code	Value ($)
D358–I	Cup and Saucer	N	300
D361–I	Slop, large size	N	450
D362–I	Sugar, large size	N	375
D363–I	Cream, large size	N	475
D364–I	Teapot, large size	N	900

SHAMROCK TEA WARE

Degenhardt No.	Item	Code	Value ($)
D366–II	Tea and Saucer, low shape	E	150
D366–III	Tea and Saucer, low shape	E	110
D367–II	Teapot, middle size	E	475
D368–II	Sugar, small size	E	120
D369–II	Cream, small size	E	135
D370–II	Tray	E	1,200
D371–II	Set complete (4 T&S)	E	2,650
D372–II	Coffee and Saucer	E	145
D373–II	Breakfast and Saucer	E	180
D374–II	Moustache and Saucer	E	375
D375–III	Tea and Saucer, tall shape	E	110
D376–II	Plate, 5	E	80
D377–III	Plate, 7	E	70
D378–III	Plate, 8	E	75
D379–III	Bread Plate	E	165
D379–V	Bread Plate	E	85
D380–III	Slop, large size	E	75
D381–II	Slop, middle size	E	90
D382–VI	Cream, large size	E	50
D383–VI	Sugar, large size	E	45
D384–III	Teapot, large size	E	325
D384–IV	Teapot, large size	E	250
D386–II	Kettle, large size	E	500
D387–II	Kettle, small size	E	525
D388–III	Covered Muffin Dish	E	400
D389–II	Egg Cup	E	50
D390–II	Milk Jug	E	275

HEXAGON TEA WARE

Degenhardt No.	Item	Code	Value ($)
D391–II	Tea and Saucer	C	200
D392–II	Teapot, middle size	C	550
D393–II	Cream, small size	C	175
D394–II	Sugar, small size	C	150
D395–II	Tray	C	1,450
D396–II	Set complete (4 T&S)	C	3,300
D397–II	Coffee and Saucer	C	175
D399–II	Moustache and Saucer	C	425
D401–II	Plate, 6 in.	C	110
D405–II	Sugar, large size	A	140
D406–II	Cream, large size	C	180
D409–II	Kettle, large size	C	575

NEPTUNE TEA WARE

Degenhardt No.	Item	Code	Value ($)
D414–II	Tea and Saucer	C	185
D415–II	Teapot, middle size	C	525
D416–II	Sugar, small size	C	150
D417–II	Cream, small size	C	160
D418–II	Tray	C	1,200
D419–II	Set Complete (2 T&S)	C	2,700
D420–II	Coffee and Saucer	C	150
D422–II	Plate, 6 in.	B	95
D423–III	Plate, 7 in.	B	70
D424–III	Plate, 8 in.	C	85
D425–VI	Bread Plate	B	75
D426–II	Slop, large size	C	175
D427–II	Sugar, large size	C	145
D428–II	Cream, large size	C	170

Degenhardt No.	Item	Code	Value ($)
D429–V	Teapot, large size	B	300
D431–VI	Kettle, large size	B	300

CONE TEA WARE

Degenhardt No.	Item	Code	Value ($)
D432–II	Tea and Saucer	C	210
D433–II	Teapot	C	650
D434–II	Sugar, small size	C	160
D435–II	Cream, small size	C	185
D436–II	Tray	A	1,400
D437–II	Set complete (4 T&S)	C	3,450
D441–II	Sugar, large size	C	225

ERNE TEA WARE

Degenhardt No.	Item	Code	Value ($)
D445–II	Tea and saucer	C	225
D446–II	Teapot	G	750
D447–II	Sugar	B	165
D448–II	Cream	B	190
D448–II	Cream	G	200
D449–II	Tray	B	1,450
D450–II	Set complete (4 T&S)	B	3,600
D451–II	Plate, 5 in.	G	95
D453–II	Kettle	B	825

TRIDACNA TEA WARE

Degenhardt No.	Item	Code	Value ($)
D454–I	Tea and Saucer	C	165
D454–I	Tea and Saucer	G	185
D455–I	Teapot, middle size	C	500
D456–II	Sugar, small size	C	135
D457–II	Cream, small size	C	160
D458–I	Tray	G	1,200
D459–II	Set complete (2 T&S)	G	2,600
D461–II	Moustache and Saucer	G	325
D462–II	Coffee and Saucer	B	135
D464–III	Plate, 5 in.	B	55
D464–VI	Plate, 5 in.	B	35
D465–III	Plate, 6 in.	A	80
D466–II	Plate, 7 in.	C	110
D468–I	Bread Plate	C	425
D469–VI	Slop, large size	B	38
D470–III	Slop, middle size	B	120
D472–II	Sugar, large size	B	125
D474–II	Cream, large size	B	150
D475–II	Teapot, large size	B	375
D476–I	Teapot, small size	A	475
D477–II	Kettle, large size	A	425
D479–II	Covered Muffin Dish	B	250
D480–V	Milk Jug	B	75

CHINESE TEA WARE

Degenhardt No.	Item	Code	Value ($)
D482–I	Chinese Tea Urn, large size	K	12,000
D483–I	Tea and Saucer	K	600
D484–I	Teapot	K	1,300
D485–I	Sugar	K	450
D486–I	Cream	K	500
D487–I	Tray	K	2,300
D488–I	Set complete (2 T&S)	K	6,000

ABERDEEN TEA WARE

Degenhardt No.	Item	Code	Value ($)
D489–II	Tea and Saucer	C	300
« »			
D496–I	Ribbon Jam Pot	B	675

Degenhardt No.	Item	Code	Value ($)
D498–II	Butter Tub	A	85
D500–III	Acorn Trinket Box	B&D	275

SCROLL TEA WARE

Degenhardt No.	Item	Code	Value ($)
D502–II	Tea and Saucer	G	250
D503–II	Teapot	G	700
D512–II	Sugar, large size	G	175
« »			
D515–I	Bamboo Teapot, large size	A	625
D516–I	Bamboo Teapot, small size	A	500

LOW LILY TEA WARE

Degenhardt No.	Item	Code	Value ($)
D518–II	Tea and Saucer	C	220
D519–II	Teapot	C	750
D520–II	Sugar	C	180
D521–II	Cream	C	200
D522–II	Tray	C	1,600

HARP SHAMROCK TEA WARE

Degenhardt No.	Item	Code	Value ($)
D524–III	Tea and Saucer	E	130
D525–III	Teapot	E	400
D525–VI	Teapot	E	200
D526–III	Sugar	E	110
D527–III	Cream	E	120
D528–II	Tray	E	1,050
D529–II	Set complete (4 T&S)	E	2,500
« »			
D530–II	Shamrock Honey Pot on Stand	E	475
D531–VI	Shamrock Biscuit Jar	E	135
D532–III	Rathmore Biscuit Jar	K	425
D533–VII	Sardine Box and Stand	D&G	185

LILY TEA WARE

Degenhardt No.	Item	Code	Value ($)
D536–II	Tea and Saucer	C	200
D537–II	Teapot	C	700
D538–II	Sugar, small size	C	180
D539–II	Cream, small size	C	200
D540–II	Tray	C	1,650
D541–II	Set complete (4 T&S)	C	3,750
D542–II	Plate, 5-in.	G	125
D543–II	Bread Plate	G	275

LIMPET TEA WARE

Degenhardt No.	Item	Code	Value ($)
D549–II	Tea and Saucer	B	120
D549–III	Tea and Saucer	B	95
D551–V	Sugar, small size	B	30
D552–V	Cream, small size	B	40
D555–III	Coffee and Saucer	B	100
D557–III	Plate, 5-in.	B	55
D558–III	Bread Plate	B	175
D559–VI	Slop, large size	B	36
D560–II	Sugar, large size	B	150
D561–III	Cream, large size	C	95
D564–VI	Milk Jug	B	55
D565–III	Teapot, large size	B	350

BLARNEY TEA WARE

Degenhardt No.	Item	Code	Value ($)
D567–II	Tea and Saucer	G	300
D568–II	Teapot	G	700

Degen-hardt No.	Item	Code	Value ($)
D571–II	Tray	G	1,400
« »			
D582–II	Slater Sweet	A	250
D584–II	Harp Jug, 30's	D	325
D585–I	Harp Jug, 24's	A	375
D586–I	Harp Jug, 12's	A	450

SHELL TEA WARE

D587–II	Tea and Saucer	D	425
D588–II	Teapot	D	800
D589–II	Sugar	D	375
D590–II	Cream	D	400
D591–II	Tray	D	1,950
D592–II	Set complete (4 T&S)	D	5,400

VICTORIA TEA WARE

D593–II	Tea and Saucer	C	350
D594–II	Teapot	C	850
D595–II	Sugar	C	325
D596–II	Cream	C	350
D597–II	Tray	C	1,500
D598–II	Set complete (4 T&S)	C	4,550
« »			
D599–II	Shell Biscuit Jar	C	900
D600–I	Diamond Biscuit Jar	A	950
D600–I	Diamond Biscuit Jar	D	1,050
D601–I	Shell Cream, large size	A	650
D602–I	Shell Sugar, large size	A	575
D603–VI	Crate Match Box	B	95
D604–II	Oval Shamrock Box	E&D	350
D604–III	Oval Shamrock Box	B,E&J	300
D605–II	Round Shamrock Box	E	300

SYDNEY TEA WARE

D607–II	Tea and Saucer	C	325
D608–II	Teapot	C	700
D609–II	Sugar, small size	C	300
D610–II	Cream, small size	C	350
D611–II	Tray	C	1,450
D612–II	Set complete (4 T&S)	C	4,250
« »			
D621–VI	Egg Frame and Cups (6)	G	350

HEXAGON TEA WARE
(Hand Painted Flowers)

D622–II	Tea and Saucer	N	300
D623–II	Teapot	N	800
D624–II	Sugar	N	275
D625–II	Cream	N	300
D626–II	Tray	N	1,700
D627–II	Set complete (4 T&S)	N	4,300
« »			
D628–II	Leaf Plate, size 1	C	125
D629–II	Leaf Plate, size 2	C	140
D632–II	Leaf Plate, size 5	C	200
D634–V	Heart Plate, size 1	B	32
D635–V	Heart Plate, size 2	B	34
D636–IV	Heart Plate, size 3	B	37
D637–V	Shell Butter Plate	B	42
D639–VI	Erne Leaf Plate, size 2	B	45
D640–VI	Erne Leaf Plate, size 3	B	50

Degen-hardt No.	Item	Code	Value ($)
D641–V	Sycamore Plate, size 1	B	35
D642–IV	Sycamore Plate, size 2	B	42

ECHINUS TEA WARE

D645–I	Tea and Saucer	F	300
D646–I	Teapot, middle size	F	750
D647–I	Sugar, small size	F	300
D648–I	Cream, small size	F	350
D649–I	Tray	A	1,250
D649–I	Tray	C	1,475
D650–I	Set complete (4 T&S)	A	3,650
D650–II	Set complete (4 T&S)	N	4,800
D652–II	Plate, 6-in.	B	110
D654–I	Bread Plate	N	425
D656–I	Sugar, large size	B	350
D657–I	Cream, large size	B	375
D658–I	Teapot, large size	F	850
D659–I	Teapot, small size	B	700
D664–I	Moustache and Saucer	G	425
D666–VI	Egg Cup	B	35

FINNER TEA WARE

D669–II	Tea and Saucer	K	325
« »			
D680–I	Custard Cup and Saucer	A	195
D685–I	Shell Plate, large size	G	300
D689–II	Oval Plate, size 2	C	150

FAN TEA WARE

D694–I	Tea and Saucer	K	300
D695–I	Teapot	K	800
D696–I	Sugar	K	325
D697–I	Cream	K	350
D698–I	Tray	K	2,000
D699–I	Set complete (4 T&S)	K	4,800
D700–I	Coffee and Saucer	B	250
« »			
D707–I	Crate Biscuit Box	A	1,500

ARTICHOKE TEA WARE

D709–I	Tea and Saucer	F	350
D711–I	Sugar Box	F	450
D712–I	Cream	F	450
D713–I	Tray	G	2,000
D715–I	Plate, 5-in.	F	150
D716–I	Bread Plate	F	400
D719–I	Cream	F	475
D720–I	Covered Muffin Dish	F	700

INSTITUTE TEA WARE

D722–I	Tea and Saucer	B	200
D723–I	Breakfast and Saucer	J	300
D724–I	Plate, 6-in.	A	100
D725–I	Plate, 7-in.	B	125
D726–I	Bread Plate	B	225
D727–II	Slop	K	200
D728–I	Sugar Box	F	425
D729–II	Cream	A	375
D731–I	Covered Muffin	D&J	600
D731–I	Covered Muffin	K	500

9

Degenhardt No.	Item	Code	Value ($)
	GRASS TEA WARE		
D732–I	Tea and Saucer	D	300
D733–I	Teapot, middle size	D	750
D734–I	Sugar Box, small size	D	350
D735–I	Cream, small size	D	325
D736–I	Tray	D	1,350
D737–I	Set complete (2 T&S)	D	3,500
D741–I	Plate, 6-in.	D	150
D742–I	Plate, 7-in.	K	200
D743–I	Bread Plate	K	450
D744–I	Slop, large size	K	275
D748–I	Cream, middle size	K	335
D750–I	Teapot, small size	D	650
D751–I	Kettle, large size	K	850
D752–I	Covered Muffin Dish	K	775
D753–I	Milk Jug	K	450
D755–I	Honey Pot on Stand	K	775
	THORN TEA WARE		
D758–II	Tea and Saucer	K	500
D759–II	Teapot	K	950
D760–II	Sugar, small size	K	450
D761–II	Cream, small size	K	500
D762–I	Tray	K	2,000
D763–II	Set complete (2 T&S)	K	5,000
D764–I	Breakfast and Saucer	D	575
D767–II	Bread Plate	K	600
D768–I	Slop, large size	K	475
D771–I	Teapot, large size	A	775
D774–I	Kettle, large size	D	900
« »	Triple Bucket, large size	J	1,500
D778–I			
	THISTLE TEA WARE		
D779–I	Tea and Saucer	G	350
D780–I	Teapot	G	800
D781–I	Sugar	G	325
D782–I	Cream	G	350
D783–I	Tray	G	1,500
D784–II	Set complete (2 T&S)	G	3,200
« »	Shell Plateaux, 4½-in.	B	90
D790–III			
D791–I	Shell Plateaux, 7-in.	A	300
D792–I	Shell Plateau, 9-in.	A	350
D794–II	Shell Biscuit Box, 7-in.	B	1,600
D795–I	Shell Biscuit Box, 9-in.	B	2,200
D798–I	Oblong Shell Jelly	D	425
	LACE TEA WARE		
D799–II	Tea and Saucer	K	525
D800–I	Teapot	K	1,000
D801–I	Sugar	K	450
D802–I	Cream	K	500
D803–I	Tray	K	2,200
D804–I	Set complete (2 T&S)	K	5,500
D805–I	Coffee and Saucer	K	475
D806–I	Plate, 6-in.	K	325
« »	Florence Jug, 30's	K	95
D813–VII			

Degenhardt No.	Item	Code	Value ($)
	RING HANDLE IVORY (Belleek Shape)		
D820–II	Coffee and Saucer	A	140
D823–II	Plate, 7-in.	K	75
D824–I	Bread Plate	K	300
D825–II	Slop	K	150
D826–II	Sugar	N	400
D827–II	Cream	K	150
D832–I	Jug, 30's, Stoneware	F	225
	EARTHENWARE		
	Tea Ware, etc.		
D843–II	Creams	T&F	100
D845–I	Teapots, 18's	F	135
D857–I	Bowls, 24's	T&F	125
D858–I	Mugs, 24's	T	150
D859–II	Covered Muffin Dish	A	175
D862–I	Triple Bread and Cheese Tray	A	325
D865–I	Plain Jug, 30's	K	200
D866–I	Fluted Jugs, 12's	T&F	250
	Dinner Ware		
D878–I	Salad Plates, large size	A	75
D880–II	Jelly Moulds, 6-in.	A	55
D881–I	Jelly Moulds, 7-in.	A	80
D882–II	Jelly Moulds, 8-in.	A	75
D883–I	Jelly Moulds, 9-in.	A	100
D885–I	Hot Water Cover Dish, 10-in.	A	175
D886–I	Hot Water Plate	A	125
D887–I	Plate, 10-in.	N	110
D888–I	Soup Plate, 10-in.	T	55
D889–I	Plate, 9-in.	T	40
D890–I	Plate, 8-in.	T	30
D891–I	Plate, 7-in.	T	30
D894–I	Plate, 4-in.	A	18
D899–II	Flat Dish, 12-in.	T	80
D900–I	Flat Dish, 14-in.	T	120
D901–I	Flat Dish, 16-in.	T	140
D902–I	Flat Dish, 18-in.	T	155
D903–I	Flat Dish, 20-in.	T	175
D906–I	Gravy Dish, 20-in.	T	225
D912–I	Sauce Tureen and Stand	A	200
D914–I	Sauce Boat	T&D	225
D915–I	Cover Dish, 10-in. and Liner	T	250
D916–I	Cover Dish, 8-in. and Liner	T	185
	Toilet Ware		
D932–I	Covered Brush Tray, 6's	T	165
D939–I	Ewers, 6's	F	750
D950–II	Italian Basin, 6's	T	225
D951–I	Eldon Ewer, 12's	T	450
D953–I	Etruscan Ewer, 6's	N	900
	Assorted Ware		
D977–I	Milk Pans, 14-in.	A	175
D980–II	Milk Pans, 20-in.	A	200
D1014–II	Round Bed Pan, small size	A	180
D1017–I	Urinals (Female), Handled	A	300

Degenhardt No.	Item	Code	Value ($)
D1021–I	Foot Bath, best shape, 16-in.	F	350
D1033–I	Italian Ewer	K	575
D1035–I	Minton Shop Ewer	A	250
D1049–I	Pub Barrel–Brandy	K&T	1,400
D1050–I	Publ Barrel–Gin	K&T	1,250
D1051–I	Pub Barrel–Port	K&T	1,250
D1052–I	Pub Barrel–Rum	K&T	1,250
D1053–I	Pub Barrel–S. Whisky	K,N&T	1,500
D1055–II	Telegraph Insulator	A	45
D1056–I	Vegetable Bowl with Cover	K	750
D1057–I	Well and Tree Platter, 20L	A	150

STATUES AND HOLY WATER FONTS

Degenhardt No.	Item	Code	Value ($)
D1103–II	Angel Font Kneeling, large size	L	825
D1105–IV	Blessed Virgin Mary, large size	L	800
D1108–IV	Celtic Font No. 6	B&D	60
D1110–III	Cherub Font, large size	A	300
D1111–VI	Coral and Shell Font Wall Bracket	B	175
D1115–III	Sacred Heart Font No. 4	D	175
D1116–II	Sacred Heart Statue, large size	L	1,200

FIGURES AND BUSTS

Degenhardt No.	Item	Code	Value ($)
D1125–I	Basket Flower Carrier (version of D1141 with flowers in basket)	L	6,000
D1126–I	Boy Candlestick, Pierced	D	2,000
D1127–I	Bust of Charles Dickens	L	8,500
D1128–I	Bust of Lord James Butler	L	2,800
D1129–IV	Bust of Joy (made with and without cross necklace)	L	750
D1130–I	Bust of Queen of the Hops	L	4,500
D1131–VII	Bust of Shakespeare	A	175
D1132–II	Bust of Sorrow	L	3,000
D1133–I	Bust of Wesley	L	2,500
D1134–I	Figure of Affection	D	3,500
D1135–I	Figure of Bather (looking over her left shoulder)	A	2,300
D1137–I	Girl Candlestick, Pierced	D	2,000
D1138–II	Greyhound, Single	L	850
D1138–VI	Greyhound, Single	A	325
D1139–III	Horse and Snake	L	8,800
D1141–I	Italian Grape Gatherer	L	5,200
D1142–II	Leprechaun	D	550
D1142–III	Leprechaun	D	400
D1142–VI	Leprechaun	K	175
D1143–II	Man With Cat and Puppies	D	2,900
D1145–I	Minstrel With Flute Pipe Paperweight	A	2,300

CENTRES AND COMPORTS

Degenhardt No.	Item	Code	Value ($)
D1160–I	Tazza on Flowered Pedestal Centre	L	3,800
D1161–II	Triboy Woven Basket Comport, large size	J	4,700
D1164–I	Triboy Comport, small size	D	1,500
D1165–I	Tridolphin Comport	A	3,000
D1166–I	Vine Comport Pierced, 3¾ x 10	K	2,200
D1169–III	Woven Basket Comport, small size, 5¾ x 8½	A	1,750

FLOWER HOLDERS AND POTS

Degenhardt No.	Item	Code	Value ($)
D1170–II	Angel Flower Pot, Footed	A	2,500
D1172–II	Belleek Flower Pot, small size	B	135
D1176–I	Nautilus On Shells	C	950
D1179–II	Pierced Spill, Flowered, small size	A	300
D1180–II	Ram's Head Flower Holder	A	1,200
D1181–II	Shell Flower Pot, Footed	A	2,200
D1183–I	Swan Flower Holder	A	1,250
D1185–I	Violet Holder	C	850

VASES AND SPILLS

Degenhardt No.	Item	Code	Value ($)
D1198–VI	Celtic Tara Vase	K	220
D1204–I	Double Fish Vase	D	2,500
D1205–II	Double Root Spill	D	950
D1209–III	Finner Vase, Flowered	A	500
D1213–II	Harp Vase	E	250
D1215–I	Lizzard Vase	K	1,700
D1217–II	Pierced Shamrock Vase	H	225
D1218–II	Prince Arthur Vase, Flowered	J	950
D1219–IV	Rathmore Vase	B	80
D1220–III	Ribbon Vase, Flowered	A	300
D1221–VI	Roscor Vase	D	250
D1222–VI	Rose Isle Vase	D	950
D1224–II	Shamrock Trunk Stump Spill	E	200
D1226–II	Shell Spill, Double	A	375
D1229–II	Tara Vase	A	1,200
D1230–I	Triboy Vase	J	6,500
D1231–I	Triple Fish Vase	D	4,000
D1232–I	Triple Hippiritus	A	2,750
D1233–II	Vase of Masks	J	1850
D1235–II	Water Lily Vase On Rocks	D	2,800

HAND WOVEN BASKETS, PLATES AND TRAYS

Degenhardt No.	Item	Code	Value ($)
D1245–5	A.M. Round Basket, Round Rod, Edged	A	950
D1246–4	A.O. Oval Basket, Round Rod, Edged	A	1,250
D1249–5	Boston Basket, Flowered	D	2,400
D1250–3	Cake Plate, Round Edge	A	1,200
D1253–5	Forget-Me-Not Basket	D	550
D1255–4	Hand-woven Tray	A	2,200
D1258–6	Heart Shape Basket, Flowered, large size	D	475
D1259–6	Heart Shape Basket, Flowered, small size	A	400
D1261–10	Henshall's Twig Basket, middle size	J	2,600

Degenhardt No.	Item	Code	Value ($)
D1262–4	Hexagon Basket, Plaited and Flowered	D	2,800
D1262–3	Hexagon Cake Plate, Unhandled	A	1,000
D1264–3	Hexagon Twig Cake Plate, Handled	A	1,100
D1266–3	Hexagon Woven Fruit Basket, Flat Rod	J	1,800
D1269–2	Lily Basket, Flowered	J	2,600
D1270–6	Oval A. I. Basket, Flowered	D	600
D1274–5	Round Basket, Centre Handled and Flowered	D	2,800
D1277–6	Round Covered Basket, large size	D	4,000
D1279–6	Spider's Web Cake Plate	D	3,900
D1281–1	Twig Special Two Strand Basket	A	2,300
D1282–4	Twig Cake Plate, Handled	J	950
D1283–4	Twig Handled Oblong Tray, 6¾ x 14½	A	900
D1284–4	Woven Plain Heart Shape Basket	A	450
D1286–3	Flat Rod Round Basket, 6½	A	1,500

SUGARS, CREAMS, AND JUGS

Degenhardt No.	Item	Code	Value ($)
D1291–I	Ampanida Open Cream	A	325
D1294–I	Bearded Mask Cream, small size	A	185
D1301–VI	Double Shell Sugar	B	35
D1302–I	Fluted Cream	A	225
D1304–III	Irish Pot Cream, Shamrocks, Size 1	E	125
D1305–II	Irish Pot Sugar, Shamrocks, Size 1	E	150
D1306–I	Lily Jug, 24's, Stoneware	A	450
D1310–I	Rope Handled Jug, 5½	A	375
D1314–VI	Vine Tankard Jug	D	140

SHAMROCK WARE

Degenhardt No.	Item	Code	Value ($)
D1316–VI	Berry Dish, small size	E	50
D1317–VI	Bouillon Cup and Saucer	E	85
D1318–III	Butter Plate	E	75
D1319–III	Coffee Pot	E	375
D1323–VI	Cup Marmalade Jar	E	50
D1325–II	Marmalade Jar	E	135
D1326–IV	Milk Jug, Flat, small size	E	85
D1327–III	Milk Jug, Round, small size	E	125
D1328–IV	Mug, large size	E	55
D1330–II	Plate	E	165

TRIDACNA TEA WARE

Degenhardt No.	Item	Code	Value ($)
D1344–II	Brush Tray	C	325
D1345–IV	Butter Plate	B	45
D1346–III	Coffee Pot	B	325
D1348–III	Mustard	B	55
D1349–III	Open Salt	A	45
D1352–VI	TV Set	B	90

HARP SHAMROCK TEA WARE

Degenhardt No.	Item	Code	Value ($)
D1355–V	Bread Plate	E	85
D1356–VI	Butter Plate	E	75
D1357–VI	Coffee Pot	E	220
D1358–VI	Cream, large size	E	42
D1359–VI	Kettle	E	275
D1360–VI	Plate, 7	E	40
D1361–VI	Slop Bowl	E	45
D1362–VI	Sugar, large size	E	40
D1364–VI	Bell	E	60
D1365–VI	Coffee Cup	E	40
D1366–VI	Coffee Saucer	E	30
D1367–II	Plate, 5	E	85

LIMPET TEA WARE

(Early ware was coral branch footed)

Degenhardt No.	Item	Code	Value ($)
D1371–III	Covered Sugar, small size	B	150
D1371–V	Covered Sugar, small size	B	43
D1372–III	Plate, 7	B	75
D1373–III	Teapot, middle size	B	175
D1374–VI	Plate, 10	B	70
D1375–VI	TV Set	B	85

NEW SHELL TEA WARE

(Adaptation of Shell Tea Ware and Echinus Tea Ware designs)

Degenhardt No.	Item	Code	Value ($)
D1380–V	Bread Plate	B	95
D1381–VI	Butter Plate	B	35
D1382–VI	Cream, large size	B	40
D1383–VI	Open Sugar, large size	B	35
D1384–III	Plate, 7	G	120
D1385–V	Tea Cup	B	38
D1386–V	Tea Saucer	B	28
D1388–VI	Plate, 6	B	40

INSTITUTE TEA WARE

Degenhardt No.	Item	Code	Value ($)
D1390–I	Butter and Stand	A	400
D1391–I	Butter and Stand, Scalloped	A	450
D1393–I	Platter	A	375
D1394–I	Steak Dish, 3 Pieces	A	1,500

CHINESE TEA WARE

Degenhardt No.	Item	Code	Value ($)
D1397–II	Plate, 5¼	D	200

IVY TEA WARE

Body design similar to Shamrock Tea Ware, but decorated with sprigs of ivy)

Degenhardt No.	Item	Code	Value ($)
D1413–III	Plate	B	80
D1415–III	Tea Cup	B	75
D1416–III	Tea Saucer	B	50

Degenhardt No.	Item	Code	Value ($)
	CELTIC DESIGN TEA WARE		
	(Same basic body as Ring Handle Ivory Tea Ware, but with designs adapted from the Book of Kells engraved in bands and painted in brilliant colors)		
D1425–III	Bread Plate	K	250
D1428–III	Coffee Cup	K&B	95
D1429–III	Coffee Pot	K	750
D1430–III	Coffee Saucer	K&B	75
D1431–III	Covered Sugar, large size	K	200
D1432–III	Cream, large size	K&B	200
D1435–III	Plate, 5	K	95
D1436–III	Slop Bowl	K&B	125
D1437–III	Tea Cup	K&B	110
D1438–III	Tea Saucer	K&B	90
D1440–III	Teapot, middle size	K	725
D1442–III	Cream, tall shape	K&B	190
D1443–III	Open Sugar, large size	K&B	165
	CELTIC LOW SHAPE TEA WARE		
D1452–VI	Cream	B	50
D1455–V	Sugar, Covered	B	60
D1456–VI	Tea Cup	B	50
D1457–VI	Tea Saucer	B	30
	ARTICHOKE TEA WARE		
D1461–I	Breakfast Cup	F	200
D1462–I	Breakfast Saucer	F	175
D1463–I	Milk Jug	F	525
	MASK TEA WARE		
D1474–VII	Hurricane Lamp	A	75
D1475–III	Bread Plate	B	200
D1476–VI	Coffee Cup	A	25
D1478–VI	Coffee Saucer	A	25
D1479–VI	Covered Sugar, large size	A	45
D1481–VI	Cream, Low Shape, large size	A	40
D1482–III	Cream, Low Shape, small size	B	80
D1483–I	Cream, Tall Shape, large size	A	180
D1483–II	Cream, Tall Shape, large size	A	140
D1484–III	Cream, Tall Shape, small size	B	90
D1485–VI	Milk Jug	A	60
D1486–III	Open Sugar, large size	B	100
D1487–III	Open Sugar, small size	A	70
D1490–III	Plate, 6 in.	B	100
D1491–III	Plate, 7 in.	B	125
D1492–III	Sandwich Tray	B	275
D1493–III	Tea Cup	B	60
D1494–III	Tea Saucer	B	50
D1495–III	Teapot	B	375
D1495–VI	Teapot	A	185
	RING HANDLE IVORY WARE		
D1500–II	Tray	N	1,500
	MISCELLANEOUS		
D1502–I	Amphora Lamp	D	1,850
D1506–I	Boudoir Candlestick, Flowered	J	1,250
D1507–I	Calawite Candle Extinguisher and Stand	A	850
D1510–VI	Celtic Bowl of Roses	D	2,450
D1511–VI	Celtic Candlestick, Low	B	155
D1512–II	Celtic Fruit Dish	K	450
D1513–III	Celtic Salad Bowl and Stand	K	750
D1514–II	Cheese Cover and Stand	D	1,450
D1516–I	Chinese Tea Urn, small size	A	8,500
D1517–I	Clam Salt	J	285
D1518–VI	Coral and Shell Wall Bracket	B	175
D1519–I	Double Bucket, large size	A	950
D1521–I	Echinus Footed Bowl	B	1,075
D1521–VI	Echinus Footed Bowl	G	475
D1523–I	Flask	F	1,650
D1524–II	Flowered Frame, Footed	J	9,500
D1526–I	Frog Lily Pad Paperweight	D	1,450
D1526–VI	Frog Lily Pad Paperweight	D	75
D1530–I	Gothic Candlestick	A	1,000
D1531–I	Harp, Hound and Tower Commemorative Plate	A	1,250
D1533–I	Hunter's Wall Plaque, Hand Painted Centre	K	4,200
D1534–I	Individual Egg Holder	A	450
D1535–I	Lily of the Valley Frame, large size	J	3,900
D1537–VI	Lithophane—Farm Girl with Goat	A	600
D1538–VI	Lithophane—Girl at Wall	A	600
D1539–VI	Lithophane—Child Looking in Mirror	A	600
D1540–NM	Lithophane—Lovers at Table	A	200
D1542–NM	Lithophane—Ladies with Pigeon	A	200
D1544–III	Lithophane—Madonna, Child and Angel	A	4,000
D1546–I	Lyre Wall Bracket	F	1,400
D1547–III	Mask Ware Powder Bowl, large size	D	375
D1549–III	Mask Ware Tobacco Box	B	375
D1550–I	Menu Tablet	D	900
D1551–I	Napkin Ring—Egyptian	F	500
D1554–III	Primrose Butter Plate	B	75
D1555–VI	Prince Charles Dog (Spaniel) on Cushion Paperweight	L	100
D1559–III	Shamrock Ashtray	E	55
D1561–III	Shamrock Barrel Marmalade Jar	E	125
D1562–II	Shamrock Covered Butter Tub	E	300
D1563–V	Shamrock Pin Tray	E	85
D1564–III	Shamrock Salt Tub No. 2, large size	E	70
D1565–III	Shamrock Salt Tub No. 1, small size	E	55
D1567–VI	Shell Muffineer Shaker	B	35
D1570–I	Terrier Dog (Boxer) on Cushion Paperweight	L	475
D1571–II	Thorn Flowered Bowl	J	1,250

Degenhardt No.	Item	Code	Value ($)
	CANDLE ITEMS		
D1601–I	Papal Candle Lamp	K	5,000
	CENTRES AND COMPORTS		
D1613–I	Tri Dolphin Comport, 5"H	J	700
D1614–I	Triple Root Centre	D	2,000
D1616–II	Victoria Triple Shell Centre	C	1,800
	COVERED BOXES AND JARS		
D1621–VI	Cherub Trinket Box	D	120
D1622–VII	Devenish Covered Box	D	95
D1624–VII	Hexagon Covered Box	D	63
D1626–VII	Melvin Candy Jar	G	110
D1629–VII	Thorn Covered Box	D	65
	DECORATIVE ITEMS		
D1632–VI	Belleek Easter Egg, 1972	B	200
D1636–III	Celtic Bowl of Flowers	J	1,750
D1639–I	Harp Brooch, Flowered	A	500
D1640–VII	Harp with Applied Shamrocks, 8⅝"H	K	280
	FIGURES AND BUSTS		
D1650–I	Bust of Gladstone	L	3,500
D1653–VI	Collie (Male)	A	150
D1662–VI	Terrier	A	35
	FLOWER HOLDERS AND POTS		
D1670–II	Basket Flower Pot, Flowered, 3"H	J	425
D1674–II	Double Shell Flower Pot, Flowered	J	550
D1678–I	Four Section Flower Holder	F	1,300
	HANDWOVEN BASKETS, PLATES AND TRAYS		
D1683–4	Boat Shaped Basket, Footed & Plaited	L	4,400
D1684–3	Boat Shaped Basket, large size	A	4,800
D1685–6	Cherry Blossom Plate, Three Strand, Flowered	D	650
D1688–5	Erne Basket	D	575
D1689–2	Henshall Flat Rod Basket, small size	A	1,200
D1690–6	Melvin Basket	D	900
D1692–3	Round Flat Rod Basket, 6¾"D	A	1,700
D1693–3	Scalloped Basket, Flat Rod, Two Strands	A	2,600
D1695–5	United States Bicentennial Plate, Flowered	K	6,000
	LAMPS – ELECTRIC		
D1700–VII	Armstrong Lamp	F	375
D1704–VII	Killarney Biscuit Jar	D	260

Degenhardt No.	Item	Code	Value ($)
	MIRROR FRAMES		
D1720–I	Lily of the Valley Frame, small size	J	2,000
D1721–NM	Queen Victoria Frame, Flowered	J	18,000
D1723–II	Shell Frame, large size	A	3,000
	MUSIC BOXES		
D1729-VII	Enchanted Holly	D	55
	STATUES AND CROSSES		
D1746–VI	Celtic Cross, large size	B	300
	VASES AND SPILLS		
D1751–VII	Armstrong Vase	F	300
D1773–II	Michael Collins Vase	K	600
D1774–VI	Owl Spill	B	75
D1777–VI	Round Tower Vase	D&E	485
D1780–VI	Shamrock Scent Spill	E	45
D1781–VII	Sheerin Vase	K	60
D1782–V	Thistle Top Vase, Flowered	D	110
D1783–VII	Thorn Vase, large size	D	65
D1784–VII	Thorn Vase, small size	D	45
D1785–VI	Toy Panel Vase	G	35
D1786–VI	Tree Trunk Vase	B	48
D1791–VII	Tyrone Vase	K	52
D1792–II	Ulster Vase	G	1,050
D1793–II	Vase with Bird, Flowered	A	1,000
	WALL BRACKETS AND PLAQUES		
D1802–I	Fern and Flower Wall Bracket	A	1,250
D1803–I	Irish Squirrel Wall Bracket	A	5,500
D1804–I	Melon Vine Wall Bracket	D	1,600
D1805–I	Thistle Flowered Wall Bracket	G	2,400
D1807–I	Wall Plaque, "Praise Ye the Lord," (earthenware)	D	650
	BELLEEK COLLECTORS' SOCIETY EXCLUSIVE LIMITED EDITIONS		
	(All limited edition items for the collectors' society have special marks)		
D1810–VI	1979, Charter Member Trademark Plaque	K	125
D1811–VI	1979, St. Matthew Gospel Plate	M&F	125
D1812–VII	1980, Bonbonniere, Flowered	K	160
D1813–VII	1981, St. Mark Gospel Plate	M&F	125
D1814–VII	1982, Institute Cream and Sugar	F	95
D1815–VII	1982, St. Luke Gospel Plate	M&F	125
D1816–VII	1983, Wild Irish Rose Candlesticks (pair)	D	110
D1817–VII	1984, St. John Gospel Plate	M&F	200
D1818–VII	1984, Wild Irish Rose Bell	D	82

Degenhardt No.	Item	Code	Value ($)
KILLARNEY COLLECTION			
(Painted and embossed pattern features rose, thistle, and shamrocks)			
D1980–VII	Bell	D	77
D1981–VII	Biscuit Jar	D	110
D1982–VII	Candlestick	D	75
D1983–VII	Creamer	D	66
D1984–VII	Flower Bowl	D	70
D1985–VII	Sugar	D	60
D1986–VII	Spill	D	77
D1987–VII	Vase	D	77
SHAMROCK WARE			
D2000–VII	Beer Stein	E	72
D2003–VII	Candy Jar	E	83
D2005–III	Dresser Tray	E	225
D2006–II	Flower Pot, Pierced	E	185
D2007–VI	Gaelic Coffee Cup	E	55
D2008–VI	Gaelic Coffee Saucer	E	35
D2009–VI	Honey Pot	E	95
D2010–VII	Hurricane Lamp	E	85
D2015–III	Soup Bowl, 8D	E	120
D2017–VII	TV Set	E	85
D2018–VII	Two Tier Cake Plate	E	135
SPIRAL SHELL COLLECTION			
(Diagonal swirls radiate from the base to the top of each piece)			
D2025–VII	Biscuit Jar	A	93
D2026–VII	Butter Dish	A	45
D2027–VII	Candlestick	A	52
D2028–VII	Creamer	A	44
D2030–VII	Sugar	A	52
SPRINGTIME COLLECTION			
(Pink flowers with four petals on a diagonal grooved background)			
D2037–VII	Bud Vase	D	69
D2040–VII	Creamer	D	50
D2042–VII	Sugar	D	60

Degenhardt No.	Item	Code	Value ($)
SUMMER BRIAR COLLECTION			
(Five-petal pink flowers with yellow centers, green leaves and black berries on a basket weave pattern background)			
D2050–VII	Covered Sugar	D	65
D2051–VII	Creamer	D	55
THISTLE TEA WARE			
D2061–VII	Two Tier Cake Plate	G	130
THORN WARE			
D2067–VII	Napkin Ring	D	25
D2068–I	Tea Stand	K	750
MISCELLANEOUS			
D2078–VI	Coral Bell	D	60
D2079–V	Cottage Cheese Dish	B	125
D2079–VI	Cottage Cheese Dish	D	175
D2081–I	"Give Us This Day Our Daily Bread" Tray (earthenware)	A	550
D2082–I	Gladstone Chamber Pot	T	1,250
D2083–VII	Gravy Boat, 5 L	C	60
D2085–VII	Heart Cup and Tray	B	60
D2086–VII	Honey Pot, Flowered	D	150
D2087–VI	Horseshoe Ashtray	E	37
D2092–VI	Lattice Ashtray	B	30
D2097–I	Pocket Watch Stand	A	850
D2098–VII	Pottery Scene Plate, 6	G&M	61
D2108–I	Stilton Cheese Dish and Stand	A	1,250
D2110–VII	Thimble—Wild Irish Rose	D	27

RICHARD K. DEGENHARDT

BELLEEK

THE COMPLETE

COLLECTOR'S

GUIDE AND

ILLUSTRATED

REFERENCE

SECOND EDITION

WALLACE-HOMESTEAD

BOOK COMPANY

Radnor, Pennsylvania

Copyright © 1993 by Richard K. Degenhardt
Second Edition   All Rights Reserved
Published in Radnor, Pennsylvania 19089, by Wallace-Homestead,
a division of Chilton Book Company
No part of this book may be reproduced, transmitted, or stored
in any form or by any means, electronic or mechanical,
without prior written permission from the publisher.

Designed by Adrianne Onderdonk Dudden

Credits: p. i, Woodcut of the Pottery as it appeared in 1883
(Evan Bracken photo); pp. ii–iii, modern-day Pottery (Allen
Markley, LBIPP/Gary Parrott photo); p. v., D16-I Crouching
Venus, gilt (Del. E. Domke Collection, Hiroko Saita photo)

Manufactured in the United States of America

Library of Congress Cataloging in Publication Data

Degenhardt, Richard K.
    Belleek : the complete collector's guide and illustrated
    reference / Richard K. Degenhardt. — 2nd ed.
       p.   cm.
    Includes bibliographical references and index.
    ISBN 0-87069-698-X
    1. Belleek Pottery, ltd.—Catalogs.   2. Parian porcelain—
Northern Ireland—Belleek—Catalogs.   I. Title.
NK4210.B4A4   1993
738.2'09416'3—dc20   *93-30049*
                                                          CIP

1 2 3 4 5 6 7 8 9 0   2 1 0 9 8 7 6 5 4 3

To the memory of Tommy Campbell (1913–1986)
and to his colleagues, the skilled men and women who
—as did their predecessors, and as their successors will in their time—
give enduring craftsmanship to the world.

CONTENTS

FOREWORD

In 1978, Richard K. Degenhardt made a great tribute to the Belleek Pottery and its wares with his comprehensive book *Belleek: The Complete Collector's Guide and Illustrated Reference*. This scholarly work quickly became the bible of Belleek collectors, and it has proven to be a collector's item in its own right. Degenhardt's work demonstrated his zeal, fervor, and dedication to that great institution we call Belleek Pottery.

Fifteen years later, it is with great pride that I introduce Richard's completely updated, enhanced, and expanded reference book on Belleek pottery. He pursued this work unfettered by the past, and its thoroughness ensures it will become a major addition for every Belleek collector.

Since the publication of Richard's original book in 1978, the recent history of Belleek can only be described as checkered, at best. The past five years have witnessed the beginning of an era of rejuvenation and renaissance; we are currently experiencing a period of great financial stability and great quality, as well as a focus on our customer that has never been witnessed at Belleek before. Above all, those involved with the pottery share a common vision that Belleek can achieve great heights, and the realization of that vision has begun in every aspect of Belleek's business.

The publication of Richard's new book coincides with the first major expansion and development of the Pottery since its founding in 1857. The expansion program, which began in 1993 and will conclude in 1998, will position the Belleek Pottery for the demands beyond the year 2000.

Richard must be commended by all the patrons of Belleek for his loyalty and dedication to the Pottery; he is truly one of our greatest ambassadors. This second edition of *Belleek: The Complete Collector's Guide and Illustrated Reference* again demonstrates his scholarship and diligence.

On behalf of the Belleek Pottery, its management, and its employees, and on behalf of all of the patrons and collectors of Belleek worldwide, I would like to thank Richard for another great contribution to our heritage.

George G. Moore
Owner and Chairman
The Belleek Pottery Limited
Belleek, County Fermanagh, Ireland

PREFACE

I have had a lifelong love affair with Ireland, the Irish, and things Irish. My grandparents, with the exception of my paternal grandfather, came from County Cork. It may be prejudice based on my heritage, but from the Cliffs of Moher in the west to the east where the mountains of Mourne come down to the sea, and from the Giants Causeway in the far north to my Grandfather Kennedy's town of Cobh on the southern shore, I find that each county has a unique charm, and each shares a common stellar asset: the Irish people. Their warmth, wit, and interest in their fellow man is infectious. Visitor beware, lest your heart be captured, as mine has been.

Among the things Irish I most appreciate is the exquisite work of The Belleek Pottery Limited. Such words as *leprechaun* and *magic* come to mind when viewing the results of Belleek craftsmanship. The creamy texture, the gossamer appearance, and the translucent quality of the ware conspire to suggest mirage rather than fact.

Magic is partially defined as "the practice of using rituals . . . to attempt to control events in nature." Perhaps reading the pages that follow will assist you in arriving at your own conclusions as to Belleek's ability to produce what is yet another definition of magic, a "mysterious and overpowering quality."

My intention, in this book, is to offer beginning collectors a "feel" for Belleek, as well as to include the sort of definitive information that advanced collectors expect. I also hope that advanced collectors will gain a more thorough understanding of Belleek through the detailed discussion of how Parian is created.

Finally, I have sought to develop a close emotional tie with those persons who matter so much, the craftsmen and women of Belleek, who have made collecting possible.

Whether you are a seasoned collector, have but a single piece, or simply have an interest in Belleek, this book is written for you.

"Happy Belleeking!"

ACKNOWLEDGMENTS

Rarely is a book written without assistance from a number of individuals who provide information, direction, and encouragement. The first and second editions of this book are no exception. In 1978 it was my pleasure to thank and salute, with particular emphasis, Sean O'Loughlin, Kevin McCann, Eamon Ferguson, Philip Cleary, and John P. McCann. My heartfelt appreciation was also extended to directors of The Belleek Pottery Limited, Chairman Clinton O'Rourke, Managing Director Patrick O'Neill, and Commercial Director Jim O'Mahony, for their splendid cooperation. The help of two of the sons of board members, Bernard O'Rourke and Stephen O'Neill, was of particular benefit. The fine aid of Miss Jannette Thompson, of the Museum of Applied Arts and Sciences, Sydney, Australia, brought to light invaluable copies of eight diaries written by Robert Williams Armstrong during the pottery's important early years of 1862–1881. In closing my previous expression of appreciation I stated: "It would have been extremely difficult—if not impossible—to have completed the requisite research without the generous assistance of Pottery Manager Tommy Campbell, without doubt the leading authority of his time on the history of the pottery and the techniques of its handcrafting process." That was an understatement.

The current edition was based not only upon all the assistance showered on me in the past, but was additionally made possible by the superb support of the Belleek Pottery Chairman, George G. Moore. My genuine thanks to Managing Director John Maguire; Chief Modeler Fergus Cleary; Marie McGrellis, Patricia McCauley, and all the members of the pottery staff whose cooperation has been beyond measure. Allen Markley went far beyond the "extra mile" to be of help. Old friends in Ireland, Sean O'Loughlin, Mairead Dunlevy Reynolds, Clinton O'Rourke, Joe O'Loughlin—and in the United States Bernard O'Rourke—again came to my aid by giving of their knowledge, as well as by helping to secure data and old photographs.

Finally, I salute the collectors—lovers of Belleek—who generously shared their collections to make this edition a reality. Acknowledgment of their magnificent contributions and support gives me particular pleasure.

PART ONE

BELLEEK

A HISTORY OF

THE POTTERY

AND ITS WARE

CHAPTER ONE

THE BEGINNING

FOUNDERS AND EARLY YEARS

"More important to the buyers of Belleek than even the quality of the body is the fine detail of the patterns, and if this detail is diminished or destroyed by bad molds or bad workmanship, the demand for Belleek will decrease. Therefore, it is important that cases are kept touched up and that the fettler, in taking off seams, does not destroy the adjoining pattern. Quality and good craftsmanship should be the watchword."

These words spoken to me by Tommy Campbell, manager of The Belleek Pottery from 1966 to 1978, echo the commitment of skill and dedication to artistry that have been synonymous with Belleek since it was born on the banks of the River Erne in 1858.

Artistry and craftsmanship are not strangers to this lovely land of mountains and valleys that comprises the western portion of County Fermanagh and embraces Lower Lough Erne. On the islands of Lough Erne, minutes from Belleek, strange enigmatic stone figures were found; the oldest of these is believed to have been carved long before the birth of Christ. Later examples, dating from the twelfth century, show the transition from a pagan past to Christian influence.

More than three and one-half centuries ago Attorney General John Davies scribed, "The natives of this [Fermanagh] county are reputed to be the worst swordsmen in the north, being inclined to be scholars or craftsmen."

It was here, in the shadow of the village once called Wellsboro, that the gifts of nature joined with men's skill and determination to chart a new destiny for the region, and a new expression of art for the world.

There is little doubt that a pottery would one day have operated at Belleek, because of available material and trainable labor. That the pottery was started when it was offers the collector two additional reasons for interest. First, the pottery began when Ireland was in one of the most disastrous periods of her sad history. Second, Belleek of the first period meets the general requirement of being 100 years old or older, to qualify as truly antique. Had production begun at an even earlier date there would, of course, be more ware of antique vintage.

Fate determined that the founding of the pottery would follow an event of dire magnitude. Seumas MacManus in *The Story of the Irish Race,* 4th ed., (New York: The Devin-Adair Company, 1944) states:

The Great Famine, usually known as the famine of '47, really began in 1845, with the blighting and failure of the potato crop, the people's chief means of sustenance. The loss that year amounted to nine million pounds sterling. A worse failure occurred in '46. But by far the most traumatic was in '47, when suffering reached its climax. The terrible famine of '47 and '48 proved to be the most stunning blow that the Irish nation received in a century. It is calculated that about a million people died—either of direct starvation, or of the diseases introduced by the famine, and nearly another million fled to foreign lands between 1846 and 1850.

MacManus quotes Lord Broughan, speaking of Ireland's sufferings at the time: "They surpass anything on the pages of Thucydides—on the canvass of Poussin—in the dismal chant of Dante."

The Village's Natural Advantages

Fig. 1-1 *John Caldwell Bloomfield, one of three founders of the pottery. The pottery site was carved from his Castle Caldwell estate. (Allen Markley, LBIPP/Gary Parrott photo.)*

Under the shadow of the famine in 1849, John Caldwell Bloomfield (Figure 1-1) inherited the Castle Caldwell estate from his father, John Colpoys Bloomfield, of County Wicklow. In 1817 the elder Bloomfield had married Frances Arbella Caldwell, daughter of the Sixth Baron Caldwell. The Castle Caldwell estate encompassed the village of Belleek. Between 1841 and 1851, County Fermanagh lost 25 percent of its population through migration and starvation. According to a paper written by Bloomfield in 1884 to the Royal Irish Academy in Dublin, at the time he inherited the estate, he was concerned about the plight of the tenants, as the property was "quite run down." Fortunately, he was an amateur mineralogist, with a particular interest in ceramics. This background caused him to take more than passing notice of the unique, glistening white finish on the exterior walls of the thatched roofed homes in the area. Of course, he knew the coating was limestone, which still remains the common exterior surfacing in that area. Limestone, yes, but it was the rare sparkle that tugged at his mind. The source of the coating was said to be "naturally burnt lime." He reasoned that the "lime" was feldspar, which it proved to be, and it existed in large quantities on his estate!

Bloomfield was thus prompted to survey his lands to determine what minerals might be present, and how they might be utilized to offer employment. Though he may have held his own interest paramount, it cannot be disputed that, unlike many landlords of the time, he was not unmindful of the peril of his tenants. At one point, he even tried to establish a cement-making concern to provide employment.

Happily, his surveys revealed the presence of both feldspar and kaolin approximately five miles from what was to become the site of the pottery. Bloomfield vowed he would start a pottery in Belleek, whose name in Gaelic, *beal leice*, translates to "Flagstone Ford." The village was a natural choice, especially the part of the village known as Rose Isle. This small isle, one of Lough Erne's reputed 365 islands, provided the best opportunity to leash the power of River Erne, power to provide a mill race with sufficient flow to work a mill wheel capable of grinding the components used in the making of pottery into slip (liquid potter's clay).

Excitement must surely have attended his "find!" All the necessary ingredients to make pottery, with three exceptions, were present on the estate: feldspar, kaolin, flint, clay, shale, peat, power, and trainable labor. The missing components for success, capital, expertise, and coal to supplement the firing ability of turf, had to be secured, and in that order.

Callers at Castle Caldwell (Figure 1-2) took an interest in Bloomfield's project. Late in 1853 a doctor friend, Sir Charles Cameron of Dublin, sent samples of the Irish clay and feldspar to the Royal Porcelain Works, Worcester, England, to be tested. The English firm was then owned by partners, Kerr and Binns. W. H. Kerr, a native of County Tyrone only 20 miles from Belleek, had used Irish materials to produce a dessert service, "Midsummer Night's Dream," which Bloomfield had seen on display in Dublin in 1851.

Sir Charles, in his book *Reminiscences of Sir Charles Cameron, C.B.*, published by Hodges and Figgis in 1913, tells a slightly different version of the find.

In the '50's [1850s] I spent my Christmas holidays with the late Mr. John Caldwell Bloomfield, D.L., and his first wife at Castle Caldwell, on Lough Erne, County Fermanagh. One day when out shooting along with my host, we noticed a white patch of clay, and took a portion of it to the castle. I heated it to redness in the dining room fireplace, and on removing it from the fire, and allowing it to cool, I found that it remained quite white, which proved the absence of iron oxide. I brought a portion of it to Dublin, and gave it to Mr. Kerr, who had a porcelain shop in Capel Street in connection with the Royal Porcelain Works, Worcester. He sent it to the Works, and it was returned in the shape of a saucer which I have, at present, labeled first article made from Belleek clay. At that time the Reverend Joseph Galbraith, F.T.C.D., was Professor of Geology in Trinity College, and he doubted the existance of real china clay in the County Fermanagh, and addressed a letter to that effect to the Editor of 'Saunder's News Letter', a daily paper since extinct. I, of course, replied, and others joined in the discussion, which continued for many days, and the controversy was humorously referred to as the 'China War'. That I was right was, however, proved by a factory being started to work the clay.

Robert Williams Armstrong (Figure 1-3), an architect from London who had an abiding interest in ceramics, was working for Kerr at Worcester at the time of the tests. One report tells of a meeting which was said to have taken place between Bloomfield and Armstrong, both of whom, by chance, were visiting the same Dublin antique shop. They struck up a conversation concerning the tests, the making of pottery, and the need for capital to begin the venture. At Bloomfield's suggestion, Armstrong accompanied him to call on Bloomfield's friend, David McBirney, to discuss the possibilities and the need for capital. McBirney, owner of an emporium on Ashton Quay, was a Dublin merchant of considerable means.

Whether the sequence of events occurred in this manner cannot be verified. It is known that neither Bloomfield nor Armstrong was wealthy. (Bloomfield later claimed he lost 2000 pounds sterling in the venture.) In any event, McBirney expressed interest

Fig. 1-2 Castle Caldwell. This old photograph of the Bloomfield residence is not dated. (National Library of Ireland, Dublin.)

CASTLE CALDWELL. Co.DONEGAL. 1580. W.L.

Fig. 1-3 Robert Williams Armstrong, the pottery's first manager and art director was one of the three founders of the pottery. (Allen Markley, LBIPP/ Gary Parrott photo.)

and was persuaded to invest in the undertaking after traveling to Worcester with Armstrong. At Worcester, according to the Dublin Exhibition's Catalogue of 1865, McBirney was "wholeheartedly assisted by W. H. Kerr in his research on the commercial possibilities of the pottery." S. McCrum, in *The Belleek Pottery* (Belfast: *Ulster Museum Botanic Gardens*), states, "A number of trial pieces were submitted to him [to McBirney, from Kerr]. After a visit to Castle Caldwell, and a careful examination of the possible site and the deposits of raw materials, McBirney offered to supply the entire capital necessary for building the factory and starting and running the business, which was to trade as "McBirney and Company," with Armstrong as Art Director." Armstrong also served as the pottery's first manager.

The particular advantages of Belleek as the site for the pottery was later commented on in the *Dublin Builder,*

But it strikes the visitor with amazement to learn the extraordinary variety of ingredients and facilities which the favoured district affords for this manufacture. Not only is there almost unlimited water power, but there is found within a limited radius, not only the kaolin, flint and feldspar, which are essential ingredients of stone china and parian ware, but also the shale from which are constructed the fire clay saggers in which the ware is fired. The firing of kilns up to an advanced stage is effected with the peat, which is abundant in the neighborhood, leaving nothing to be imported but a modest quantity of coal, where with to complete the process.

The last major hurdle that remained was the absence of a railway station at Belleek, the nearest being twenty-three miles away. As Bloomfield saw it, "This [the lack of rail service] involved the question of ruin, or abandonment of the project." So Bloomfield pulled strings, lobbied hard, and practically paved the way single-handedly. Rail service came to Belleek.

Eventually the Belleek location offered splendid transportation opportunities for the marketing of the ware. Lower and Upper Lough Erne provided a water avenue to Enniskillen, with Belfast accessible by canal. Derry—and the whole world from its port—could be reached by rail. Rail to the east coast of Ireland tied Dublin and Dundalk to Belleek, and on the west coast, Ballyshannon, just six miles from the pottery, sat serenely near the shores of the Atlantic.

Improved transportation, available materials, and the key advantage of sober, God-loving, genuine, properly proud, and industrious people! Names like Flannigan, Cleary, Keown, McCauley, McGuire, and O'Shea are listed on today's roster of employees, and on the rolls of an old "hedge school" dating back more than 150 years. To generations of craftsmen Belleek has offered more than employment; it has offered, too, a way of life and the respected tradition of previous generations. Many were then, as they are now, farmers who tend their land and their stock, as well as their prized craft. Ireland's long late spring and summer evenings (sunset in June lingers until midnight) are particularly suitable to this change of pace for the craftsmen. The Fermanagh and Donegal farm is, basically, a family enterprise. Each family member has the privilege and responsibility of doing his or her share. Add *work* to the saying, "The family that plays together and prays together, stays together," and it aptly applies to Belleek.

Building the Pottery

With materials tested, the specific site selected, and capital invested, the time was at hand to commence building the pottery. Though there are no written records of construction, it is believed that Bloomfield utilized Armstrong's architectural talents in designing the structure.

The *Impartial Reporter* of November 25, 1858, stated,

On Thursday last [November 18th] the principal foundation stone was laid by Mrs. J. C. Bloomfield . . . [S]ome coins of the present year of her Majesty's reign, the *Impartial Reporter*, and *Fermanagh Farmer's Journal* of the day, together with a neatly engrossed document descriptive of the undertaking, were duly deposited in a thick glass bottle which fitted into a cavity cut for the purpose . . . at the northeast corner of the building.

The principal building, as well as the house occupied by the Armstrongs (Figure 1-4), was constructed of the finest materials. Bricks for building the kilns were made locally. Actually, Bloomfield was making bricks with his "C.C." designation before plans to go ahead with the pottery had been completed. Both firebrick and ornamental brick were produced at his Castle Caldwell estate. Limestone was quarried in the vicinity and cut by area stonemasons on the premises. The main structure is a testimonial to their skill: it is three stories, 56 feet in height, 160 feet in length, and 33 feet in width. Walls and staircases are made of the native stone. Today, traveling those same steps, thoughts come to mind of the artisans past and present whose feet have carved design and character into their stone surfaces. The original windows, though painted countless times during the past century, are still serviceable.

The Business Underway

The pottery opened with much of the interior construction yet to be completed. A carpenter was retained for several years just to build the large oak-paneled doors. They are works of art, as beautiful as they are durable.

What a grand and memorable day it must have been, when the large water wheel began its long journey, turning to power the machinery then used in the making of Belleek. Several years later, in 1864, the *Dublin Builder* offered this comment: "The visitor, with a mechanical turn of mind may inspect the [Belleek] water wheel worthy of attention. This admirably constructed piece of machinery is one of the last erected by Fairbairn. It is of the ventilating system and is of 100 horsepower."

The importance of the water wheel in those days cannot be overstated. It was the water wheel's job to drive the machinery used in earthenware production. There were pans for mixing the clay; presses; and machines for making cups, mugs, plate molds, and thrown pieces. All this heavy machinery was pressed into work by the stroke of the wheel. Food for thought: Though the world has become more mechanized in each decade during the past century, the Belleek Pottery, in its change from the making of

Fig. 1-4 Historic photograph of pottery with bottle kilns in operation. The Armstrong residence is seen in front of the main building to the right. (Pottery Photographic Library.)

earthenware to the exclusive production of Parian china, has become more reliant on the skill of the craftsman. Today only two types of power-driven machines are used at the pottery, the slip mixing cylinders and the vibro energy mill. Every other step in production reflects the caress of the craftsman.

The ordinary domestic ware of early production was of high quality and extreme beauty. Pestles, mortars, washstands (Figure 1-5), hospital pans, floor tiles, telegraph insulators, and tableware are representative of the broad scope of diversification. Earthenware cups and mugs were particularly difficult to fashion, as they had to be turned on a lathe to sculpt the exterior and shaped on the inside by a machine called a jolley.

What of Bloomfield and his relationship to the pottery during the beginning years? Tommy Campbell, former manager of the pottery and a devotee of its history, told me in 1976 that the evidence he had seen or heard of indicating that Bloomfield was directly

Fig. 1-5 D1040-I, Wash Basin, Slop Bowl, and Wooden Stand; 32⅝" H. (Ulster Museum, Belfast.)

involved in the day-to-day affairs of the pottery was the first indenture, which was signed by Bloomfield, Armstrong, and McBirney. In those days it was common practice in Europe to indenture boys and girls to the trades for five years, for which time they were bound to remain. The second indenture has not been located. But the third indenture is in hand, and it is not signed by Bloomfield.

John J. Treacy, author of *The Interacting Influences of Belleek Pottery and its Environment*, refers to McBirney and Armstrong as joint owners of the pottery. In any event, it seems apparent that Bloomfield's interest was, at best, silent, just as it is reasonable to assume that Armstrong, the architect with pottery experience gained through his association with Kerr, influenced the pottery's basic structural design. It may even be conjectured,

This Indenture made the *First* day of *October* in the year of our Lord one thousand eight hundred and *twenty two* BETWEEN *James Slevin* of *Rathmore* in the Parish of *Belleek* in the County of *Fermanagh* an Infant of the age of years (hereinafter called the said Apprentice) of the first part *James Slevin* of *Rathmore Belleek* aforesaid *Father* of the said *Apprentice* of the second part, and DAVID McBIRNEY, and ROBERT WILLIAMS ARMSTRONG, of Belleek, in the said County of Fermanagh, Potters and Co-partners (hereinafter called the said Masters) of the third part WITNESSETH that the said *Apprentice* of *his* own free will and with the consent of the said *James Slevin his Father* Doth by these Presents put place and bind *himself* Apprentice unto the said DAVID McBIRNEY and ROBERT WILLIAMS ARMSTRONG, to learn that branch of a Potter's art or business called *Presser and Mould Maker* and them to serve after the manner of an Apprentice from the *First* day of *October 1872* for the term of *Four* years (the usual holidays excepted) from thence next ensuing, and fully to be complete and ended, during all which term the said Apprentice shall and will faithfully honestly and diligently serve and obey said Masters as a good and faithful Apprentice ought to do And the said Masters do hereby covenant for themselves their executors and administrators to and with the said *Apprentice and his Father* *his* executors and administrators that they the said Masters shall and will teach and instruct the said Apprentice or cause to be taught and instructed in the said branch of the Potter's art or business called *Presser and Mould Maker* in the best manner they can during the said term And also shall and will find the said Apprentice fair and reasonable work during the said term And also shall and will pay the said Apprentice for said work and services during the said term (the usual holidays excepted) such wages as are hereinafter mentioned, that is to say

At the rate of *6/—* per week for the first six months from this date
At the rate of *6/—* for the remaining six months of the first year of said Apprenticeship
At the rate of *8/—* per week for the second year „ „ „
At the rate of *10/—* per week for the third year „ „ „
At the rate of *11/—* per week for the fourth year *Twelve Shillings* „ „
And the rate of *12/—* per week for the fifth year „ „

But should the said Masters consider it right or fitting to pay the said Apprentice on the piece-work principle then it shall be at the following rates or proportion of a journeyman's wages viz.—For all work done during the first year of the said Apprenticeship *one fourth* journeyman's wages For all work done during the second year *one third* said rates or wages For the work done during the third year *one half* said rates For the work done during the fourth year *three fourths* said rates And for the fifth year said rates and wages

And the said *Apprentice and his Father* and do hereby severally covenant and agree with and to the said Masters their executors and administrators that the said Apprentice shall during the said term honestly and faithfully serve *his* said Masters and well and truly perform the Conditions and Agreements herein contained on the part of the said Apprentice to be done and performed The said Masters shall be at liberty to put an end to and determine this Indenture and to cease to teach or instruct the said Apprentice during all or any part of the then residue of the said term And further that the said Masters shall not be liable or called upon to pay any wages to the said Apprentice should the Works be stopped abandoned or ceased to be carried on by the said Masters their executors and administrators or should the said Apprentice wilfully neglect said Master's work or refuse to faithfully and fully carry out and perform said Masters' instructions.

In witness whereof the said parties have hereunto set their hands and seals the day and year first above written.

Signed Sealed and delivered by the above named *Apprentice*
and *his Father*
in the presence
of *James Aiken*

James Slevin
James X Slevin his mark
D. McBirney &
Robt W Armstrong.

with some foundation in fact, that he was the sole architect. Actually, Armstrong continued to practice his profession while manager of the pottery. The Manor House in Enniskillen, the Presbyterian Church in Ballyshannon, and his son-in-law's house on Belleek Island are examples of his architectural skill. Armstrong did diligently research the possibilities of the area, and the design of the pottery indicates a definite understanding of ceramic production, coupled with architectural skills. For example, heavy machinery was housed quite apart from the manufacturing section, thus minimizing the effects of vibration. The drying areas and mold rooms also reflect a depth of knowledge in their design and placement.

Armstrong, as the pottery's first manager, looked to his experience in England to attract the talent needed to start production. It was not an easy task! Potters of the period were almost prisoners of their employers, because of the grave concern that if the employee would leave, the secrets of the pottery would depart with him "packed" in his knowledge of his trade. At Belleek, skilled potters would be required to fashion the willing hands and capable minds of the Irish workers into those of craftsmen. Armstrong's choice for this job was excellent. William Bromley, a foreman at Goss' Stoke-on-

Fig. 1-6 D1127-I, *Bust of Charles Dickens; 18" H. William Gallimore, the pottery's first chief modeler, designed this exquisite piece. (Donald & Victoria Quinn Collection. Chris T. Vleisides photo.)*

Trent Pottery, and William Gallimore, its chief modeler, were influenced to come to Belleek. Additional potters, numbering perhaps twelve, were recruited from Stoke-on-Trent and Worcester.

Bromley was appointed manager of the Parian section, and Gallimore was named chief modeler. Perhaps the most famous of Gallimore's designs, which are reported to have numbered in the hundreds, is D1127-I, Bust of Charles Dickens (Figure 1-6). Bromley returned to his former position with W. H. Goss in 1866.

McBirney built two housing areas in the village for employees; many of these homes still stand. English Row, now Rathmore Terrace, is of typically English two-story, red brick design, and Irish Row is of traditional Irish design, featuring semi-detached houses with whitewashed walls.

Early Designers and Designs

Very few of the English potters remained at Belleek permanently; most either returned to England or eventually emigrated to the United States to continue their trade at such American potteries as Ceramic Art Company (Lenox), Ott and Brewer, and Willets. A notable exception was William Henshall, who came from Stoke-on-Trent to Ireland and Belleek in 1865 to become manager of Basket and Flower Making. He is the craftsman credited with the introduction of Belleek's world famous basketwork (Figure 1-7). His name designates the lovely baskets that display the flowing, flowered rims. These include the delightful small #572, Henshall basket, with the unique rectangular base, and the medium D120, Henshall basket, graced by the applied handle. Henshall lived and died in Belleek, leaving not only the making of baskets but also the gorgeous Belleek flowers (Figure 1-8) as a timeless legacy. Rose Montgomery, née Henshall, was wed to a Belleek boy, and is apparently the only descendant of the English potters who married locally.

From the very beginning, McBirney and Armstrong wished to make porcelain, not only to utilize to the full the mineral wealth around the pottery but also to give full scope to the craftsmanship and skill now being developed by them within the pottery. Further-more, Armstrong knew that if the company were to achieve an international reputation and status for its products it could only be through the medium of porcelain. Their early attempts at the manufacture of porcelain failed, however, and it was not until 1863, after six years of experimentation, that a small amount of Parian was produced.

Fig. 1-7 Early craftsman skillfully creates one of Belleek's world-famous baskets. (Pottery Photographic Library.)

Fig. 1-8 *Craftsman at work, during the pottery's embryonic years, applying the talent taught by William Henshall to create Belleek's beautiful flowers. (Pottery Photographic Library.)*

This was by no means the end of Parian experimentation and trials, which are recorded throughout Armstrong's diaries. One very interesting example from the diaries appears in a March 22, 1864, entry: "For Parian Trials—For the coming exhibition in Dublin I consider the best compound will be found as follows [formula described]. The above composition, being very plastic and workable, might do to produce, *"Ivory tinted china"* like *the Worcester* and would take well with gold line i.e. Tea Pot Stands."

Even though the knowledge and skill to create Parian had been gained, earthenware remained the principal product at Belleek until 1920. "Of fifty-three indentures of apprenticeship, in the possession of the present company, out of 100 issued between 1865 and 1900 only six related to Parian making. All the others were for earthenware" (Campbell, 1957). According to Williams (1975), "Seventy workers were employed in 1865, increasing to 180 in 1869. Thirty of the aforementioned seventy were boys and girls, and twenty-seven of the latter 180 were hired from abroad." The pottery ceased earthenware production entirely in 1946 with the introduction of new kilns which the designer claimed would reach and hold an even temperature of 1150°C.

Through Armstrong's influence, or perhaps that of his wife, Annie Langley Nairn (Figure 1-9), whom he married in 1848, the subjects for much of the pottery's ware were devised. Mrs. Armstrong was an accomplished watercolorist who painted marine and botanic subjects, as well as landscapes. Armstrong definitely designed the artichoke "family" of Parian, and it is believed that he also created D758-D777, the Thorn Pattern. "Designed by Robert Williams Armstrong" does appear at the bottom of the registered designs of D645-D668, Echinus Tea Ware. A plate in this pattern used for Queen Victoria's tea and breakfast service, register number 221217, was the first design registered by Belleek. The date was 5 September 1868. (Design registration marks are discussed in Chapter 5. Examples of designs submitted by Belleek and given registration approval are shown in Figures 5-3 and 5-4.) McCrum states:

Mrs. Armstrong exhibited at the Royal Hibernian Academy from 1844–1847. She designed much early ornamental porcelain, with marine subjects, such as sea-weeds, shells, sea urchins, rock work and corals. Again, attribution is difficult. It is impossible to say how far her work, [that of her husband], and Gallimore's overlapped, although she has always been given credit for the entire production in this field of design. An important aspect of the treatment of animals, plants, and marine and botanical subjects, was the precision and accuracy of their modeling. This feature is generally said to be due mainly to Mrs. Armstrong's influence, although, if what is suggested about Armstrong is correct, he may have had some importance in this. Besides, it is not unlikely that they influenced each other. The effectiveness of such modeling . . . in giving a sense of texture and form, was also heavily dependent on the use of dark, cream coloured, smooth, iridescent glaze, and the varying thicknesses of the bodies themselves.

The Armstrongs lived in a two story limestone house, ''Melrose,'' standing only steps south of the pottery's main entrance, as shown in Figure 1-4, being the white building to right of entrance. This building, in later years used as a repository for old molds, remained until the mid 1980s when it was damaged during construction work. A decision was then made to completely remove the structure.

The pottery's earthenware decorations were applied by transfer printing (Figure 1-10). Volume and variety required the company to have its own full-time staff engravers. The quality of the printing of the applied designs was good, even on common ware (Figure 1-11), with few missing sections or improper joining of design run. Smearing of design features was negligible. A wide range of designs was used, basically featuring flowers, birds, butterflies, and fish. Predominant colors, one to each piece, were brown, black, and green. Blue and dark red were used more sparingly. Pieces with handpainted decoration, overglazed, were also produced in multi-colors (Figure 1-12). The latter, it is believed, were representative of the fervent wishes of McBirney and Armstrong that the pottery gain international acclaim.

In referring to the pottery's display at the Dublin International Exposition of 1865, the *Art Journal* of July 1865, observed, ''This is a promising collection of earthenware, the issue of a factory on Loch Erne.'' It was at the Dublin Exposition that Belleek won its first gold medal. In December, 1865, the *Art Journal* reported an award to the pottery, ''For productions that give good promise of future excellence.'' Prior to this acclaim, McBirney and Armstrong were exporting pieces to the United States, Canada, and

Fig. 1-9 Annie Langley Nairn, wife of Robert Williams Armstrong, an accomplished artist who was influential in the design of many of the pottery's marine subjects. (Allen Markley, LBIPP/Gary Parrott photo.)

Fig. 1-10 Printing transfer designs from engraved copper plate. (Pottery Photographic Library.)

Fig. 1-11 D915-II, Cover Dish, "Ulster" pattern, earthenware. (Lauresa Stillwell Collection.) D887-I, Plate 10", earthenware. (Berdell L. Dickinson Collection. Berdell L. Dickinson photo.)

Australia, not to mention the "large quantities of goods daily to different towns in England and Ireland, including London."

By 1869 the pottery's Parian creations warranted an article in the *Art Journal* which observed, referring to the 1865 exhibition, "They then furnished very inconclusive signs of the perfection to which they have since advanced." Orders of tremendous prestige were being received from Queen Victoria, the Prince of Wales, Prince Tech, the Duke of Abercorn, and the Earls of Arran, Erne, and Enniskillen, as well as other nobility. The small earthenware factory had been touched by royalty! Since 1869, Belleek's earned reputation as creator of artistic ware for the discerning buyer and collector has remained international in dimension.

Erin was awakening from slumbers imposed by centuries of conquest and oppression and by lack of high-temperature-producing fuels and ore-bearing minerals. Now Parian of aesthetic value, in addition to that of utilitarian importance, was being produced. Parian in perfection is exemplified by the statue which commemorates Ireland's embryonic entry into the world of industry. Appropriately titled, "Erin Awakening from Her Slumbers," or simply, D1, Figure of Erin, the piece is 17½ inches tall and 11½ inches at the widest point of the base, which represents the flagstone ford of the River Erne's falls at Belleek. This lovely figure of a colleen, designed by William Boyden Kirk (1824–1900), stands in strap sandals, the back of her gown flowing over an Irish harp embossed with Celtic designs. Shamrocks lace her hair, and her fingers gently remove the drape covering an urn on which the words "Belleek Pottery" are inscribed. The drape, harp, her belt, shamrocks, and the waves lapping at the flagstone are glazed. The remainder of the piece is unglazed. In addition to the one described above, statues of Erin may also be found which include a glazed Celtic cross resting on its side, below and slightly behind the urn (Figure 1-13). The largest statue produced to date, "Prisoner of Love," which is approximately 26 inches tall, was also introduced in the First Mark Period (Figure 1-14).

Fig. 1-12 D1034-I, Rathmore Ewer, painted, 13½" H., earthenware. D950-I, Rathmore Basin, painted, 15½" D., earthenware. D940-I, Chamber, painted, 5¾" H., earthenware. D1047-I, Candlestick, tall, painted, 8⅛" H., earthenware. (Donald & Victoria Quinn Collection. Chris T. Vleisides photo.)

The *Art Journal* of 1870 noted the workmanship, design, and skill by which the dimensions of the original statue by Fontana had been reduced. Attention was called to the quality of material with its marble-like appearance. No minor feat! The clay experienced, at the least, sixteen percent shrinkage in biscuit kiln firing. All parts (many of which had to be molded separately and joined to form the whole before firing) must share a common percentage of shrinkage. Thus, a finger or toe would make the piece unacceptable if it experienced more or less shrinkage than the torso or base. Quite a critical demand, and another testimonial to the quality of the materials and the skill of the craftsmen!

Regardless of costs or complexity, the pottery remained committed to the highest of artistic principles. The Belleek statue "parade" began, joined by the Belgian Hawkers, Blessed Virgin, Sacred Heart, Affection, Meditation, Basket Carrying Boy and Girl, Cavalier, Roundhead, Crouching Venus, and others. Busts included Clytie, Joy, Sorrow, Dickens, Parnell, Shakespeare, Wesley, and Queen of the Hops. Nacreous glaze was used to accentuate highlights on many of these pieces.

Fortunately, Belleek secured the nacreous glaze patent of a Frenchman, J. J. H. Brianchon. The time of this acquisition cannot be accurately ascertained. However, Brianchon's patent was granted in England on July 8, 1857. McCrum states: "Although Belleek's porcelain was of high quality, its surface in the biscuit-fired (unglazed) state was granular and became easily dirtied, two problems which were generally found in manufacturing Parian, and which are sources of contemporary complaint about the material. To cover these defects, Staffordshire manufacturers had used a lead glaze, but this tended to follow the unevenness of the granulation." Brianchon's glaze offered a smooth surface, not susceptible to hairline cracking, and dust-resistant. McCrum continues, "The glaze was made by melting thirty parts of resin, then stirring in ten parts of bismuth nitrate, followed by forty-five parts of lavender oil added. Lustres of different tints could be produced by using different metallic nitrates."

Armstrong, speaking to the Belfast Naturalists' Field Club in 1870, stressed the antiquity and high distinction of ceramic ware using, as his evidence, quotes from

oriental and classical material, as well as the Bible. Belleek Parian, he claimed, was "a real porcelain, in contradistinction to the phosphate of lime, or 'bone' body used in England."

In January 1870, D. McBirney and Company, Proprietors, produced price scales listing white and ivory china vitrified and semi-vitrified goods. Dinner pieces of semi-vitrified body with ordinary gilding on knobs and handles included forty-four standard items, in sixteen separate price levels, ranging in cost from five pence to two shillings for a 10-inch dinner plate. Ungilded pieces of the same variety were presented in eight price

OPPOSITE PAGE:
Fig. 1-13 D1-I, Figure of Erin, 17½" H. William Boyden Kirk designed this beautiful figure of a colleen. (Marie Bain Collection. Mark Donovan photo.)

Fig. 1-14 D18-I, Prisoner of Love, 25½" H. The largest statue crafted in the history of the pottery. (Del E. Domke Collection. Hiroko Saita photo.)

structures, six of which also provided the increased price for gilding. Dinner plates of 10-inch dimension, not gilded, spanned a rate range from two pence to four and one-half pence. A dinner service for twelve cost from fifty shillings and five pence to 324 shillings and six pence, a dinner service for eighteen cost sixty-four shillings and three pence to 430 shillings, and a twenty-four person dinner service cost from eighty-eight shillings and one pence to 575 shillings and six pence. To put these prices in perspective: The average weekly wage paid factory workers in Ireland and England in those days was fifteen to eighteen shillings, or about $3.75 to $4.50 (U.S. dollars). The pound sterling was made up of twenty shillings, and each shilling equaled twelve pence. Thus, one pound sterling equaled about five U.S. dollars.

The variety of popular pieces included 10-inch dinner plates; salad plates (no measurements given); 8-inch pie plates; 6- and 7-inch muffin plates; 12-, 18-, 20-, and 22-inch gravy dishes; flat dishes ranging from 9 to 22 inches; pie dishes from 9 to 12 inches; 8- and 11-inch soup tureens and stands; 10-inch soup ladles; sauce tureens and stands; sauce ladles; 8-, 9-, and 10-inch covered dishes; 10-inch oval root dishes, same with two or with three compartments; 12-inch round root dishes, same with two or with three compartments; 10-inch steak dishes; salad bowls; cheese stands; pickle dishes; sauce boats; sauce stands; 10-inch hot water plates; and two sizes of broth bowls with stands.

Additional, or occasional pieces, were offered as follows: fish drainers, pearl white, same price as the dishes they fit. Drainers for covered dishes, half price of the covered dish. Drainers with divisions cost extra. Round dishes, one size higher than price of oval dishes. Pie dishes, extra deep, price and a half. Round or deep baking dishes, one size higher, and round and deep baking dishes, two sizes higher.

Porcelain was featured by Belleek for the first time at the Dublin Exposition of 1872. The display was the largest in the Irish and English industrial areas of the Exposition. Among the more prestigious pieces, the catalog listed nine Parian statues and busts, ice buckets, compotes, centerpieces, Pope's tiara cheese covers, and D482, Chinese Tea Urn, large size (Figure 1-15). In 1880 the pottery was awarded its second gold medal, this time at the Melbourne International Exposition. Ware with Sheffield silver mountings was shown for the first time at the Cork International Exposition of 1883.

Without doubt the most gifted painter in the pottery's history was Eugene Sheerin (1855–1915). Sheerin grew up in a small whitewashed cottage in Drumbinnion, County Tyrone. Partially paralyzed at the age of four, he was unable to attend school. Mairead Reynolds (née Dunlevy), Assistant Keeper, National Museum of Ireland, writing in *The Clogher Record*, 1980 states:

> Such a handicap might be expected to have restricted his education and opportunities were it not for the interest and determination of his mother and family. His mother taught Eugene to write and draw using Vere Foster's copy-books. . . . His talent was noticed and he was encouraged to enter works in the Annual Exhibition of Drawings in Belfast.

A certificate of merit was awarded to him at that exhibition, and his talent came to the attention of Robert Williams Armstrong. Armstrong gave him a position in the Painting and Decorating Department, where his instruction in painting on porcelain began on May 2, 1878. Sheerin's nephew, Thomas McCallen, an apprentice in the Parian Casting Department, pushed Eugene to and from work each day in his bath-chair.

Reynolds continues,

> At age twenty-two Eugene was about twice as old as the other apprentices. . . . [He] did the usual job-lot work such as painting shamrocks. . . . [E]ncouraged by Armstrong his enthusiasm for creative work and his painting skill developed. . . . His disappointment must have been great when he found that due to the intense cold in the large stone-built factory, he could not work during the winter. . . . [D]uring 1879–1880, he was singled out to work on wall placques. The subjects which he painted varied widely. . . . From October 1880 to July 1881 Eugene stayed with his brother, Joseph, in Dublin. They both attended the Dublin Metropolitan School of Art. Eugene took classes

in free-hand, perspective and modelling and he won a prize at the end of his course. . . . [H]e entered paintings and painted placques (Figure 1-16), in the Exhibition of Irish Arts and Manufactures in Dublin, 1882. The painted placques sold for about 16 pence each. He returned to the school for extra tuition in the winter of 1884–1885. Formal training developed his technique of miniature painting.

Perhaps the most famous work of Sheerin's Belleek art legacy is the lovely Ring Handle Ivory service, depicting a different prominent Irish landscape scene on each piece—be it the small, D830, Egg Cup, or the sizeable, D829, Covered Muffin Dish. Figure 1-17 shows examples from an exquisite service of this type attributed to him. Sheerin often signed or initialed his work, but it appears this was not a steadfast rule. It is my belief that his work was no longer signed after he returned to the pottery. His exceptional talent was apparently lost to Belleek with the reduction in employment following the sale of the pottery in 1884. At that time the services of all engravers, decorative designers and fine painters was ended. I should note that another version of

Fig. 1-15 D482-I, Chinese Tea Urn, large size, painted, 14″ H. (Marie Bain Collection. Mark Donovan photo.)

his leaving the pottery attributes it to the premature death of his nephew, which deeply affected him. The exact time of his return to pottery employment is uncertain. He was definitely back in service by 1893 and remained until late 1895, when he was offered the opportunity to work at home. On January 5, 1896, Sheerin wrote a letter to management wherein it was apparent that he did not have suitable facilities at home to allow him to accept the Pottery's offer.

The Founders Pass Away

Ironically, during the pottery's height of success and international acclaim, McBirney passed away in October 1882 at age seventy-eight. The partnership agreement between McBirney and Armstrong had never been put in written form. McBirney's heirs would not recognize Armstrong's rights of partnership and ordered the property to be sold.

Fig. 1-16 D1557-I, Round Wall Plaque, hand-painted, 14³/₁₆″ D. Titled "Innocence" by the artist, Eugene Sheerin, this is an excellent example of his work. (Donald & Victoria Quinn Collection. Chris T. Vleisides photo.)

Fig. 1-17 Ring Handle Ivory Tea Ware (Belleek Shape). Hand-painted in a variety of Irish scenes, this ware is attributed to the talent of Eugene Sheerin. (Berdell L. Dickinson Collection. Berdell L. Dickinson photo.)

Certainly Armstrong must have resisted this decision by McBirney's heirs. The sequence of events which followed comprise one of the most crucial periods in the history of the pottery.

In the February 21, 1883, issue, the *Dublin Telegraph* commented,

It is surely not true that the potteries at Belleek are to be abandoned! A Belfast paper states that since the death of the founder of the works the trade has fallen off, in consequence of the apathy of the present owner [McBirney's son, Robert, who had emigrated to Charleston, South Carolina], who resides in America, to such a degree as to make the closing of the potteries only a matter of a few months. The abandonment of the industry supplied by the manufacture of this beautiful ware, which has attained for itself a world-wide fame, would be simply a national disgrace, and we trust the people of Fermanagh and of Ulster generally will not suffer one of the few productions peculiar to Ireland to fall off. If Ulster does not take the matter up, then we think the forthcoming Exhibition in Cork should not open without some effort being made by the promoters to raise as much capital as would float the potteries as a Limited Company. Mr. J. G. V. Porter is in season and out of season holding forth on the industrial resources of Ireland and the necessity for drainage. Could he not emerge from Lisbellaw and do something in the matter of Belleek? Whoever does it, something ought to be done, and the sooner the better.

In his January 2, 1884 issue of *Ireland's Gazette, Loyal and National,* J. G. V. Porter did try to help. On January 4, 1884, Porter wrote as follows,

To Robert Armstrong, Esq., C.E., Dear Sir, You have several times spoken to me about the bad prospects of your China Factory, which my family have tried to help from its beginning. It is not easy now for any man outside to be of use when its part owner, with you, is in United States, and of course in legal possession; but I have taken advantage of a letter in the morning post to add a few notes. You will see both in *Ireland's Gazette* of January 2nd, now sent; and if on that groundwork you will write further to me I will publish your letter in the next *Gazette*. I could not write further without perhaps harm, but you can write fully. Yours faithfully, J. G. V. Porter.

On January 27, 1884, Robert Williams Armstrong died at his home on the pottery grounds at age fifty-nine. His tombstone, in the Church of Ireland Graveyard at Belleek, features a broken column, formerly placed by him on the grave of one of his children who had previously passed away. The marker also designates the resting place of his wife and three of his children. In recent years a copper tablet was erected at the grave site by Tommy Campbell. The tablet carries the following inscription written by Jim Flanagan who has worked at the pottery since 1953:

Fig. 1-18 Mrs. Maude Cassidy, great-granddaughter of Robert Williams and Annie Nairn Armstrong, visits with the author at the pottery. (Allen Markley, LBIPP/Gary Parrott photo.)

> Here lies Robert Williams Armstrong C. Engineer,
> Architect, Inventor, and Ceramic Historian.
> Through his zeal and endeavor the name Belleek
> is renowned throughout the world.
> The people of the locality owe much to this great man.
>
> The first manager of Belleek Pottery.
> Born London 1824 of Co. Longford parents. Died 1884.

It is said that one of Armstrong's sons, David, emigrated to Australia. This could account for a fact I mentioned in the first edition of this book:

A particularly exciting revelation occurred during the final weeks of writing this manuscript when I received, through the splendid efforts of Miss Janette Thompson, Museum of Applied Arts and Sciences, Sydney, Australia, copies of eight diaries written by Robert Williams Armstrong during the pottery's important early years of 1862–1881, in which he recorded countless Parian, earthenware, caneware and china recipes, and the results of trials of slips, bodies, glazes and lustres.

In the late summer of 1992, while I was at the pottery working on this present edition of my book, it was my pleasure to meet Mrs. Maude Cassidy, great-grand-daughter of Robert Williams Armstrong and Annie Langley Nairn Armstrong (Figure 1-18). Mrs. Cassidy had learned that I was at the pottery, and she came over from a neighboring county to meet me. My pleasure was multiplied by the fact that she brought

Fig. 1-19 *Katherine Cecelia Armstrong, daughter of Robert Williams and Annie Nairn Armstrong. (Allen Markley, LBIPP/Gary Parrott photo.)*

photographs of her great-grandmother Armstrong (Figure 1-9) and of her grandmother, Robert and Annie's daughter, Katherine Cecelia (Figure 1-19).

The last of the three original founders of the pottery, John Caldwell Bloomfield, died in Enniskillen, County Fermanagh, in 1897. He is buried on the Castle Caldwell estate.

In spite of the finding of Armstrong's diaries, one of the mysteries that has permeated the years, defying answer, is the absence of early pottery records, such as records of design, design approval, and of the quantities of various ware produced. There is no doubt that records were kept. The founders of the pottery, it is evident, were sticklers for detail, just as their contemporary counterparts are. Molds were exceedingly well kept, and properly classified. The molds of Erin, of which there were twenty separate and distinct molds, serve as an example. Each mold was labeled and carefully placed in the old mold store. The practice of explicit and detailed marking of molds ceased in 1884, and those made after that time were not as scrupulously identified. But what of the pottery's records? Some speculate they may have been Armstrong's sole tangible "memento," beyond the above-mentioned diaries, of his investment of heart and talent. Perhaps an overzealous "spring cleaning" took place, and the priceless records gave way to something far less important. Should they turn up someday, no doubt they would be material for a new book on Belleek. Unquestionably, they would be a splendid addition to the pottery's scant annals of its early, and especially important, formulative years.

On February 28, 1884, the following notice appeared in *The Fermanagh Times:*

LANDED ESTATES COURT TITLE
Valuable Fee-Simple Estate
in The
County Of Farmanagh
being part of the Estate of
David M'Birney, Esq., J. P., Deceased
To Be Sold By Public Auction
in Two Lots,
At The Auction Rooms of Messrs. Bennet & Son,
No. 6 Ormond Quay,
in the City of Dublin,
on
THURSDAY, The 28th Day of February, 1884
At the Hour of One O'Clock, P.M.

LOT 1.—Part of the Lands of Finner, containing 95a or 18½p, statute measure, or thereabouts, situate in the Barony of Lurg, and County of Fermanagh; held in Fee-simple, under Landed Estates Court conveyance, dated the 26th day of November, 1878, subject to £150 per annum, portion of the annual rent charge of £230. 15s.5d, terminating on the death of the survivor of three lives, now aged respectively 61, 59 and 51 years, as set forth in the conditions of Sale, in indemnification of all other lands liable thereto, producing the gross annual rent of £306.5s.4d, subject to said sum of £150 per annum. The Government Valuation of this Lot is £339.10s. per annum.

LOT 2.—The Lands of Rathmore, Including White Island, containing 74a and 15p, statute measure, or thereabouts, situate in the Barony of Lurg, and County of Farmanagh, held in Fee-simple, subject to £80.15s.3d. per annum, portion of the annual rent charge or sum of £230.15s.4d, for certain lives terminating as above stated, and producing the gross annual rent of £237.1s is, subject to said sum of £80.15s.3d. The Government Valuation of this Lot is £445.5s per annum.

Private Proposals for the purchase of both or either of the foregoing Lots will be received by Messrs. Michael Larkin and Co., Solicitors, having Carriage of the Sale, up to the 23rd day of February, 1884:

DESCRIPTIVE PARTICULARS.
There is a Railway Station on the property at Belleek, on the Enniskillen and Bundoran Railway, which intersects it, also water carriage to Belfast and Limerick by the Ulster and Shannon Canals. The water power at Belleek is very extensive. There is excellent fishing in the district and the lands are situate in one of the most beautiful localities in Ireland. The well-known and successful China and Pottery Works of Belleek are situated on this property. The tenants are respectable, and pay their rents punctually, and a great number of them have valuable interests in their holdings, and the estate is one capable of considerable development.

CHAPTER TWO

THE MIDDLE YEARS

CHANGE AND SUCCESS

New Owners, Managers, and Modelers

The *Donegal Independent* reported on May 3, 1884, that a meeting was held in the Townhall, Ballyshannon, of those interested in the purchase and reopening of the Belleek Potteries. Mr. Robert Sweeny, Chairman Town Commission, Ballyshannon, rendered an account of his stewardship, having been deputed at a previous meeting.

Mr. Sweeny, representing the interested local group of potential investors, had proceeded to Dublin to negotiate with Mr. Robert Gardiner, J. P., Administrator of the estate of the late David McBirney, who represented Mr. Robert McBirney, residing at Charleston, South Carolina, United States, residuary legate of David McBirney.

The amount the investors were prepared to pay for the property, 4,500 pounds sterling, was offered, and the bargain was closed with Sweeny paying a deposit and obtaining a draft agreement. He reported further as follows:

> For this 4,500 pounds we get works leased for 999 years from 1858, subject to 50 pounds sterling rent; the machinery, the two water rights, and all the plants, moulds, models and engravings, the rights of fishing from the plot of ground known as Feely Stephen's mill and the right of water way—in fact everything but the book debts and stock. As to certain patents claimed by Mrs. Armstrong's representatives, we of course do not get them. We get possession of the works on June 1.

The share list was then opened at the meeting and 8,000 shares, at one pound sterling per share, were subscribed, "a number of which were by operatives of the factory."

The new venture was to trade as "The Belleek Pottery Works Company (Limited)," and its prospectus for an issue of 25,000 pounds sterling was advertised in the *Donegal Independent* on May 24, 1884. Among the assets noted in the prospectus, one is of particular interest; "The extensive Buildings designed by the late Robert Armstrong, C. E., and erected under his personal supervision, at a cost exceeding 10,000 pounds sterling have been added to each succeeding year to meet the growing requirements of the trade and they are in a thorough state of repair." The prospectus listed a number of advantages that the directors of the new company were confident would insure its success. Two should be mentioned: "The Cheap Rate at which the entire Plant and Machinery, Manager's Residence, Garden, Right of Fishing, etc., have been secured—the price paid (4,500 pounds sterling) being less than one-tenth of their actual cost," and

"The Reputation already secured for the Belleek Pottery—the demand for which has always been far in advance of the supply." Finally, the document stated that none of the directors would receive any renumeration until "the Company shall have out of Profits paid a Dividend of at least 5 percent to the Shareholders, and then it will be for the Shareholders themselves to decide whether any, and if so what renumeration, shall be paid to the Directors, or any of them."

Also, in May 1884, *Ireland's Gazette* called attention to the purchase, wished the new owners success, and observed, "Their sale now, after 25 years trial, at one-tenth of their original cost, and with all their acquired name and prestige, can be regarded from two points of view. But many prosperous enterprises are built on the ruins of their original shareholders or founders." Later, in the same month, the same publication reported an interlocutory injunction had been applied for on behalf of the plantiff, Mrs. Armstrong, to restrain the defendant, administrator Robert Gardiner, from proceeding with the sale. "The Vice-Chancellor, after hearing the voluminous affidavits filed on both sides, directed the case stand for a week, to allow the plantiff and the defendant to come to some arrangement with regard to getting a correct valuation of the premises, the plant and the machinery."

On July 3, 1884, the *Daily Express,* reporting on the case of *Armstrong v. Gardiner,* advised: "The terms of a consent had been drawn up, but there was a disagreement as to the costs which the plantiff required defendant to pay." The defendant waived his objection to pay the plantiff's cost of "250 pounds sterling," as well as, "release her from a bill of exchange for 200 pounds," incurred by the late Robert Armstrong.

Ireland's Gazette announced the formal opening of the pottery (Figure 2-1), on September 15, 1884 under its new ownership, commenting,

This company has got all the substantial Buildings and Machinery, that cost Messrs. M'Birney and Armstrong 40,000 pounds, well laid out, for above trifle, besides all the prestige acquired by

Fig. 2-1 *View of pottery and village prior to 1892. (National Library of Ireland, Dublin.)*

the last Mr. Robert Armstrong's artistic skill, and all the valuable experience learnt, and workmen taught and trained, in a quite new enterprise; so we can see good reason to hope that Mr. Sweeny's Company, making prudent use both of prestige and experience, will be a commercial success.

The first general meeting of the new company on November 7, 1884, advised the shareholders that the property had finally been acquired in August, at which time the company also

succeeded in purchasing the entire stock in trade, including the green wares and finished stock, at a figure less than one fourth of the original cost of production. By this we not only effected a considerable savings to your company, but also we were able to send out without delay orders which we had already received from the old customers of the firm. Being convinced that above everything else, the future success of the works must depend on a competent manager, we made the appointment to that office the object of our chief concern. And of the numerous applications which came in reply to our advertisement we made selection, after careful scrutiny, of Mr. Poole, a gentleman whose high recommendations and whose great and varied experience in the Stafford-shire Potteries, convinced us of his thorough fitness for the office.

Despite this accolade, Joshua Poole's services could hardly have continued past Christmastime 1884, as two local brothers, James and Edward Cleary, managed the pottery from 1884 to 1920. James was a modeler of great ability. Examples of his skills include: D218, Cleary Mug; D249, Cleary Sugar and Cream; D193, Cleary Spill, large size; and D194, Cleary Spill, small size. In 1887, during James's management, the pottery was presented with a third gold medal, this time at the International Exposition at Adelaide, Australia. Edward, who succeeded his brother as pottery manager in 1900, had been employed as a painter of the ware. Desmond Cleary, a Belleek hotel operator until his death in 1974, was a son of James. Five of James's grandchildren still live in Belleek. One grandson, Fergus Cleary, is the pottery's chief modeler.

In 1904 Belleek issued what is believed to be the pottery's first illustrated catalogue. The illustrated section is not only reproduced in its entirety following the Part Two "Gallery," (page 179) it forms the basis of the Degenhardt, "D," numbering system of antique ware and other pieces not in current production. (This is the same "D" prefix numbering system I employed in the first edition of this book.) The collector will quickly recognize several of Belleek's most prestigious pieces.

James Cleary and Michael Maguire, also a native of Belleek, were trained by Gallimore. Maguire modeled the shamrock ware, which is listed in the current catalog as items #1 through #49. Tommy Campbell told me that unmarked, unpainted examples of the shamrock pattern, which occasionally show up, are representative of "bad lots" which were not placed on the market. Perhaps these were given to employees for home use, or saved from destruction at the request of large purchasers who noticed them while at the pottery. In any event, Maguire's shamrocks have survived through the years, and the shamrocks are today's most popular pattern. Maguire's contribution to the offerings of the pottery was not limited to shamrock ware. Attention is called to his skill as the pottery's figure maker. D1134-I, Figure of Affection, painted; D20-I, Figure of Meditation, painted (Figure 2-3); and D1138, Greyhound, Single, speak with more authority than can words to Michael Maguire's imprint on Belleek. Relatives of Maguire also continue to reside in Belleek. Some, as is the case with Cleary's descendants, are currently employed at the pottery.

Frederick Slater moved to Belleek from England in 1893, married a local girl, and spent the remainder of his life in the village. Slater was from a prominent English family that, for four generations, had served in important positions at Derby, Doulton and Stoke-on-Trent. According to William Scarratt (1906),

The third son of Joseph Slater, who is named Mr. Albert Slater, has also two sons. Walter, the oldest of these served his apprenticeship at Minton's, Stoke, after going [on] to Doulton's where he stayed twenty years. In 1905 he accepted an appointment at Wileman's of Foley as pottery's

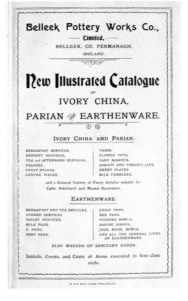

Fig. 2-2 *Title page from the 1904 catalogue, the first illustrated offering by the pottery.*

designer. Frederick, the younger son, a modeler, became a designer of shapes, etc. to the famous Belleek Pottery, County Fermanagh, Ireland, celebrated for its imitation of pearl on their lustres.

It is believed that Slater modeled the honored D2, International Centrepiece (Figure 2-4). The vase, which is 28 inches in height and 16 inches at its point of greatest span, was awarded Belleek's fourth gold medal at the Paris Exhibition of 1900. This striking piece, beyond doubt the most elaborate in the pottery's history, is, perhaps, also the most revered. Urn shaped, it rests on a scrolled base which also supports three Irish Wolfhounds chained by Parian links to a belt which surrounds the lower one-third of the body. The design of the belt appears to be from the tenth century at the time of King Brian, having its origin with the invading Vikings. Hand-applied flowers lavishly cover the upper two thirds of the vase's body. Three Irish harps, with Celtic designs decorating their frames, are mounted on the shoulder of the body. The top is trumpet-shaped with a fluted lip and intricate, open filigreed base. In 1967 a version of this spendid piece with maple leaves included in the flowered areas was crafted to commemorate the Centenary of the Canadian Confederation. This beautiful piece is on permanent display at the Manitoba Centenniel Centre, Winnipeg.

Late in the 1800s some of the pottery's craftsmen went to Coalisland Pottery in neighboring County Tyrone. Coalisland's trademark was the red hand of Ulster—an extended, raised hand with the inscription in Gaelic, ''Red Hand Forever.'' Principal production prior to that pottery's closing, over eighty years ago, was drainage pipe, brick, and fire clay, although some porcelain was made.

The Possel Pottery in Glasgow, Scotland, was expanded by a Belleek native named Boyle, who inherited that firm upon the death of the owner. A number of Belleek potters worked in what they called ''Boyle's Pottery.''

One of the most pleasant memories created during research for the earlier edition of this book was a visit with ninety-two-year-old John Dolan, who worked for Belleek from ages fourteen to twenty. He then went to work for Possel Pottery in Scotland, where he lived for fifty-seven years prior to returning to Belleek to retire. Only during his early years in Scotland did he work at the potters trade. With a twinkle in his blue eyes and a smile tugging at the corners of his mouth, he observed, ''The pottery [Belleek] is a convalescent home now.'' Looking at a picture of his fellow craftsmen, of whom he was the only one still living, taken some eighty years before in front of the main building (Figure 2-5), he reminisced. Well he might have considered the fine working conditions of modern employees as being enviable. His starting wage was three shillings per week. After seven years, at the time of his departure to Scotland, he had advanced in pay to a weekly scale of twelve shillings. Winter hours were 6:30 A.M. to 6:00 P.M., and on Saturday until 2:00 P.M.; the summer schedule was somewhat shorter. Allowance was made for a breakfast and dinner period.

John Dolan began his apprenticeship making saucers, and progressed, after two years at his trade, to basket and flower making. In 1975, encouraged by the manager of the Flowering and Basket Shop at that time, Mr. Dolan crafted a basket at his home using a false teeth receptacle as his working base. In his first effort at basket making in seventy-one years, he instinctively employed the three-strand design. He states that three-strand weaving of the plaited bases of basket work was replaced by four-strand plaiting in 1921. It was my privilege to see his basket, which had been taken to the pottery for glazing and firing. Who else had a ''false teeth'' basket!

John Dolan's father, his mother after she became a widow, and five brothers worked at the pottery, and his daughter continued the family tradition. It was she who showed me one of her father's favorite possessions—a Belleek second period black mark spittoon.

An early photograph, impossible to date, is of particular interest, as it shows women

Fig. 2-3 D1134-I, *Figure of Affection, painted, 14¹/₂″ H. D20-I, Figure of Meditation, painted, 14″ H. Michael Maguire, who modeled the pottery's famous Shamrock Ware, created these lovely pieces. Trained by William Gallimore, Maguire became one of the most accomplished modelers in the annals of the pottery. (Miriam & Aaron Levine Collection. Mark Donovan photo.)*

Fig. 2-4 Craftsman of bygone days admiring D2-II, International Centrepiece, no doubt the most elaborate offering ever crafted by the pottery. One wonders if the pictured craftsman might be Frederick Slater, its creator.*

Fig. 2-5 *Craftsmen of The Belleek Pottery Limited, Belleek, County Fermanagh, Ireland, 1901. John Dolan, now deceased, began his apprenticeship at the pottery at age fourteen. In the picture he is seated third from the left, in the first row. The picture of Mr. Dolan at age ninety-two was taken by the author during his interview. Dolan's father, mother, and five brothers worked at the pottery. His daughter retired as head of the Painting and Decorating Department a few years ago.*

who worked at the Pottery, no doubt in the Painting and Descorating Shop, and their charge hand (Figure 2-6).

The Effects of World War I

The years marched on, and so did the affairs of nations, leading to World War I. The pottery, again the victim of troubled times, struggled through the war years, with restrictions on exports taking their toll. Examples of the beautiful pieces crafted during the period prior to World War I are shown in Figure 2-7.

Writing in the *Irish Independent* on October 7, 1919, Cahir Healy referred to "the announcement made only a few days ago that the Belleek Pottery (Figure 2-8) was for sale," and he observed,

They [the current owners] won gold medals for their exhibits at Paris in 1900, Adelaide in 1887, Melbourne 1880, Dublin in 1865; they have made tea sets for princes of blood and princes of commerce, like Lipton, Indian Rajahs, and so forth. Their fame is worldwide. The five directors are shop-keepers in Fermanagh, Derry, Donegal and Tyrone, but none of them possess any practical experience of pottery work or management. A local company was formed (1884) to carry on the work. From that time until the present the pottery has been run by the company after an old-fashioned easy-going manner. The directors have had more money, seemingly, than they could utilize, for a recent balance sheet shows an investment of over 1,000 pounds in Great Northern Railway 4 P.C. stock! They did not advertise, for they were in the happy position of having more orders than they could execute. Wherever the blame lies, the fact stands out that the 200 workers who found employment there 30 years ago have dwindled down to 60 today. I think the directors have grown "tired" in an industrial sense, for it seems ironical to find a concern with more orders than it needs, a dwindling output, and a considerable sum invested elsewhere at 4 percent. The truth, perhaps, is that the directors only took up the burthen from a sense of duty to the locality and the workers. What is needed now is a "live" man or syndicate who will renovate the place, scrap a very little of the plant, add to it a few modern machines for producing the commoner wares speedier and cheaper than they can be turned out today entirely by hand. Some offers for purchase are being considered, but the proprietors do not want the concern to drift into rival hands, who might close it up, or utilize it for quartz crushing or something different from its present purpose to the great detriment of the locality. The directors, with their own affairs and places to superintend personally, have discharged an obvious duty for many years; they feel, with some reluctance, perhaps, that the time has come for a change. Anyhow, the Belleek Pottery is for sale.

Fig. 2-6 This early photograph of women employed at the pottery is impossible to date. It is believed that they were paintresses in the Painting and Decorating Department, shown with their charge hand on the right.

Fig. 2-7 From the Belleek Pottery Old Photograph Album, this shows the pottery display area. The top circle, on the left, indicates D1140, Hound and Stag. This piece is known to have existed only by virtue of its appearance in this photograph. Many other pieces of particular interest are shown. Next to D1311, Rope Handled Jug (on the table, lower right), is D1611, Pierced Reticulated Covered Comport; and four items further to the right is D1203, Dolphin Vase.

Fig. 2-8 *Though not dated, this old photograph of the pottery and village of Belleek was taken no earlier than 1892. This is confirmed by the fact that St. Patrick's Church, built in 1892, can be seen on the distant hill. (National Library of Ireland, Dublin.)*

Eleven days later the *Fermanagh Herald* quoted the *Irish Times:*

The Belleek Pottery is one of those institutions—like Guinness's Brewery and the Belfast shipyards—which the mention of Ireland's name brings into the minds of men of all nations. The Belleek ware has ranked for generations in the first flight of the achievements of the plastic art. Its grace of design and delicacy of texture are an advertisement throughout the world of the skill and taste of Irish craftsmanship. We know nothing of the circumstances in which the pottery is advertised for sale as a "going concern." It is possible to speculate that, like other "luxury trades," it has suffered through the war and through the prolonged absence of the English and American tourist traffic. Be that as it may, all Irishmen must hope that this famous and long established industry will be maintained in its existing excellence and will not pass out of Irish control.

CHAPTER THREE

1920 TO TODAY

THE BELLEEK POTTERY IN MODERN TIMES

The *Donegal Independent* of January 17, 1920, announced,

We are pleased to learn that at a meeting of the directors of the Belleek Pottery held in Bundoran on Thursday a tender was received for its sale. The tender (10,000 pounds) was sent in by Mr. Bernard O'Rourke, Dundalk, a prominent merchant connected with the milling industry and associated with several very successful business concerns as director. The conditions of purchase are that it must be carried on as a pottery and not converted to any other industrial use. This ends a very lamentable situation as the pottery has been a decaying concern for many years there being now only about forty hands employed. We congratulate Belleek and might safely say the same to the new owner or owners since there is no doubt that with keen business management it will prove a great success. The meeting decided that Mr. O'Rourke's offer should be placed before an extraordinary general meeting of the shareholders. Mr. O'Rourke five years ago bought the Milling Company's properties in Dundalk, and it is now being carried on by him.

The *Donegal Independent* continued:

The sale of the Belleek Pottery, to use a much abused phrase, marks an era in the history of the famous village. Marks, I should think, the beginning of a new era of prosperity, unspoiled by the efforts of public auditors and other persons. It is probably the only industry that has not benefitted by the Irish Revival, that has sunk down under the tide of prosperity flooding the country. Consumption, or tuberculosis, or anemia, or some other disease laid its fangs on the throat of Belleek Pottery. It was in its last gasp and about to give its last kick. Now there is every reason to hope that if a man with the driving power, energy and money—a live wire as the Yankees would say—of Mr. Bernard O'Rourke, Dundalk, takes a grip that things will happen. The cobwebs of the roof will come down with a dull thud and life and animation will replace the stagnant atmosphere of the Pottery City. I look upon the acquisition of the Belleek Pottery by such a man as one of the blessings of the year, of many years in fact.

By the end of January 1920, the directors and principal shareholders of the Belleek Pottery Works Company, Ltd., had met and agreed to accept the offer of Mr. O'Rourke and the Irish syndicate he represented. The *Fermanagh Herald* reported:

An extraordinary general meeting of the shareholders held on February 18, 1920 passed three resolutions: "That the two offers of Bernard O'Rourke, Esq., dated 11th November 1919 and 14th January, 1920, respectively, to the Belleek Pottery Works Company, Ltd., be, and the same are hereby accepted, and it is ordered that the said offers be accepted under the Seal of the Company. That it is desirable to wind up the Company, and accordingly that the Company be wound up voluntarily. That Mr. David Telford, of Trinity Chambers, Dame Street, Dublin, be appointed liquidator at the renumeration of one hundred guineas and out of pocket expenses.

Legal ratification of the sale was completed in mid-March, 1920, and the "new owners of this ancient ceramic industry" were announced in the March 13th *Fermanagh*

No. 4972.

Certificate of Incorporation.

———

I hereby certify that THE BELLEEK POTTERY, LIMITED, is this day incorporated under the Companies Acts, 1908 to 1917, and that the Company is limited.

Given under my hand, at Dublin, this 26th day of April, 1920.

Fees and Stamps	.. ..	£11 10 0
Stamp Duty on Capital	..	£62 10 0

(Signed), A. W. BEATTY,
*Assistant Registrar of Joint Stock Companies
for Ireland.*

WE, the several persons whose names, addresses, and descriptions are subscribed, are desirous of being formed into a Company in pursuance of this Memorandum of Association, and we respectively agree to take the number of shares in the Capital of the Company set opposite our respective names.

Names, Addresses, and Descriptions of Subscribers.	Number of Shares taken by each Subscriber.
JOSEPH DOLAN, Ardee, Co. Louth, Merchant.	One.
JAMES KEOWN, 28 Bachelor's Walk, Dublin, Merchant.	One.
JOHN O'NEILL, 13 and 14 South King Street, Dublin, Merchant.	One.
BERNARD O'ROURKE, Iniskeen, Dundalk, Co. Louth, Merchant.	One.
Total number of shares taken	Four.

Witness to signatures of Joseph Dolan, James Keown, John O'Neill, and Bernard O'Rourke (the word " acquired " having been substituted for " required " on last line of Clause 7, and " charged " substituted for " charges " on third line of Clause 18)—

MICHAEL MAGUIRE,
Solicitor,
Ballyshannon,
Co. Donegal.

Dated 22nd day of April, 1920.

Fig. 3-1 *Copy of the Certificate of Incorporation issued April 26, 1920.*

Herald: "Messrs. Bernard O'Rourke, millowner, Inniskeen and Dundalk; Jos. T. Dolan, M.A., merchant, Ardee [succeeded by Neil McMahon prior to the close of 1920]; John O'Neill, manufacturer, Dublin; and J. Keown, of the firm of Begg and Co., whiskey and wine merchants, Dublin." Figure 3-1 shows a copy of the Certificate of Incorporation. A new name—The Belleek Pottery Ltd.—and a new vision had come to the pottery.

A potter named P. J. Derrigan was appointed as the new owners' first manager. He came from a Stoke-on-Trent Pottery and remained at Belleek for two years. Derrigan was succeeded in 1922 by a Hungarian, K. E'Loyd, who introduced some new designs. He is credited with the revival of the U.S. and Canadian markets lost during World War I. E'Loyd tried many new ventures which he believed would be profitable. Fancy earthenware and the further development of Parian are examples. Unfortunately, the market at the time did not support his ideas.

A representative who traveled for the pottery in Ireland during those years observed, "It was very difficult to convince a shop owner to stock Belleek china. They'd take earthenware, but not china, because there was no market for it. No point to even display it in their windows as no one could afford to buy the Parian pieces as they were considered to be too expensive." A cup and saucer would have cost about five shillings—25 pence in the coin of today!

Steps were taken to effect economy. The making of figures and ornate centerpieces was curtailed. The wide offering of dinner services was reduced; other items entirely disappeared from the line. In spite of the curtailment, a new pattern in tea ware, the Celtic Design, was added. This design was created by Madam Bereniux, a Hungarian, who worked under Slater's direction. One wonders if she had been induced to come to Ireland by fellow Hungarian E'Loyd. Earthenware remained the mainstay and principal product.

F. J. Dolan, a Belleek native, managed the pottery from 1925 until his death in 1931—the same year that Frederick Slater passed away. It is apparent that Dolan soon achieved great success, and that Parian offerings began to take a more prominent position in total crafting.

The pottery's booth at the British Empire Exhibition at Wembley, England, in 1925 featured exquisite and, today, rare, Parian offerings (Figure 3-2). The booth was tended by Bernard O'Rourke (foreground), his sister, Eileen (wearing the hat), and two assistants. Note the figural piece with two seated children to the right of the Rose Isle Vase. Using a magnifying glass, move to the right to the shelf immediately below the Bust of Clytie and you will find a child kneeling in prayer. Three items to the right is D160, Hand and Shell vase. Sharp eyes will discover another exceedingly rare item in two sizes. Hint—they are figural pieces!

In 1927 the *Irish Times* stated,

A coal stoppage in Great Britain has had its reaction on one of Ireland's best known industries—the manufacture of Parian China at Belleek in Co. Fermanagh. For twelve weeks the pottery hands have been idle, because there is no Scotch coal to be had for the firing of the kilns. The stoppage is unfortunate both for the workers and the proprietors of the pottery for never before has there been such a keen demand for Belleek ware. By its lightness of body, its rich, delicate cream-like or ivory tint, and the glittering iridescence of its glaze, it has forced itself on the attention of people of taste in all the Continents. The enforced stoppage is the more regrettable as there are ready for the kilns a variety of new designs which, it is expected, will lift the artistic fame of the pottery even higher. Along with Mr. Fred J. Slater, the designer, Mr. (F. J.) Dolan has created fresh forms of the expression of beauty that is in Belleek-made Parian. It was by the exquisite delicacy of its tea and dessert services that Belleek ware first came to be known to connoisseurs. It is, however, in its basket-plaited designs that Belleek stands out preeminently in the whole pottery world. Every woman who loves beauty in the home would like to be able to afford [D1167] the open work basket compote, hand-woven, without floral decoration. Fourteen inches in diameter and twelve inches high, it will be retailed at about two pounds sterling. Hand-woven cake plates [D1279] look almost as fine as the spider's web from which they are designed. Their price will be 12 shillings, 6

Fig. 3-2 The Belleek Pottery Limited booth at the 1925 British Empire Exhibition, Wembley, England, features rare Parian offerings. (Photo courtesy Clinton O'Rourke; Allen Markley, LBIPP/Gary Parrott photo.)

Fig. 3-3 An example of superb basket crafting. (Ulster Museum, Belfast.)

pence each. The new company of which Senator B. O'Rourke is Chairman, appears to have well and truly laid the foundation of a world-flung business for this, Ireland's only pottery.

Michael Dolan moved from his position in the Basket and Flowering Shop to assume his deceased brother's responsibilities for a few months until a Dubliner, P. McCormack, was hired for the post.

Prior to the close of 1931, A. Upton, an Englishman, was employed to follow McCormack's short stay. Upton was an "earthenware man," and under his direction Belleek's production of Parian was severely curtailed. It was during this time that the name "Melvin Ware" was added to the earthenware trademark. Upton left Belleek in 1933, accepting an appointment as manager of a pottery in Arklow, County Wicklow, Ireland. Harry Arnold was named manager and was succeeded by his son, Eric, in 1940.

Adapting to Economic Conditions and World War II

World War II brought traumatic times to Belleek, just as the earlier war had. Not only were her Fermanagh sons in military service, but coal for firing the kilns was rationed and difficult to obtain. Bernard O'Rourke, writing to Belleek's distributor in the United States, Gilbert Pitcairn, on December 16, 1939, gives a dramatic glimpse of the period.

I have yours of 24th alt. Your order reached the Pottery on 8th inst. but I fear there is not much chance of early shipment as all these goods must be manufactured and as you know Mr. Arnold wants 3 months to get out orders. I am pressing him to send you all he can of your order early in the new year. Shipping delays here are appalling: goods that took 4 days to reach their destination between Ireland and England now take 4 to 6 weeks. Even when we ship goods from here you may expect them to be held up at Liverpool for a month. If your stock is so very low try and send us orders very long in advance as we cannot supply now as promptly as before the war. Best regards and a very happy Christmas.

Through skillful management the pottery did remain in operation during the war years. The few craftsmen who were employed devoted their skills to the making of earthenware, which required far less china clay than Parian and could be produced at a lower kiln temperature. A small kiln was used for firing, again to conserve precious fuel. To further ration china clay, no cups or mugs requiring handles were produced. Basic utility ware, which demanded the least commitment of craftsmanship, china clay, and fuel, sustained the pottery through the long war years. The single exception was basketwork, crafted in very limited quantities. "Hot spots" in the kiln during earthenware firing were capable of reaching the necessary temperature for basket firing. By their very nature these articles placed no inordinate demand on the precious reserve of china clay. Thus, fortunately, this exquisite art continued without serious interruption, allowing the most skilled of the workers to pursue their trade. During these years, and until his death in January 1976, the pottery was operated under the direction of partner and chairman of the board, Patrick Keown. Clinton O'Rourke, son of The Belleek Pottery Limited founder Bernard O'Rourke, was selected to succeed Keown. He served as Chairman until the spring of 1983.

Modernizing Belleek Kilns and Pottery Operation

In the very beginning, the pottery was able to reach a temperature of up to 1200°C in certain parts of the higher sections of the 50-foot-tall, brick, bottle-shaped kilns (Figure 3-4). Basically, however, these kilns produced a temperature high of 1050°C, suitable to fire earthenware, but too low for the firing of porcelain. Thus, only those sections of the

Fig. 3-4 *The 50-foot-tall bottle-shaped kilns that served to fire Belleek Parian and earthenware throughout the early history of the pottery. (Pottery Photographic Library.)*

kiln that achieved the maximum temperature could be used for porcelain. The old kilns would hold about two weeks' production. Initial fuel was peat and wood, with coal added during the latter part of the "firing up" process to attain the required temperature. Beginning in 1936 coal only was used for firing the big kilns which continued in service until 1945.

Belleek ceased earthenware production entirely in 1946 with the introduction of two kilns patented and designed by Allport of Stoke. The Allport kilns were constructed and successfully used until 1952 when the first electric kiln was installed. Fired by coal, the Allport kilns did not differ in size from the old bottle kilns. Their chief feature was a flue built 50 feet up the center of the structure, allowing the heat to be more evenly distributed. This was a temporary flue which was removed during unloading, or "drawing out," the kilns. The ware to be fired was placed in sagers and built up to the "crown" of the kiln, approximately 25 feet. The sagers were made of refractory clay, each about 8 inches tall, and could withstand a very high temperature. Stacked around the ware, twenty-five to thirty high, they offered protection from the fumes, smoke and flame created by the burning coal.

Occasionally a piece of old Belleek is seen with soot spots embedded therein. The Allport kilns measurably corrected this problem of firing. Now and then a kiln, or a part of a kiln, would become "sulfered," giving the ware a blue or grey color, and causing a partial or complete loss of the ware being fired. It is believed that this condition was caused by a severe downdraft in the kiln. Again, the Allport kilns greatly reduced this cause of loss. Not only did the Allport kilns have the capability of reaching and maintaining a firing temperature of over 1100°C throughout the kiln, but they were far more economical to operate. Aggregate firing time was reduced from fifty-six to nineteen hours, and coal requirements per firing were reduced from 17 to only 9 tons.

For the first time in the pottery's history, a sufficient temperature could be maintained throughout the kilns for the firing of Parian. Even with this tremendous increase in Parian production capability, the pottery, as in 1865, could not satisfy the ever growing export demand.

In 1976 Patrick J. O'Neill, who served as Managing Director from 1967 to 1983, told me that he attributed the postwar increase in U.S. and Canadian exports in large measure to the servicemen who took Belleek back home with them. They bought the pieces, in many instances, while on leave in Northern Ireland. The exclusive production of Parian china proved to be the final step which firmly established the enviable universal reputation of Belleek.

The first electric kiln, the Litherland Electric Oven, was put into service in 1952 as an enamel kiln. This signaled the beginning of a new era in the crafting of Belleek. No longer would the pottery be dependent upon imported fossil fuel for its production. The electric enamel kiln proved so satisfactory that similar kilns for "biscuit," or first, firing were erected. Total firing time was again reduced. No longer do the tall brick kilns with their smoking chimneys look down on railway cars supplying the coal they required. Even the pits of burned cinders have been erased by the years. The famous water wheel yielded to a water turbine in 1930, which likewise gave way to a diesel generator.

Electric lights pierced the Irish night from the windows of homes in Belleek long before electricity became available as a public service. There was no further need for the pottery to make candleholders and oil lamps to chase the hours of darkness from the village.

For a brief period in mid-1966 Cyril Arnold followed his brother, Eric, as pottery manager. He was especially noted for hand painting scenes on plates (see, for example, D1527-IV in Figure 3-5 and the earthenware placques in Figure 3-6).

Tommy Campbell was appointed manager in 1966 (Figure 3-7). Tommy had begun his outstanding career years earlier as a young apprentice, working his way along the path of promotion via the common ware (earthenware) and Parian crafting benches. His steady and capable hand guided all phases of pottery crafting. Tommy retired in 1978 and was succeeded by his assistant, Sean O'Loughlin. Sean came to the position equipped with an in-depth knowledge of all phases of pottery operation, and with a particular talent for teaching apprentices, as well as an inordinate skill in correcting problems inherent in Parian slip.

Activities of the Belleek Pottery in Recent Years— A Firsthand View

For some time I had been campaigning for an official Belleek collector's society under pottery sponsorship. The first edition of my book, *Belleek: The Complete Collector's Guide and Illustrated Reference*, was published in the autumn of 1978. The book proved to be the perfect launch. Charter membership included an introductory piece of Belleek. The latter, D1810-VII, is a miniature of the Belleek Trademark Plaque which is above the pottery's main entrance doors (Figure 3-8). The painted and gilt piece features the traditional Irish wolfhound, Celtic round tower, Irish harp, and sprigs of shamrocks.

An invitation was extended by the pottery for my wife, Margaret, and me to spend three weeks in Ireland in the spring of 1979. The purpose of the trip was to make in-store appearances, under the pottery's sponsorship, discussing Belleek and autographing my book. Our schedule began at a press reception in Clery's Department Store, Dublin, on May 24, 1979. During the following two days, time was devoted to autograph sessions in Dublin; similar sessions followed in Carlow, Waterford, Cork, Ennis, Galway, Belfast, Sligo, Belleek, Longford, Dun Laoghaire, and Limerick.

A petrol shortage was then being experienced in Ireland. Each retailer along the way took the responsibility of seeing that we had the necessary fuel to reach our next destination. I admit I still chuckle when I think of Billy Kehoe, owner of Knox Store in Waterford town, filling our tank from a can with no spout, using an improvised funnel made out of cardboard. More petrol soaked through the funnel than went down it into the tank! Billy, holding the can in one hand and the funnel in the other, did a jig of such perfection that not a drop spotted his suit.

Fig. **3-5** *D1527-IV, Gilt Scenic Plates, 9" D. Hand-painted by former pottery manager Cyril Arnold. (Jean & Max Norman Collection. Chris T. Vleisides photo.)*

Fig. **3-6** *This Cyril Arnold hand-painted plaque, D1557-III, 14" H. × 10½" W., is an example of his work on earthenware. (Miriam & Aaron Levine Collection. Mark Donovan photo.)*

Fig. **3-7** *Tommy Campbell proudly shows one of his cattle in this photo taken in 1976 while he was manager of the pottery. (Richard K. Degenhardt photo.)*

Warm memories vividly remain of the many courtesies we were extended by customers and store personnel.

At Liam and Angela Cahir's Belleek Shop in Ennis, a sweet lady with silver hair brought in a piece of antique Belleek. She inquired if it had a name and any value. At the end of our visit she politely asked, "Degenhardt, now that's not Irish, is it?" When I explained that my other three grandparents were born in County Cork, she replied, "I might have known. I can see why you love Belleek, as do we."

During our stay in Belfast I was scheduled to speak to a luncheon meeting of the Belfast Rotary Club at the Europa Hotel. Here I was, a Missourian with a German surname, proporting to speak with authority on a world famous product of Northern Ireland! What gall—no, what trepidation! My reception was cordial and the appreciation expressed most sincere. How friendly and gracious the Irish!

James F. O'Mahony, Commercial Director of the pottery, invited me to meet with him in New York during a trip he was to take to the United States in September 1979. Jim surprised me by asking that I accept the position of executive vice president of Belleek Ireland Incorporated, a soon-to-be-chartered U.S. subsidiary of The Belleek Pottery, Limited. Bernard O'Rourke, grandson of the principal founder of the present [1979] company, was at the time an executive of the Industrial Development Authority of Ireland in New York. Bernard was to begin with the new United States subsidiary in October as executive vice president, responsible for liaison with Waterford Glass Inc. in New York, Belleek's U.S. distributor. This was to be a new relationship, whereby Belleek would assume greater participation in the U.S. distribution of the product. I accepted Belleek's offer in December 1979 and retired from thirty years in Chamber of Commerce management. I was fortunate that my avocation would now be a vocation, and I could work with Belleek on a full-time basis.

Bernard and I belonged to the five-member board of directors of Belleek Ireland Incorporated. The remaining members were in Ireland, and were also members of the board of The Belleek Pottery Limited. They were Clinton O'Rourke, chairman; Patrick J. O'Neill, managing director; and James F. O'Mahony, commercial director. Reporting to Jim O'Mahony, my principal charge was to build a membership base and establish a headquarters for the embryonic Belleek Collector's Society, make in-store appearances for Belleek throughout the United States and Canada, chair the New Product Selection Committee, and answer mail inquiries from collectors. It was my privilege, during the more than four years that followed, to meet Belleek collectors in practically every major city in the United States and in Toronto. Fourteen local chapters of the Society were formed in as many principal cities from coast to coast, and more than 8,000 members were enrolled in The Belleek Collector's Society!

In New York, under Bernard O'Rourke's direction, steps were being taken positioning Belleek to do its own U.S. warehousing, distribution, and billing. In Ireland, expansion was under way to enlarge the Painting and Decorating Shop; limited space and personnel in this important area had long been a bottleneck in the smooth flow of ware through the crafting process. Progress seemed to be assured at last, but such was not the case.

A myriad of economic factors conspired to cause a change in pottery ownership in April 1983. The Northern Ireland Industrial Development Board offered financial assistance. Roger Troughton, an Englishman living in Dublin, was appointed managing director. In 1984 the pottery was offered for sale with the proviso that ownership be based in Northern Ireland. Gerald Investments Limited, with Roger Troughton as principal, was the successful bidder. A change in management took place at the end of September 1985 when my friend, Sean O'Loughlin, resigned to establish a new pottery in County Donegal near Ballyshannon. Sean was succeeded as manager by his assistant, the long-time craftsman Gerry McCauley, who continues to serve in that capacity. (I pleasantly remember the day in June 1976 when I met Gerry, who was at his bench deftly "sticking up" the winkle shell feet on D429-VI, Neptune Tea Ware Teapot, large size.) Troughton continued as Managing Director until he sold the pottery in January 1988.

The next buyer was Powerscreen International Plc, a Dungannon-based engineering company. Soon afterwards, in May 1988 Bernard O'Rourke resigned his position, in which he had been charged with all aspects of Belleek's U.S. operation. Thus a period of sixty-eight years during which the O'Rourke family was closely associated with the pottery ended. During Powerscreen's brief ownership, a grant from the International Fund for Ireland was used to establish a modern Visitors Center at the pottery. This beautiful, award-winning facility includes a reception area, museum, audio visual theatre, cafeteria, show room, and retail sales shop (Figures 3-9 and 3-10).

Powerscreen's Managing Director, Pat Dougan, came to the United States in the spring of 1989, to develop a new U.S. distribution system for Belleek. The plan was to divide the United States into specific geographic markets. One of his stops was a call on Mrs. George G. Moore in California, who had advanced definite thoughts concerning the development of Belleek in the U.S. market.

Angela Hughes Moore, a native of Northern Ireland, had long possessed an interest in Belleek china, an interest born during class trips to the pottery when she was a schoolgirl. She believed deeply in Belleek and its future. Angela was prepared for Dougan's visit. Backing her expressed interest in a distribution franchise was a study of the market, warehousing, and so on. Powerscreen approved, and she was given the franchise to develop and expand retail outlets west of the Mississippi River in the United States. Moving forward as president of the newly formed Belleek West, Inc., she secured warehousing facilities in San Marcos, California. During the summer of 1989 substantial orders for ware were placed with the pottery.

Apparently differences of opinion among Powerscreen officials as to how the product would be distributed in the United States resulted in what, for all practical purposes, amounted to a halt of shipments to U.S. distributors. A change in Powerscreen's executive management occurred in early August 1989, after which Belleek West received little to no information concerning plans and shipments. George G. Moore contacted Powerscreen's new chief executive officer and arranged a meeting to sort out problems, with particular emphasis on ware acquisition. At the meeting, which was held at Belleek in September 1989, a hint was dropped that Powerscreen might wish to divest themselves of Belleek to permit concentration on the company's principal activity, engineering. A subsequent meeting was held in Ireland at Powerscreen's Dungannon headquarters in November 1989. The terms of an agreement for Moore's acquisition of Belleek was reached. Throughout the remaining fall and winter of 1989–1990 major decisions concerning the pottery were reviewed by Moore.

The formal agreement to purchase Belleek was signed in January 1990. Erne Heritage Investments, owned by George G. Moore, who serves as chairman, officially received ownership of Belleek on March 29, 1990. A schoolgirl's love affair with an Irish institution was a dream come true!

Once again, in my opinion, the pottery has reached a time of stability, evidenced by the strong commitment of direct family involvement. George G. Moore is listed on the

BELOW:

Fig. 3-9 *The Belleek Pottery's reception area features an example of D2, International Centrepiece. (Allen Markley, LBIPP/Gary Parrott photo.)*

OPPOSITE PAGE:

Fig. 3-10 *Of special interest to all visiting collectors is the "not to be missed" Belleek Pottery Museum. (Allen Markley, LBIPP/Gary Parrott photo.)*

1990–1992 directories of the top 100 Irish-American business leaders. A native of Dundalk, he is the 1992 recipient of the University College, Dublin, Outstanding Alumnus Award. His father-in-law, Michael Hughes of Newry, is a member of the Erne Heritage Investments Board of Directors. Angela Moore serves as President of the International Belleek Collector's Society. The addition of "International" to the title is well deserved; the Society has a growing membership and a total of eighteen local chapters in Canada, England, Northern Ireland, and the United States. The first International Belleek Collectors' Convention was held in Burbank, California, on February 5 & 6, 1993.

John Maguire, a County Fermanagh native from Marlbank, Florencecourt, is managing director at an especially important time in the pottery's history. This year, with assistance from the Industrial Development Board for Northern Ireland, the pottery has embarked on a five-year expansion program which will create sixty new pottery jobs. Total employment will thus increase nearly 50 percent—from the present approximately 130 people to nearly 200. Phase one of the five-phase plan, a new Casting Shop, is now complete. Members of the Casting and Fettling Shop team were involved in planning all aspects of this facility: bench styles, heating systems, workstations, etc. This effort helps to assure collectors that the hand-crafted and hand-painted qualities of Belleek that are intrinsic to the ware will never change.

The Village of Belleek and Its People

The pottery at Belleek and the village of Belleek are synonymous, a dramatic departure from crowded pottery cities like Stoke-on-Trent. The craftsmen and craftswomen of Belleek are individuals, part of the pottery and part of the countryside. Nearly all have a bit of a farm, grow their own vegetables, cut their turf, and care for livestock. Practically all own their homes and care for and about each other. The pottery, with its 130 craftsmen and craftswomen in the village of 600, is a living part of the community, a fact realized and appreciated by both employee and employer. Most employees reside within a ten-mile radius of the pottery, and the 50 percent who live within a mile of the main entrance have a pleasant walk or bicycle ride to work. Even the children are "pottery minded." The schools in Fermanagh, Donegal, and nearby Tyrone schedule annual outings to the pottery. Students write essays or theses on Belleek.

The border between Northern Ireland and the Republic of Ireland is a mere twenty yards from the main gate.

Many of the village men play Irish football, or hurling, and are members of the Gaelic Athletic Association. The Belleek Club, with the assistance of grants from the Gaelic Athletic Association (G.A.A.) and the government, bought seven acres of land on which to build a recreation center and playing fields. Despite the grants, the bulk of the funds had to be raised by club members. They struck upon the idea of a commemorative plate which might be designed and sold with the proceeds directed to the fund. Club member and then pottery manager, Tommy Campbell, was approached. Campbell liked the idea and secured approval to move forward with the project. The renown Kilkenny Design Center was contacted. Noted Irish sculptor Oisin Kelly was asked to design and model the plate along lines proposed by Tommy, with the G.A.A. crest in the center, surrounded by eight profiles of the most outstanding Association leaders since its founding in 1884. The motto of the Fianna, named for the legendary Finn MacCool, leader of the Fian in the third century, is inscribed in Gaelic around the entire rim of the plate: "Repeal not the Union, but the Conquest." The managing director at the time the plate was made, Patrick J. O'Neill, offered to have the pottery market the plate, with all proceeds directed to the Belleek Club.

The G.A.A. plate (Figure 3-11) introduced in late 1976, is an example of the close relationship between the pottery and the people. The G.A.A. Vase, D1766-VII, was issued in 1984 on the observance of the centennial of the founding of the association. The five side panels portray the coats of arms of the four provinces of Ireland—Munster, Leinster, Connaught, and Ulster, plus the G.A.A. crest (Figure 3-12). In 1992 the proceeds from the sale of a special trophy were directed to the recreation project, which is now complete.

One might imagine that crafting Belleek day in and day out would cause further exposure to the ware to be considered a "postman's holiday." Not so. Articles are proudly displayed and used in the homes of the workers. When visiting towns and cities away from home, they delight in searching out stores that carry the Parian to see "what is on hand." Their pride in their craft makes their job more than a day's work. They know that collectors and collections begin with one piece. Belleek is a very real part of their heritage, as is the well known friendliness of the Irish. Put the two together, and they conspire for the grandest form of conversation about the ware.

This brings to mind the tale of the man who secured an automobile in Enniskillen to drive along Lower Lough Erne to Belleek. As he left the town limits he was preceded by another automobile. Throughout the trip, people along the road would wave to the passengers in the first vehicle and then to him. His curiousity was sparked, as he was confident there must be some notable in the car ahead and that he had been assumed to be with that party. Upon arriving in Belleek he eagerly inquired, only to learn that those in the other vehicle were as much visitors as himself!

BELOW:
Fig. 3-11 D1883-VII, Gaelic Athletic Association Commemorative Plate, painted, 8⅞" D. Limited edition issued in 1976 to assist in raising funds to build playing fields and a recreation center at Belleek. (Richard & Margaret Degenhardt Collection. Evan Bracken photo.)

RIGHT:
Fig. 3-12 D1766-VII, Gaelic Athletic Association Centennial Vase. Issued in 1984 to commemorate the 100th Anniversary of the Gaelic Athletic Association. (Belleek Pottery photo.)

Visiting the Pottery and Its Surrounds

The pottery's reception center, museum, audiovisual theatre, cafeteria, showroom, and retail sales shop are open Monday through Friday from 9:00 A.M. until 6:00 P.M. Saturday hours are 10:00 A.M. till 6:00 P.M., and Sunday hours are 2:00 P.M. to 6:00 P.M. These facilities are closed on weekends from the end of October to the beginning of March. Principal holidays are Christmastime, approximately December 22nd to January 4th; March 17th, St. Patrick's Day; Good Friday; and Easter Monday. It is advisable, upon arrival in Ireland, to telephone Belleek (036 56) 58501 to make certain that your visit will be on a day of pottery operation. Guided tours are conducted Monday through Friday beginning at 9:00 A.M., with the last tour before lunch at 12:15 P.M. Tours start again at 2:15 P.M. The last tour of the day begins at 4:15 P.M. (3:15 P.M. on Fridays). Tours are available year-round on weekdays of pottery operation. A nominal fee is charged adults; children twelve years of age and younger are admitted at no charge when accompanied by an adult. Belleek tours are quite special, as the visitor is treated to a view of each aspect of the crafting process—not the case in many potteries!

Pottery visitors doubled in number from 8,000 in 1962 to 16,000 in 1968. The total reached 65,000 in 1990 and 70,000 in 1991. In 1992, 90,000 visitors experienced a personal view of the amazing process that creates Belleek.

The visitor should allow time for touring the pottery and a stroll through the village of Belleek. Castle Caldwell is now a bird sanctuary on the north shore of Lough Erne. Little remains of the castle structure; however, the short trip is, in itself, a delight. Though much of the forests of Ireland were cut down (the British were accused, but this was also done in England and, sadly, in many of the states in the United States), the Forestry Department is engaged in a broad reforestation program. The Department of the Environment has constructed a boat marina on the Erne River near the pottery. The river and her lakes are navigable from Belleek to their source in County Cavan, 60 miles to the east and south. The Ballyshannon hydroelectric scheme makes passage impossible along the Erne west to Ballyshannon and the Atlantic Ocean.

The fisherman will delight in the trout, salmon, and coarse fishing offered in lakes, rivers, and streams of the area. Fishing has been a favorite pastime of local residents for generations. The Erne was quite a salmon river prior to the hydroelectric project, which caused the river to drop 100 feet between Belleek and Ballyshannon. One of the falls was 16 feet high.

Nearby Ballyshannon and Bundoran are part of the area's seaside resort advantage. Donegal town, less than an hour's drive from Belleek, provides interesting shopping with particular emphasis on fine tweeds and Irish sweaters, many of which are handcrafted in the cottages scattered over the surrounding hills of County Donegal.

A variety of accommodations are available in the area. Peter Clark's Chalets, immediately across from the pottery, are on the bank of the River Erne. I have also enjoyed my stays at Mary Brennan's "Erneville." Located a short distance from Belleek, out the Garrison Road on the left, it is a most pleasant and neat bed and breakfast.

Determination, dedication, artistry and craftsmanship have prevailed through more than a century, melding their attributes into a love which is proclaimed by each representative of the pottery's family of products. Perhaps it is this quality, more than any other, which places Belleek apart from the world's china, and Parian in a class unto itself!

Standing on the uplands across from St. Patrick's Church, at the eastern edge of the village, you can watch the sun setting behind the Donegal horizon, turning the windows of the pottery to flame. You are able to look upon the village and her people. The people who give enduring craftsmanship to the world, as did their predecessors and as will their successors.

CHAPTER FOUR

THE PROCESS

THE CREATION OF PARIAN

The handcrafting of Belleek begins with the design and continues through an intricate succession of vital steps, culminating with its wrapping and boxing for shipment. The few times during production when machinery is employed are insignificant to the true handcrafting of the ware. Briefly, the machinery includes the plunger, used to mix the slip; the kilns; the vibro energy mill, used to scour the ware; and the "dod box," which is operated by hand to extrude the Parian lattice-like rods used in fashioning basketware.

A true appreciation of Belleek is enhanced by an understanding of the process of its creation, coupled with an acquaintance with the origin and history of the ware.

Design and Modeling

The continuing and growing acceptance of Belleek Parian is, of itself, an unspoken testimonial to the timelessness of design and design concepts and a constant accolade to William Gallimore, who developed over 500 designs; Frederick Slater; Annie and Robert Armstrong; William Henshall, credited with the introduction of applied flowering and basket weaving; James Cleary; and Michael Maguire. In addition to the principal designers and modelers, others, in some way associated with Belleek, tried their hand. Excellence in design during a period when design competition was especially keen is confirmed by the pottery's four international gold medals won at Dublin in 1865, Melbourne in 1880, Adelaide, Australia in 1887, and Paris in 1900.

Simplicity of line and design elements, reminiscent of eighteenth-century work, were more commonly represented by the pottery's earthenware offerings. Born in Victorian times, contemporary design of the period keynotes the latter, more prominent category. Representatives of this division comprise the vast majority of present production. It is of interest to note the divergence from popular types of Victorian tradition, while at the same time the ware is definitely representative of the era. McCrum attributes this unique circumstance to "Belleek's physical isolation from the central potteries," i.e., England.

Certain items were designed, over the years, that proved difficult to produce, due to the problem of bringing them satisfactorily through the several stages of firing, particularly the first, or biscuit, kiln. Remedial changes in the design were ordered as requisite to

Fig. 4-1 *First step in the creation of a new Belleek introduction is the drawing of the design. (All photos in Chapter 4 are Allen Markley, LBIPP/ Gary Parrott photos.)*

Fig. 4-2 *A three-dimensional model also details the actual surface relief work called for in the design.*

prudent production. If the item still could not be crafted to allow it to be priced within the range of practical public acceptance it had to be discontinued.

Old designs are resurrected and reintroduced into the market from time to time. The successful return of Harp Shamrock Tea Ware, now simply called Harp, is an example. Many new designs have been produced during the present century; the artistic style of most is based upon early design patterns.

Design and modeling are now under the direction of chief modeler Fergus Cleary, grandson of James Cleary, pottery manager from 1884 to 1900. Among the examples of completely new designs is the series of annual Christmas plates, Christmas ornaments, #1601–1614, Butterfly pattern, and #1410, Snowflake Candleholder. Further examples include a series of clocks. Modification of existing designs has been the basis for an attractive range of lamps.

A close relationship must exist between design and sales teams to ensure the crafting of products that will receive market acceptance. Meetings, held at least quarterly, allow representatives of design, crafting, and sales to select new subjects. Sketches or drawings of potential new items offered by the design department are thoroughly studied (Figure 4-1). Once agreed upon, the design is crafted as a three-dimensional model. To make this model a block of plaster of paris is turned on a lathe until the exact form of the piece is crafted. The modeler then details the actual pattern, or surface relief work, called for in the design drawing, on the model (Figure 4-2). Each item of Belleek, other than woven baskets and applied flowers, is cast from liquid slip. Therefore, the design must allow the mold to be easily separated to enable the delicate newly cast greenware piece to be removed from the mold without its being damaged.

Molds

Without doubt, detailed records of designs were once a part of the pottery's files. This is confirmed by the fact that a competent system of numbering was used to identify the molds involved in the creation of each piece. Should the pottery decide to reintroduce, say, D34, Prince of Wales Centre, the various molds for the creation of this exquisite piece are to be found under a common base number in the mold storage area. Even the complex International Centrepiece could be crafted again using more than a score of separate molds identified as components of the overall piece. On the rare occasion when a master mold is missing, or damaged, an old Parian representative can be used as a model. Though a new master mold cannot be "pulled" from the Parian example, the example can serve as the subject from which a modeler can create the basic plaster of paris model.

Mold development, in all cases, begins with the clay model. The master mold is actually two molds: the "block" and the "case." The master block mold is crafted from the clay model and becomes the mold used exclusively in the creation of master case molds. The master case mold is the design and the master block mold is a transfer reverse impression of the design. Not only is the master block mold available for the crafting of additional master case molds as needed, but serves also as a protective covering over the companion case mold during storage.

In photographic terms, the master block mold may be likened to the negative, and the master case mold to the positive, or print. The master case mold is solely used to create the working block molds from which the ware is actually produced. To make working block molds the master case mold is removed from the master block mold and is used to create approximately twenty working block molds. The master case mold is then put back inside the master block mold for storage, keeping the pattern safe. When working block molds, possibly numbering in the hundreds, have been made from the master case mold, it begins to wear. No longer is it capable of producing a distinct working mold pattern. Therefore it is destroyed and replaced by a new master case mold. Quality of the master block mold must be superb, if a superior master case mold is to be achieved. Only then can a satisfactory working mold be cast to produce results meeting Belleek's standards. The chief modeler has the responsibility of maintaining all master blocks and cases in perfect condition. Duplicate pairs of master molds are in inventory at all times.

Master molds and working molds are made of plaster of paris in the pottery's Mold-making Shop. Master molds, since they produce no Parian, may be of a harder plaster of paris mix. To achieve this more durable quality, one part water is added to four parts plaster of paris.

Working molds must be of a softer consistency to permit proper absorption of the moisture in the slip. This is achieved by using a formula of two parts water to three parts plaster of paris.

A constant supply of working molds must be made in balance with orders for ware. Plaster of paris and water are mixed by hand in large earthenware pitchers (Figure 4-3). Since both the master case mold and the pouring for the new working mold are of plaster of paris, a "releaser" must be used to keep the surfaces from sticking together. Soft soap is boiled and made into sizing, which is thoroughly washed over the surface of the master case mold before casting. The material is then poured by the mold maker into a form which surrounds the master case mold. Fifteen to twenty minutes later sufficient drying has occurred to allow the master case mold to be removed and a new working mold is ready to begin its life in the pottery's service (Figure 4-4)—a short life, indeed, as an average of only forty Parian casts may be made from each working mold. At this point

Fig. 4-3 *Mold Shop. Pouring the plaster of paris mixture into a master case mold to make a new working block mold.*

Fig. 4-4 *Parts of a new working block mold are separated from the master case mold.*

the working mold, made from the reasonably soft mix, begins to deteriorate and the pattern starts to fade, transferring its imperfection.

Following each cast, the working mold must be thoroughly cleaned with soap and water to remove any vestige of slip remaining from the previous pouring.

Slip

The material which becomes Belleek Parian is called slip in its liquid state. Slip is the product of the pottery's Mill Room, and must be precisely formulated each working day.

Substantial improvements have been made in material processing techniques. China clay, feldspar, ground flint glass (common window pane glass), frit, and water (at the ratio of thirty-two ounces to the pint of dry ingredients) are placed in a cylinder, or drum, which holds 200 gallons of the mixture. No bone whatsoever is used in the formula.

The recent introduction of a device called a plunger allows mixing time to be reduced. A thorough blending is now accomplished in under three hours. The mixture then passes through a series of sieves and magnets used to remove unground material and any residue of tramp iron. The sieves are exceedingly fine, with 140 holes to each square inch of their surface.

The resulting finished slip, which is of the consistency of thick cream, is stored in large vats under agitation until it is needed in the Casting and Fettling Shops.

Casting and Fettling

Prepared slip is delivered directly to the Casting and Fettling Shops. Liquid slip is used in creating all ware, with the exceptions of baskets and flowers. Thus, each item that is cast in a mold is made from liquid slip. The design of the piece to be cast was embossed on the hollow inside of the working block mold at the time the mold was made.

A craftsman, called a caster, or fettler, does all the casting and fettling work required to prepare the items of his specialty for biscuit firing. The ultimate thickness of the piece is gauged at the time of casting. Slip is poured into the number of working molds (Figure 4-5), which experience has demonstrated to the craftsman may be then emptied of excess slip, still allowing the proper amount to adhere to the inside of the mold. This number varies from eight to eighteen casts at a single pouring, depending on the article being crafted. Molds are filled completely to the top with slip. Immediately on pouring, a portion of the water in the slip is drawn, or soaked, into the plaster of paris walls of the mold. As this occurs, a portion of the once-solid ingredients in the mixture sticks to the inner walls of the mold, filling in all details of the pattern to give a perfect reproduction of the design. Actually, if the slip were left in the mold long enough, it would "set up," becoming a solid article—a teapot with no room for tea, or a vase with no space for flowers! If the slip were to be poured from the mold too quickly, the piece would be so thin it would either break upon removal from the mold, or crack during firing. The translucent quality for which Belleek is justifiably famous is principally determined by the amount of slip which is allowed to cling to the walls of the working mold before the excess is removed. Whether the piece being cast is #929, Round Tower (Figure 4-6), or the small #908, Allingham Spill, experience, which determines the number of molds to be filled at a single pouring, becomes the judgment factor to gauge the correct thickness—and thus weight—of the article. (Numerous photographs in this chapter feature #929, Round Tower, as it proceeds through the crafting process.)

An average of two to three minutes, again depending on the item being cast, is all the time required before pouring excess slip from the molds, which have been filled and will

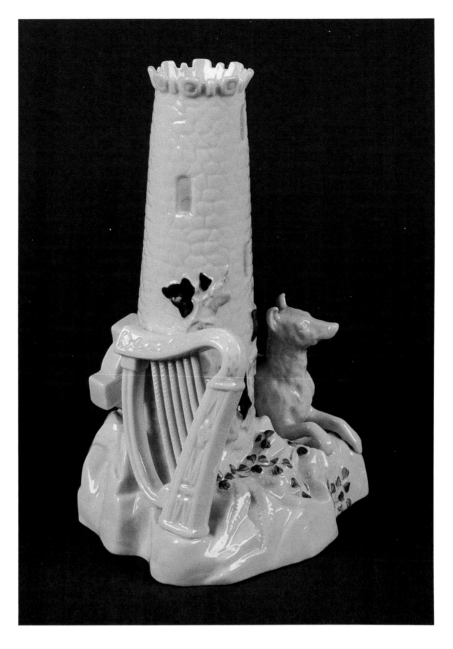

be emptied in rotation (Figure 4-7). Thus, when the last mold in the series has been filled, the first has set enough to attain the proper thickness. The caster continues to fill and pour off in rotation until the number of articles which will be required for his or her day's work have been cast. Particular care must be exercised in lifting the mold to pour off. At this point the caster must hold the top and bottom tightly to the mold walls, while tilting and pouring the excess slip from a hole in the top of the mold. The mold must be very securely held by hand as there are no vertical bands to hold top and bottom to sides. The walls of the mold are held in place by strips of automotive inner tube, or hemp twine.

After the piece has been allowed to cure in the mold for one to two hours, or more, depending on the specific article, the bands are removed and the mold sections—two, three, or four, determined by the particular item—are gently separated (Figure 4-8). The period of curing before removal from the mold is especially important. Larger pieces remain longer in the mold. Quite a bit of moisture is still present in the piece, and curing time permits the article to gain vital strength. Further, the piece shrinks slightly away from the mold walls, thereby releasing itself from the pattern and the edges of the mold. Slip has now become clay, and the piece is said to be in the greenware stage. Green

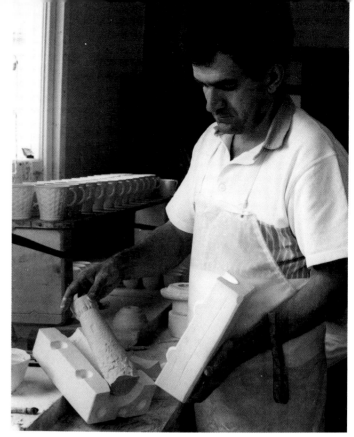

Fig. 4-7 *Excess slip is poured from the working block mold of the tower of #929, Round Tower.*

Fig. 4-8 *Working block mold sections are carefully removed from the tower of #929, Round Tower. The piece is now in the greenware stage and is very delicate.*

referring to its unseasoned state, rather than to its complexion, which is gray! If removed too soon from the mold, the article will be too soft to support itself. Left in the mold too long, it will not cooperate with the craftsmen at the time of fettling. Thus, correct timing is critical.

Greater appreciation may be gained for this important stage in the process if an example is cited here. The L/S #16, Shamrock Teapot, requires the following five separate molds: body of pot, a three-section mold; handle, a two-section mold; spout, a two-section mold; lid, a two-section mold; and finial, a two-section mold.

When the item is removed from the mold, the excess clay selvage is cut off from the top of the piece where the slip was allowed to overflow the pattern. The article is left on the bench to gain additional firmness, finally reaching a "cheese hard" stage. At this time, it may be gently held to begin fettling. If the article is a teacup, a single craftsman or craftswoman will produce about five dozen during a work day. When the selvage is removed, the cup does not have a rounded smooth lip. Also, as in all cast items, mold seams appear at each point section of the mold join. Some of the pieces have considerable spare edge, or scrap, which must be exactly removed. If there is a mitre edge in the pattern, as in #544, the Island Vase, excess material must be even more precisely removed. Twenty to thirty percent of the scrap is either remixed with slip or directed to the Basket and Flowering Shop.

The skilled handcrafting of the pattern at the point of seams, smoothing and rounding of edges, and fitting of parts together—handle to teacup, or spout and handle to coffee pot body, as well as finial to lid, and lid to coffee pot—is called fettling.

In the example of a teacup, the lip is rounded off and the seams polished with a wet sponge and a camel-hair brush. The cup handle is trimmed with a knife and smoothed to remove the seams of the two-part mold. The handle is then fitted on the cup with liquid slip, which is thickened by the addition of table salt to become the affixing agent. This procedure is referred to as sticking them up (Figure 4-9).

Fig. 4-9 *A liquid slip mixture is used for joining ("sticking up") separate parts of a greenware piece. This example shows the harp being placed on the base of #929, Round Tower.*

If the item being made is a teapot, holes are bored in the main body at the point where the spout is to be placed, to serve as a strainer and allow liquid to pour from the body through the spout. Although no mastic is added at any time, the applied pieces will adhere perfectly to the body, forming a weld during biscuit firing. This is accomplished by the strength of the slip, and a bit of suction achieved when the parts are initially fitted together. The application of various pieces to the main body must be done with great care, as they are still quite soft.

The morning after casting and fettling, the article is dry enough to be sent down to the biscuit kilns, or to the Basket and Flowering Shop. As moisture leaves the piece, in the final drying hours before biscuit firing, the color changes from gray to chalk white. It is considerably softer than blackboard chalk and extremely brittle. When touched, a powdery residue clings to the finger—a signal that extreme care must be exercised. Though the color is now white, it is still greenware.

Basket and Flower Crafting

To many, the varied examples of Belleek's basket and flowered ware represent the epitome of the pottery's offerings. Each piece bespeaks the depth of skill and artistry of its maker, the supreme care required in its firing, and the talent of the decorator, reflected from its hand-painted facets.

It is almost beyond belief that flowers and leaves, as well as baskets, take form from the most humble of beginnings. Actually, they emanate from the scrap collected from the fettler's bench; the selvage that he or she has discarded in crafting a teacup, plate, or saucer.

This scrap is mixed with slip and all the moisture removed in a drying process at 100°C. The material is then ground into a fine, white, powdery consistency with a common rolling pin. It then passes through a fine sieve or lawn to determine that it now has the required texture. After 15 to 20 pounds of this powdery substance has been produced, gum arabic, which has been prepared by melting, is poured into the finely ground clay. Prior to the introduction of gum arabic, the material is called "short" clay—china clay that lacks the degree of plasticity which will be needed. The mixture is kneaded by hand, in the same manner as one would knead bread. The dough, as it is now called, is hand-beaten on an oak block using two oak beaters (Figure 4-10). This removes all air from the mix and aids the gum arabic in giving strength to the clay. Beating and kneading continue until the bulk of the material has been considerably reduced in size and has reached the desired consistency. The mixture, brown in color, is now ready to be molded by the hands of the craftsmen into the most detailed of flowers and leaves.

That portion which is to be formed into rods (referred to as lattice work, or spaghetti strands by many collectors) is placed in the "dod box" (Figure 4-11). This device holds the distinction of being the only machine other than the vibro energy mill plunger and kilns to be found in the entire crafting process. Actually, the dod box is a cylinder-shaped extruding press which is hand operated. The box is utilized by hand turning a corkscrew that activates a piston which descends, placing pressure on the material and forcing it through a hole in a steel plate at the bottom of the cylinder (Figure 4-12). Various plates, each with a hole of a different diameter, are available to produce a variety of rods. The extruded material drops into a pail (Figure 4-13), which the craftsman carries to the workbench, removing the portion required for his immediate needs. The remainder is covered with a damp cloth to keep it moist and pliable. A knife blade or a skilled index finger is used to make flat rods when needed.

The rod material selected for immediate use is cut in single strips of the length required and then covered with a damp cloth. Next, the base of the basket is hand plaited (Figure 4-14). Each basket takes form in an inverted position over a plaster of paris mold, which is the shape of the basket's interior. Basket covers are crafted in the same manner. One by one the rods are removed from under the damp cloth and draped over the mold until they are joined with the plaited base which rests on the center of the top of the mold. Excess rod length is allowed to trail at the mold's lower edge, where it will later be cut away (Figure 4-15). Periodically, the maker will gently pat with a damp cloth the rods that he or she has placed on the mold, to keep them moist and pliable. This also enables the lower surface of overlapping rods to adhere to the upper surfaces of the lower layer. Rods that form the vertical top edge of #587, Rathmore Oval Basket, are hand-twisted; twisted rods are also used to make the basket's foot (Figure 4-16).

The gum arabic content of the material allows the article, when dried, to be handled rather firmly. While the basket is drying, required feet, handles, and the lip edge are crafted. By the time they are ready, the basket may be lifted off the inner mold and positioned to receive additional parts.

The craftsman who does the rod work to build a particular basket also makes the flowers, twigs, etc., and prepares the article for firing. Each completes the entire piece he begins (Figure 4-17).

Greenware from the fettlers' benches that is to be encrusted with flowers, such as #663, Princess Vase, #435, Birds' Nest Tree Stump Vase (which also gains a pair of birds), #668-9, #666-7 and #664-5, large, medium, and small Aberdeen Vases, and #546-7, the Rose Isle Lamp Base, are sent to the Basket and Flowering Shop to receive adornment prior to biscuit firing (Figure 4-18).

Flowers, stems, buds, twigs, and shamrocks are entirely made by hand. Petals take form in the artist's palm (Figure 4-19) and buds burst forth from his deft fingers, as do lovely shamrocks and graceful stems. Each petal is individually crafted. Should a particu-

Fig. 4-10 *The crafting of Belleek's world-renowned baskets begins in a most humble manner. A combination of dried slip and gum arabic is first kneaded into a doughlike state. This material is then placed on an oak stump and beaten by hand with oak beaters until it reaches the desired consistency.*

Fig. 4-11 *"Dough" being placed into the cylinder of a dod box.*

Fig. 4-12 *The dod box, an extruding press, is used to form the strands which the craftsman will take to his bench to weave into baskets.*

Fig. 4-13 *Extruded spaghetti-like strands are collected in a bowl—in this case an old piece of Belleek earthenware—on the floor below the dod box.*

Fig. 4-14 *Skill is evident in the weaving of a basket's plaited base.*

Fig. 4-15 *The talent of nimble fingers is revealed as rods are precisely placed downward from the basket's plaited base. All baskets are crafted in an inverted position.*

Fig. 4-16 *Rods that have been twisted by hand are fashioned to become the "foot" of a basket.*

lar flower require sixty petals, they are fashioned one at a time, until all sixty have been completed. Pinned or prop supports are not employed to build up the flower as each petal is hand applied. Literally, the crafter's hands and fingers become the molds! In the words of Master Craftsman John Doogan, "We can make anything that walks, crawls, flies, grows, or waves!"

Leaves, again one at a time, are made in a press mold, a single sided flat mold which impresses the pattern on the lower side of the clay when the upper surface is smoothed with a pen knife. As each leaf is completed, it is lifted from the mold by using the tip of a knife, turned pattern side up, and transferred to the article. The position of the leaf and graceful swags, or bends, emanate from the mind and hands of the maker. When the final touches of handles and feet have been joined, requisite props and plugs are provided at key points.

Basketware must be completely supported in a refractory basin filled with a bed of sand. This keeps the piece, as it softens, from collapsing under the high temperature of the biscuit kiln, which is especially critical at the point of firing when contraction begins. The basket's exterior is lined with paper treated with a mixture of gum arabic and water. This precaution prohibits the sand from creeping through crevices between basket rods. Were this permitted, the sand would fail to properly support the article, as well as prohibit it from contracting evenly, thereby causing the rods to break. Further, should the supporting sand make contact with the rods in their clay state, particles would adhere and be impossible to scour from the fired piece.

The paper wrapper and the gum arabic in the clay burn away during firing, leaving only the Parian (Figure 4-21). Remarkably, both remain long enough to allow the piece to contract, and the supporting sand to bond, after which it is no longer susceptible to flowing. They serve their purpose admirably!

The most difficult basket to craft is #587, the Rathmore Oval Basket. Next in complexity is #588, the Oval Covered Basket, large size. A fortnight is required to create

Fig. 4-17 An exquisite flower is placed on a nearly finished basket.

Fig. 4-18 Roses and leaves are applied to the greenware body base of #546-7, Rose Isle Lamp.

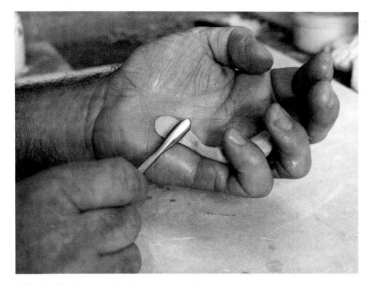

Fig. 4-19 The hand of a master craftsman becomes the ''mold'' from which a petal is formed.

Fig. 4-20 Flowers ''bloom,'' petal by petal, between the craftsman's fingers.

two of the former, and only two of the latter may be made in a week—for the world! Little wonder they are rare. Even #575, the Shamrock Basket, Flowered, small size, of which approximately twenty-three are made during a week, is not readily available on the world market.

The complexity of the work in the Basket and Flowering Shop is easier to understand if an example is considered. The #603, Birds Nest Basket, smallest of the basket family is a concoction of over 273 separate and distinct parts: twenty seven panels of four rods each, plus sixteen flowers and shamrocks of more than 165 separate segments. No wonder they are gingerly carried by their dedicated creators to the drying room for final curing prior to first firing!

Fig. 4-21 A basket is removed from the sand-filled refractory basin which supported it during biscuit (first) firing.

Biscuit Firing

Greenware is collected from the fettlers each morning by the ware carriers, who place the pieces on long, flat boards. A single board, which may accommodate as many as fifty pieces of ware, with a row of ware ''marching'' down its center, is hoisted to the carrier's shoulder and balanced; then the careful walk to the first of three kiln firings begins (Figure 4-22).

On arrival in the Biscuit Kiln Room, greenware is methodically arranged on kiln batts (Figure 4-23), a series of racks which make up the various flat levels of the kiln ''trucks.'' The trucks, prior to being stacked with ware, remind one of the old fashioned railroad hand cars, minus their seesaw propelling device. They are actually on small rail wheels and are guided along steel tracks as they are pushed by hand in and out of the kilns. When the ware is placed on the kiln batts, larger pieces are put in the center. Smaller pieces, called side ware, are used to fill in spaces between large items and around the outer margin of the kiln batt.

Although the electric kilns provide far more even temperature than their predecessors, a range from 1050°C to 1200°C may be experienced at various locations within the kiln. This fact, as well as the nature of the specific piece and its size, must be considered in determining the item's placement on the truck.

All round articles are sheltered by protective rings made of an identical mixture of slip, enabling them to experience the same degree of contraction as the ware. The ring is

Fig. 4-22 Greenware marches down a plank as it is carried from the caster's bench to the biscuit kilns.

Fig. 4-23 Greenware for #929, Round Tower is methodically placed on kiln batts, the shelves of a kiln truck.

filled with a bed of calcene alumina. The article, for instance a teacup, is gently turned in this bed to seat it in position. The calcene alumina bed not only supports the piece but also protects it from sticking to the ring. An even temperature is achieved within the confines of the ring, thereby assisting in keeping the article straight as it contracts, reducing the chance of warping. As previously mentioned, the contraction period is an especially perilous phase of the entire process. Contraction, or shrinkage, which can be as great as 16 percent of the greenware dimensions, occurs only during biscuit firing.

When visiting the pottery, the collector who views examples of greenware may immediately wonder why like items in his or her collection are not as large. Of course, normal contraction during biscuit firing is the explanation! (Figure 4-24).

A great deal happens to the ware during contraction, resulting in expected and acceptable losses of 20 to 30 percent of the articles placed in the kiln for biscuit firing. Basically, losses are attributable to warping, settling, cracking, or any combination of these things. In addition to its use as a filler in the rings previously discussed, alumina is used to combat the adverse forces of change which would be experienced by articles that do not require the ring's security. Ware such as #544, the Island Vase, is buried to about one-fourth of its height in alumina that has been spread on the flat surface of the kiln batt. Teapots of certain patterns that are prone to "squat" are placed in a bowl of alumina. Examination of the ware so protected reveals that the pieces have shrunken away from the sides of their alumina beds by ¼ inch. The bed's purpose is achieved when contraction begins. After that, the article can creep away on all sides without warping. Actually, the ware almost reaches its melting point during biscuit firing!

When firing time is at hand the biscuit kiln workers carefully lift the batts, with ware aboard, and place them on the trucks. Each layer is separated by ceramic props. Remaining gaps between articles are filled with additional ware. The doors of the biscuit kilns swing wide, and a signal for the first firing to commence is given by the kiln

Fig. 4-24 *Shrinkage, as much as 16 percent, occurs in the first (biscuit) kiln firing. This reduction must be uniform in all segments of a piece, and is dramatically portrayed by #929 Round Tower, seen here in both its greenware and finished stages.*

supervisor. The trucks, bearing their precious cargo, are pushed along the rails into the kilns. Kiln doors close, and the internal temperature begins its climb.

Trucks are loaded by 3:30 P.M., ready to replace those that are withdrawn from the kilns at 4:30 P.M. and begin their 23½ hours' residence in the biscuit kilns. Temperature at the time of changeover is 300°C, which is high enough to shorten firing time by avoiding the necessity of building back up from room temperature to this level, and low enough not to crack the ware on kiln entry.

Just before each truck is rolled into a kiln chamber, the kiln supervisor places a lighted candle and a 2¼-inch thermoscope hold croft bar, ¼-inch square, made of ceramic, into a small trap in the center of the edge of the truck facing the kiln door. The trap is directly opposite a 1-inch diameter plugged hole in the door of the kiln. After the door is closed and the plug removed, the candle will reveal whether the bar is properly centered for viewing during the firing cycle. The hold croft bar serves as a test instrument to determine if the ware has been exposed to a sufficient period of firing. The degree of bow, or kink, which develops in the bar advises the kiln supervisor that the maximum temperature of 1200°C, reached during biscuit firing, has been maintained for the requisite time to properly fire the ware.

Although the bars are indispensable aids, in addition to the kiln thermostats, they do not reflect whether a temperature above 1200°C has been experienced. Unfortunately, they would display the same degree of bow if an excess of only 10 to 20°C were encountered. Ware that has been overfired, even to this deceptively minor percentage, is pinkish in color and not nearly as beautifully translucent as properly fired ware. Consequently, thermostats must be critically adjusted to the 1200°C maximum.

A recent pottery visitor, observing a lighted candle being placed in the kiln, asked the kiln supervisor if he "started the kilns off with a candle." His innate Irish wit demanded that he reply, "Yes."

Kiln switch on time is 5:00 P.M. Initially, the dampers are opened and plugs removed to allow gasses that may be present in the ware to escape. At 6:30 P.M. the kiln supervisor closes the dampers, checks the instruments, and places the plugs in position—"bedding down for the night." The following morning at 7:30 A.M., the hold croft bars are checked, and the slight bowing which begins to appear is noted. Contraction of the bars is equal to that of the ware. Final judgment as to the time each kiln will be shut off is made when the companion bar, now glowing fire-red, has achieved the degree of bow that the kiln supervisor knows to be correct.

Temperature rises about 100°C per hour from switch on, slowing to a 50°C increase each hour during the final 200°C climb necessary to record the 1200°C maximum. Beginning about 6:00 A.M., the elements in the kilns are automatically turned on as temperature drops to 1194°C, and off again at 1200°C. This on and off adjustment, which repeats itself every three minutes for about six hours, is known as the soak. It is during the soak that the ware gains its translucent quality.

The value of the soak may be compared to the boiling of an egg. The egg is initially placed in cool water. When the boiling point is reached, it will not as yet be cooked, but must remain for additional minutes to achieve the desired soft- or hard-boiled state. The egg is, therefore, "soaked" during the boiling period. Further, if the egg were initially

Fig. 4-25 Kiln door is barely ''cracked'' to slowly start the cooling process.

Fig. 4-26 The critical temperature has now declined to a point at which the biscuit kiln door may be fully opened for the remainder of the cooling period.

placed in boiling water, it would crack, as would the ware should kiln temperature at the time of entry be too high.

When the soak has been judged to be of sufficient duration, the kilns are switched off, the dampers drawn, and the handles lifted to open the doors a fraction of an inch. Cooling commences and, unlike for the egg, it must be very gradual. A sudden change to room temperature will shatter the ware. Heat must escape and cool air enter the kiln over an extended period. At first, the doors are merely "cracked"; then, over a period of time, they are opened another 2 to 3 inches (Figure 4-25). This procedure is repeated until the kiln doors are fully opened (Figure 4-26). Soon thereafter, the trucks are drawn halfway out of the kilns, where they remain until their withdrawal is completed and changeover occurs.

The expression "too hot to handle" may be aptly applied to the ware. Now referred to as biscuit, it remains on the trucks overnight. Unloading begins at 8:00 A.M. the following day and preliminary inspection is conducted as articles of similar type or size are grouped to enable them to be more conveniently sorted in the Scouring Shop where they are delivered by the biscuit kiln workers. The workers then collect greenware from the Casting and Fettling Shops, thereby completing their daily work cycle.

Fig. 4-27 The #929, Round Tower, receives its first inspection under strong electric light. Flaws not readily apparent in prior stages are now revealed.

Scouring

Each piece is inspected again on arrival in the Scouring Shop, this time with strong electric light reflecting through the article (Figure 4-27). Flaws not apparent during the first inspection become evident. Minor imperfections may be corrected: the repair procedure is called stuffing, and applies to filling in small pinpoint-size holes, or gaps, where handles join the body of the ware. Inspection under light may also dictate a second trip through biscuit firing in a special straightening ring to correct defects, such as being out of round (for example, a teacup that is not symmetrical). Ware that fails to pass this strict inspection is destroyed (Figure 4-28).

The responsibility of the Scouring Shop is to thoroughly clean, as well as inspect, the ware received from the biscuit kilns. Removal of clinging bits of sand or calcene alumina is performed by hand and in the vibro energy mill (Figure 4-29). The mill is a circular device filled with wooden and ceramic pieces that are shaped like small eggs. The mill vibrates, and the ware is gently tumbled, cascading among the "eggs" as it completes a full 360-degree circle. The resulting rubbing action not only removes particles of clinging alumina but also acts to smooth any possible rough edges. Basket and flower ware must be scoured by hand; such ware is never placed in the vibro energy mill.

Fig. 4-28 Ware that has been rejected is immediately destroyed. "Seconds" are never offered for sale by the pottery.

Dipping

Ware that graduates from the Scouring Shop is moved to the Dipping House, the "tailor shop" of the pottery, where each item receives its permanent coat of glaze. Comprised of borax, white lead, finely ground glass, and other ingredients, the glaze is compounded to impart the pearl-like surface coating that is so typically Belleek. Forty ounces of water are mixed with each pint of dry material to develop the correct liquid glaze mixture.

Each article is dipped, just once, by hand (Figure 4-30). Should the dipper allow the piece to remain in the glaze bath too long, permitting an excessive amount of glaze to adhere, the piece would be a greenish color, or perhaps crazed—that is, faint cracks would occur in the glaze coating, which would become very apparent after gloss firing. Not spending enough time in the glaze bath results in thin, incomplete coverage. Biscuit

Fig. 4-29 *The vibro energy mill removes any remaining bits of sand or alumina and gently smoothes possible rough edges.*

Fig. 4-30 *A precise time is required in the glaze ''bath'' before the dipper removes the piece to allow it to drain.*

Fig. 4-31 *Stubbornly clinging excess glaze is blown from the piece by the dipper.*

Fig. 4-32 *Glaze must be removed from the base of each piece. If not, it would be destroyed by fusing to the kiln batt rack during gloss firing.*

ware is not porous; therefore, the glaze is not absorbed by the piece. Earthenware, on the contrary, soaks up glaze like the proverbial sponge.

Holding the article in his hand, the dipper submerges it in the glazing tub for the prescribed time known by him to be correct for the specific piece. Surplus glaze is carefully shaken from the piece—as well as the dipper's hand and lower forearm—when it is withdrawn from the bath. Particular care must be exercised to remove all surplus glaze from basketware, leaving only a thin film of the coating. Glaze has an annoying tendency to cling in the crevices formed as basket rods meet, cross and overlap. These excess droplets, which stubbornly refuse to be shaken away, are invited to "vacate the premises" by a short, strong, well-aimed breath blown from the mouth of the dipper (Figure 4-31).

Glaze is cleaned from the foot or base of each piece with a sponge, prior to sending it through a drying process (Figure 4-32). The bottom of the article is cleaned, as glaze in this area would fuse the piece to the kiln batt during gloss firing, destroying the piece. Pieces with unglazed areas, such as #645, Cherub Candelabra, must have every vestige of the coating removed from appropriate sections prior to drying. The ware passes under a battery of thirty-two 750-watt infrared electric bulbs to hasten drying, and emerges pale pink in appearance. Drying is done to enable the glazed article to be handled in preparation for the next firing.

Gloss Firing

The gloss and enamel kiln workers carry the glazed ware from the Dipping House to the Gloss Kiln Room. Like their biscuit kiln colleagues, they place the pieces on stillages that are loaded on trucks for firing.

Shrinkage and loss experienced in biscuit firing, plus the fact that rings, props, and alumina beds are not required during gloss firing, mean that fewer kilns are needed for gloss firing than for biscuit firing of the same amount of ware. Hold croft bars are not needed either, as a soak period is not part of the gloss firing procedure. Alumina could not possibly be used at this stage as it would adhere to the glazed ware in a most unattractive and unacceptable manner.

Tall pieces, such as #435, Bird's Nest Tree Stump Vase, are placed in sagers made of fine clay. Sagers are used to shield the articles, preventing them from becoming "dunted," a pottery term used to denote cracking from a sudden cold blast of air, which may occur as they are being removed from the kiln. The sager cools uniformly with the item it is charged to protect.

The gloss kilns automatically begin to fire at midnight. They reach maximum desired temperature of 1050°C and turn off at their peak of heat. Kiln doors are barely "cracked," and leisurely cooling begins. No rush, as gloss-fired ware will not be unloaded and taken to the Painting and Decorating Shop until the following morning. Gloss firing permanently bonds the glaze to the piece.

Painting and Decorating

All Belleek ware must proceed through the Painting and Decorating Shop. Some pieces arrive here merely to have the pottery's trademark applied to the base; some to receive the touches of pink, green, blue, or cob lustre, which are recognizably Belleek the world over; and the select few pieces to don the regal, multicolored attire reserved for exceptional representatives of a "royal family."

Each stroke of painting, each caress of decorating, even the placement of the trademark, is done by hand. With brushes for wands, the artists cause roses, daisies, and forget-me-nots to bloom in a burst of color (Figure 4-33). Shamrocks turn as green as Ireland (Figure 4-34), lilacs appear on the side of 420, Cottage Cheese Dish, and precious gold gilds rare pieces.

Before this "magic" occurs, every piece receives another tedious inspection under strong electric light. Only perfect Parian pieces will receive the trademark of the pottery. Unsuccessful candidates are broken. Examples of ware that receives no painting or decorating, but solely the current blue trademark, are #423, Terrier, and the lovely figures #626, Meditation and #627, Affection.

Painting and decorating are done principally by women who begin their apprentice-ship working with lustre, then proceed to shamrock leaves, next to stems, and finally to painting the handles of the ware. Raised flowers and leaves demand special skill in shading and lining. This is the most difficult skill for apprentices to acquire. Each separate color must be allowed to thoroughly air dry before a second, or third, shade may be applied over the previous hue.

Writing about Belleek in the *Irish Times,* July 30, 1974, Ronnie Hoffman observed, "Though the girls are mostly young, their skills, the patterns they follow and even their terminology is 19th Century in origin. They 'decorate' only those pieces which carry coloured flowers or leaves, they 'tint' larger areas of colour, and they 'cob lustre' those portions of china which are to be given a golden glossy look."

A single craftswoman painting, for instance, the #16 Shamrock Tea Pot, would perform all decorative steps: shamrocks, stems, twig handle, and twig finial. Likewise, a sole artist would paint all traditional parts of the #588, Oval Covered Basket, L/S. The

Fig. 4-33 *Flowers burst forth in colorful profusion in skilled hands as brushes become wands to create their magic.*

Fig. 4-34 #929, Round Tower, is adorned with ivy and shamrocks in the Painting and Decorating Shop.

#587, Rathmore Oval Basket, calls for exceptional skill and saintly patience, as it is the most difficult of the ware to decorate.

The long journey through the crafting process is now nearing an end. The final step before reaching the warehouse is about to begin in the enamel kiln—the third and final "trial by fire!"

Enamel Kiln

The gloss kiln workers also serve the enamel, or decorating kiln. During the afternoon, they collect painted ware from the decorators' benches and collect the items that are not to be painted from the section where the trademark transfer decal is applied. The latter pieces must also go through the third and final firing to permanently affix the trademark. During this firing the trademark decal backing burns off, leaving only the ink impressions, and the carefully painted, tinted, and gilt areas are permanently adhered.

As in gloss firing, alumina beds are not used in the enamel kiln. Shamrock, decorated, and painted flower items reach a maximum temperature of 750°C. Lustreware, gold-decorated items, and ware which is just to have the trademark affixed are fired to a maximum of 650°C. Separate kiln chambers permit flexibility. Depending on the ware to be fired, each chamber can be set for either requirement, or operated independently to fire both groups during one time period. When the desired temperature has been reached, the elements in the chambers automatically turn off (no soak period is needed).

Firing in the enamel kiln takes place during the normal work day, which allows the firing to be carefully watched to avoid the risk of loss should the kiln not perform properly. A loss here, with all the work invested in the pieces, would be especially costly.

Trucks, loaded with ware on the multiple levels of their kiln batts are rolled into the

Fig. 4-35 The enamel kiln firing—the third firing and final step in the crafting process—reveals the true beauty which is Belleek.

kilns, where a temperature of 650°C is reached in five hours, and 750°C in six hours. As soon as maximum firing temperature is achieved, the main switches are turned off, dampers are drawn, and doors are "cracked" slightly open to begin the cooling process.

With this final firing completed (Figure 4-35), the loveliness which is Belleek appears, and is, to say the least, breathtaking! Hand-painted shamrocks, pale green upon entering the enamel kiln, sparkle like emeralds; roses decorated in lifeless shades of pink and yellow now emerge in dazzling beauty. Even the gilding, which was drab, brown, and lifeless a few hours earlier, now sends each ray of light touching its surface back to the eye of the beholder, leaving no doubt of the piece's authenticity. Strong hands gently grasp each finished piece, placing it with others in wooden flats and grouping them to be carried to the Finished Warehouse.

Finished Warehouse

Handcrafting begins with the design of the pieces and the making of the molds. Subsequent major steps, leading along the way to the Finished Warehouse, are done by hand. There is complete justification for the resulting pottery to be labeled "handcrafted." The molds are cast by hand; the handles are applied by hand; the ware is scoured and fettled by hand, placed and removed from the biscuit kilns by hand, inspected by hand, glazed by hand, loaded and unloaded from the gloss kilns by hand, decorated by hand, loaded and removed from the enamel kilns by hand, and carried to all crafting areas by hand. Each petal and each leaf is made by hand. Even the wrapping and packing is done by hand.

The Process: The Creation of Parian

A minimum of six work days are involved in completing all except basket and flowered pieces, which require additional time. One day is needed for each of the following: casting and fettling, biscuit kiln firing, scouring and dipping, gloss kiln firing, decorating, and enamel kiln firing.

On the seventh day, upon arrival in the Finished Warehouse, each item receives its fourth and final inspection, again under strong electric light. Decorations must be complete, the trademark must be applied, and the ware must be in perfect condition. Though the percentage of rejection is much lower than in previous inspections, even at this stage, with all crafting finished, articles that exhibit a fault are shattered and discarded.

Once the ware has passed this last inspection it is wrapped in tissue paper, marked as to content, and placed in bins with like articles to await selection in the filling of orders.

Pride in their work is evidenced by the pottery's craftsmen and craftswomen throughout the process. The exclamation point to their united enthusiasm is added for all by the workers unloading the enamel kiln. "Tis a fine day, and a grand lot of Parian," they say. "God bless the work!"

CHAPTER FIVE

IDENTIFICATION

THE NAMES, THE MARKS, AND THE WARE

Names

The selection of names given specific pieces is both intriguing and enlightening. Many represent place names familiar in the locale, while others are designated by the names of the flora and fauna they portray. A few, in times past, were christened to honor personages important to the pottery. Tommy Campbell told me of one piece named after McBirney—D581, McBirney Sweet. In the spring of 1983, D1229, Tara Vase, was reintroduced, available only in gilt, and named in honor of Armstrong (D1751). This vase was adapted as a lamp, D1700, in the autumn of 1985, and offered with a shade and a brass base (Figure 5-1). Perhaps one day an item or a range of Belleek will be named after Bloomfield, even though Bloomfield—as Armstrong—did not elect to have this done when it was in his power to do so. Current pottery #1210, Caldwell Vase, recognizes Mrs. Bloomfield's family and the estate from which the pottery's site was provided. Statues and figures reflect the names appropriate to their representation, be that of a religious, mythological, or traditional derivation.

The pottery's close proximity to the sea and the interest of watercolorist Mrs. Robert Williams Armstrong in the detailed painting of marine life became the avenue for a whole spectrum of unique subjects. Her artistic skill in design, no doubt in concert with the modeling genius of William Gallimore, gave the pottery a legacy of marine subjects represented in tea services, and in elaborate ornamental Parian. Thus, the names of sea life play a prominent role in Belleek designations. Shells, corals, sea-urchins, seaweed, dolphins, and seahorses are used, at times quite lavishly, to dramatic effect.

Marks

Belleek trademarks are primarily divided into four sections—black, green, gold/brown, and blue. The first two sections each embrace three periods of the eight periods in the pottery's history.

All marks, with minor exceptions, include symbols which are unmistakably Irish, such as the Irish wolfhound with head turned to face one of Ireland's distinctive round towers: the model for this is believed to have been the Devenish Round Tower on Lower Lough Erne's Devenish Island, built in the Middle Ages to protect life, limb, and treasures

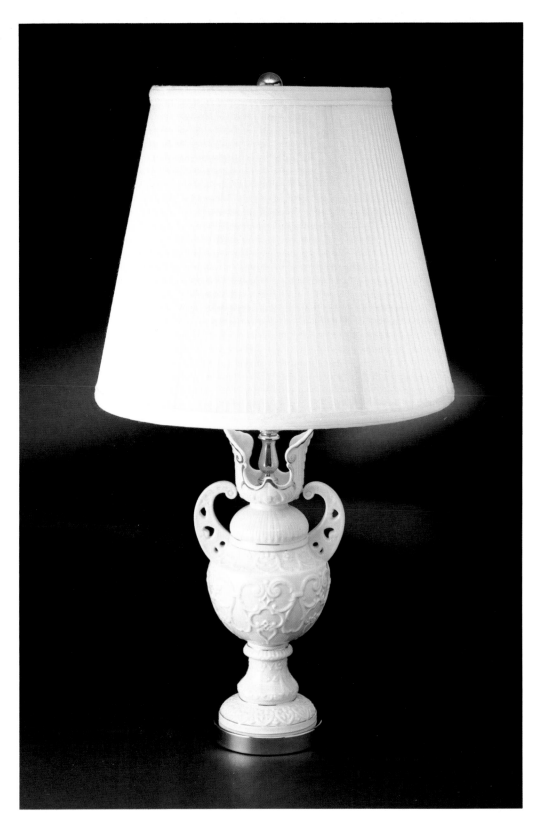

from Norman attack, is the Irish harp and two sprigs of shamrock which border the ends of a ribbon at the base of the design on which appears the single word "BELLEEK" in capital letters.

The most accurate information available has been used to provide a guide to the periods during which the principal marks were used. The absence of substantiating pottery records for the early periods, I believe, is overcome by the logical reasons for mark changes in the years indicated.

The basic trademark of the first period existed in two versions, large and small, and was most often applied as an ink transfer in black, but occasionally in red, blue, green, or brown. The latter colors were more prevalently used on earthenware. Regardless of the color, size, variation, or method of application, all are referred to as First Mark, I, ("First Black Mark") as are the impressed letters, "BELLEEK," "BELLEEK POTTERY," or "BELLEEK, CO. FERMANAGH." Impressed lettering was used at a time believed to have been quite early in the pottery's history. Occasionally, the name of a particular retail outlet and its location became a part of the ink transfer and appeared in conjunction with the trademark. Infrequently both impressed and ink transfer First Marks were used on the same article. This leads to the speculation that the impressed mark had previously been applied to a piece still awaiting shipment when the new hound, tower, and harp design copper transfer plates gave the pottery the ability to place their new logo on the piece. A single trip through the enamel kiln would do the job.

First Mark, 1863–1890

The Armstrong diaries remove any mystery concerning the Harp, and Crown Harp Marks, which were used during Belleek's early history. These marks were usually impressed, though at times transfer printed, on the bottom of the ware and, to the author's knowledge, always in connection with the trademark.

It is important to note that these are marks used to designate the composition of earthenware bodies of Armstrong's time and do not reflect a separate trademark era. Many collectors have erroneously concluded that these two marks represent the earliest period of Belleek's history. The proof that this is not the case is found in Armstrong's recently discovered diaries:

His entry for August 11, 1864, noted the formula for a Common Printing Body (earthenware on which transfer patterns would be applied) stating, "This mixture I ordered to have the Harp *Impressed* on each article." Then, on September 16, 1864, he discussed, "My Harp Body," and on November 21, 1864, he recorded, "Body rather soft in fire—prone to distort by shrinking and the hollow pieces to shrink in hard fire. I propose to alter as follows—." His Harp Body formula was refined during the years that followed. By May 30, 1868, the Harp Body had been improved to a fine point causing him to comment and decide, "Some 10-inch plates out of glost oven this day. In every way most complete and elegant. The glaze on these plates was perfect indeed in every particular, the Body excellent—so have a crown over Harp Body hence be our 'Crown Harp.'" Thus the Crown Harp Mark was introduced, replacing that of the Harp. Both referred to the body used by the pottery, and neither was adopted to replace the trademark.

In the early days, the process of affixing the trademark to each Belleek piece was far more complicated than it is today—the day of the decal.

Then, a painter's knife was used to spread the "paint," or ink substance over a copper plate (p. 13) on which up to twenty-four trademarks had been engraved. Next, the excess material was scraped off and tissue paper was placed over the plate, which was then passed between two iron rollers. The rollers were covered with flannel and were positioned to practically touch each other. Thus, the trademarks were offset onto the tissue paper. Individual marks were cut from this paper and placed on the base of the article. Heat was applied and the trademark design was transferred from the tissue paper, as it burned away, onto the ware.

The Patent Office of the Board of Trade, London, registered designs and issued a special registration mark to denote that the design was protected. This service was offered from 1842 to 1883. The registration mark, diamond in shape, provided the following information: Roman numerals in a circle at the top of the mark indicated the type of ware manufactured, IV indicating pottery, or earthenware. Additional designations appeared in each of the corners to detail, respectively, the manufacturer and the

Fig. 5-2 The First Mark, surrounded on three sides by a ribbon giving the name and location of the dealer, as well as the British registration mark on a raised Parian pad, appears on the bottom of D358-I-c, Echinus Eggshell Tea Ware Cup.

Second Mark, 1891–1926

Third Mark, 1926–1946

Fourth Mark, 1946–1955

Fifth Mark, 1955–1965

day, month, and year the design was first registered (not, as is sometimes misunderstood, the day, month, and year the article was produced). Only occasionally used by Belleek, the Registration Mark was applied in a variety of ways: impressed into the bottom of the base of the piece, impressed into a raised Parian pad applied to the base (Figure 5-2), or as an ink transfer on the base. The pottery trademark was not eliminated when the Registration Mark was used. Examples of several Belleek design registration sketches are on file in the Board of Trade, Public Record Office, Kew, London, design volumes 43 and 68 (Figures 5-3 and 5-4). Special attention is called to Design No. 258816, Variation of the Echinus Comport. I have seen no evidence that this piece was actually crafted.

As previously mentioned, the date Belleek first registered a design was September 5, 1868. The chart entitled ''The earliest designs registered for protection by D. McBirney & Co., Belleek'' that appears in Figure 5-5 was prepared by Mairead Reynolds. Important information appeared as part of her scholarly article called ''Early Belleek Designs,'' which appeared in the *Irish Art Review,* Vol. 1, No. 3, Autumn 1984.

The Second Mark, II (''Second Black Mark''), used from 1891 to 1926, reflects the addition of a ribbon surrounding the lower half of the design for the first mark, on which appears the words ''CO FERMANAGH IRELAND'' in capital letters.

This change in trademark occurred in 1891 in compliance with the United States McKinley Tariff Act of 1891 and the 1887 British Merchandise Act as amended in 1891, requiring the country of origin to be specified on the article. The mark is black, although a dark blue color of this mark has been observed (rarely). It is believed that this was actually a black Second Mark affected, in some manner, at the time of firing. Impressed lettering, though seldom used during this period, also changed from that employed during the time of the First Mark. The word *Ireland* was added to the impression; thus it became ''BELLEEK CO. FERMANAGH IRELAND.''

A round scroll, containing the three Gaelic words ''Deanta in Eirinn,'' (Made in Ireland) surrounding the upper half of a Celtic design, and ''ReG No 0857'' immediately below the scroll and following the flow of its bottom edge, was added below the design of the second mark. ''ReG No 0857'' is the registered trademark number which was actually granted in 1884. For some reason it was not deemed important to add it to the trademark until 1926. The color of this Third Mark, III (''Third Black Mark''), 1926 to 1946, was always black.

The pottery resumed full production following the Second World War. A decision was reached to change the color of the trademark from black to green. The Fourth Mark, IV (''First Green Mark''), used from 1946 to 1955, was identical to its predecessor in every way except color. Though it may be assumed that the color green was chosen because it is so identified with Ireland, the decision was actually based upon the fact that tests had proven the green trademark to be less likely to show through the translucent Parian.

A capital letter ''R'' enclosed in a circle was added to the trademark in 1955 to signify it had been registered in the United States, and the Fifth Mark, V (''Second Green Mark''), used from 1955 to 1965, came into being. This addition is immediately above the tip of the ribbon on the viewer's right. The mark is green.

In 1965, Belleek decided to reduce the size of its trademark to make it suitable on smaller articles. The ribbon itself was shortened and the words "CO. FERMANAGH" were deleted, leaving only the word "IRELAND." The U.S. trademark registry symbol was placed immediately above the Irish harp and the entire mark became smaller, and thus the Sixth Mark, VI ("Third Green Mark"), began service. This mark was still "wearin' the green."

On April 1, 1980, the enamel kiln fired the Seventh Mark, VII, for the first time (Figure 5-6). A change in both design and color was chosen. The design became the upper portion of the Sixth Mark, and it excluded the round scroll which had been an integral part of the trademark since 1926. It was used in one of the two larger sizes as shown, depending upon which best fit on the specific piece.

Seventh Mark, April 1, 1980– December 22, 1992

The Seventh Mark was introduced to commemorate the 100th anniversary of the award of a gold medal given to the pottery at the 1880 International Exposition in Melbourne, Australia. The antique gold color of the mark, during the early years of the seventh period, was selected as the appropriate color for this purpose. The original plan was that the antique gold mark—in fact the seventh mark per se—would be discontinued after one year. The fictional "Murphy" intervened, and additional supplies of the antique gold decal were ordered. Perhaps he was again present in the autumn of 1984, when a new supply of trademark decals were received that were brown in color. It is not known why this color change occurred at that time. The change to brown did remain constant through the remainder of the Seventh Mark period. At some point during the "brown mark" period a very small mark was introduced for use on pieces with a very small base. (See, for example, the foot of the Irish Setter in Figure 5-7.) Of necessity, the mark is simple in design—only the two ribbons, "BELLEEK" and "IRELAND," are used. Actually they are a smaller version of the ribbons on the larger marks of the period.

FAR LEFT:
Fig. 5-3 D23, Jack-at-Sea-Trinket Box, and D24, Jack-on-Shore Trinket Box. Designs were registered November 13, 1869. (Evan Bracken photo.)

LEFT:
Fig. 5-4 D1609, Echinus Comport Variation. Design was registered December 16, 1871. (Evan Bracken photo.)

Eighth Mark, January, 1993–

The Eighth Mark, VIII, is deep blue in color. It is quite similar in design to the Second Mark, 1891–1926, with one very important difference: the addition of the trademark registration symbol "R" above the Irish harp. This addition in design makes the Eighth Mark readily discernable from its second period "ancestor." Befittingly, this change in mark observes the 130th anniversary of the crafting of fine Parian china by Belleek (1863 to 1993).

Fig. 5-5 Earliest Designs Registered for Protection by D. McBirney & Co., Belleek

Date Registered	Design No.	Registration Description	Extra Inscription	Modern Description	Pottery Ref. No. and Richard Degenhardt[20] p. No.
Sept. 5, 1868	221217	"Plate"		Echinus plate	D360 Deg. p. 177
Sept. 5, 1868	221218	"A Vase"		Echinus footed bowl	No. 380 Deg. p. 121
Sept. 5, 1868	221219	"A Vase"		Prince of Wales Ice Pail and cover	D3-I Deg. p. 99
Oct. 22, 1868	223309	"Tea and Breakfast Service Decoration or Ornamentation"	"Signed Rob. W. Armstrong, Melrose (?) Rose Isle, Belleek"	Artichoke dejeuner set	D709-713 Deg. p. 184
Feb. 22, 1869	227409	"Decoration or ornamentation for Tea and Breakfast Service, Belleek Pottery, Co. Fermanagh, Feb. 20th, 1869, Trading as D. McBirney & Co."	"Designed by Robert Williams Armstrong Feb. 1869"	Echinus pattern tea and breakfast service	D358-365 Deg. p. 177
June 3, 1869	229837	"Design for a Dejeuner tray"	"Designed by Robt. W. Armstrong"	Echinus tray	D650 Deg. p. 94
Oct. 14, 1869	234465	"Spill Pot"		Cleary Spill Pot	No. 903 Deg. p. 103
Oct. 25, 1869	235168	"Egg Holder"		Egg Holder	D1534 Deg. p. 147
Nov. 8, 1869	235827	"Design for flower vase"	"Belleek Fermanagh Nov. 8th 1869 David McBirney & Robert Williams Armstrong, Trading as D. McBirney & Co."	Marine Vase	No. 513 Deg. p. 49
Nov. 8, 1869	235828	"Design for Water Lily Vase"	Nov. 8th 1869	Water Lily Vase	D1234 Deg. p. 134
Nov. 8, 1869	235829	"Design for Flying Fish Vase"	Nov. 8th 1869	Flying Fish Vase	No. 532 Deg. p. 98
Nov. 13, 1869	236184	"Design for Trinket Box and cover"		Jack-at-Sea Trinket box	D23 Deg. p. 169
Nov. 13, 1869	236185	"Design for Trinket Box and cover"		Jack-on-Shore Trinket box	D24 Deg. p. 169
Nov. 23, 1869	236858	"Stilton Cheese Stand and Cover"		Papal Tiara Cheese Stand and Cover	D1552, Deg. p. 108- but with stand
Dec. 18, 1869	237230	"Design for Table Jug"		Harp Jug	D586 Deg. p. 182

Reprinted by permission from Mairead Dunlevy Reynolds, "Early Belleek Designs," *Irish Art Review* (vol 1, no 3, Autumn, 1984).

Trademarks have never been changed at the pottery as a "gimmick" to promote the ware.

The word *Belleek* has been adjudged to be the exclusive property of The Belleek Pottery Limited since 1929, following a court action against Morgan Belleek China Co. of the United States.

Belleek's sole right to the name has been reaffirmed in a more recent U.S. court decision.

The defendant in the suit brought by the pottery had claimed that The Belleek Pottery Limited did not have exclusive rights to the Belleek name because ware, referred to as Belleek, had been produced for a number of years by several companies in the United States. The defendant also argued that although The Belleek Pottery Limited was entitled to use the designation, its use was generic and denoted a specific type of Parian rather than the ware of the County Fermanagh pottery.

The U.S. court ruled that The Belleek Pottery Limited was not only entitled to the trademark emblem, but also to the word *Belleek*, in connection with the sale of chinaware and pottery in the U.S. market. The pottery is similarly protected in all its markets.

Fig. 5-6 The Seventh Mark, VII, was first fired on April 1, 1980, in an antique gold color. This example of D221, Belleek Flower Pot, middle size, was presented to me by staff members at the pottery. On this piece, "1st 1980," in gilt, designates it was among the first group of Seventh Mark pieces to be fired in the enamel kiln. (Richard & Margaret Degenhardt Collection.)

Basketware Identification

Prior to 1989, Belleek's basketware was never marked by ink transfer or decals unless the basket was combined with a cast base, or pedestal (Figure 5-8). The method of marking was with a Parian pad affixed to the bottom of the base. During the early years of the pottery, the single word "BELLEEK" was impressed into the pad. Later, "CO FERMANAGH" was added and, after 1890, the word "IRELAND" was included. The registration symbol ® is followed by the word "BELLEEK."

The custom of using three strands in fashioning each row of the plaited basket base was changed in 1921. For some reason lost in time, four-strand plaiting became the standard. On certain baskets the four strands were used as two twisted strands of two rows.

Fig. 5-7 Seventh Mark Trial Pieces. D1659-VII, Irish Setter. D1653-VII, Collie, male. D1652-VII, Collie, female. D1661-VII, Spaniel. These are all "one of a kind." Perhaps some or all of these pieces will be offered in the future; interested collectors may express their wishes to the pottery. (Richard & Margaret Degenhardt Collection. Evan Bracken photo.)

Hand painting of the flowered areas of baskets, when done, was in mother-of-pearl lustre. Pastel colors were not offered until approximately 1946, following World War II.

From 1955 to 1985, a capital letter and a number were impressed into the Parian pad following the word "IRELAND." Starting in 1989 a Parian pad with the trademark, in the color used at the time of crafting, was placed on the bottom of the basket's base, replacing the impressed Parian pad.

Prior to the mid-1980s, the general statement, "If a piece displays three-strand plaiting it was crafted prior to 1921, and if it displays four-strand plaiting it was crafted after 1921," could be used with reasonable certainty. This is no longer the case. In the mid-1980s some baskets with a three-strand plaited base were made. Of course, they bore the period designation of their time of crafting. Beginning in 1989 it was decided to use various numbers of strands in the rows of the plaited base. The old adage that "A picture is worth a thousand words" is certainly true in identifying baskets!

Our thanks to the talent and assistance of Marie McGrellis, of Belleek's Design and Modeling Department, whose excellent drawings are reproduced herein. Studying her drawings will provide the clearest understanding of the period when a specific basket was crafted. This is especially important for the time since 1989.

Baskets, like other members of the Belleek Parian "family," received the new blue trademark on their Parian pads beginning with the enamel kiln firing on January 4, 1993.

Fig. 5-8 D1612-I, Triboy Woven Basket Comport, middle size, 8⅞" H., 9" D. The cast base permitted this basketware piece to be identified with a black mark transfer. (Berdell L. Dickinson Collection and photo.)

Identification: The Names, the Marks, and the Ware

1. "Belleek" 3-strand, 1865–1890

2. "Belleek/Co Fermanagh" 3-strand, 1865–1890

3. "Belleek/Co Fermanagh/Ireland" 3-strand, 1891–1920

4. "Belleek/Co Fermanagh/Ireland" 4-strand, 1921–1954

5. "Belleek®/Co Fermanagh/Ireland" 4-strand, 1955–1979

6. "Belleek®/Ireland" 4-strand, 1980–1985

BELLEEK BASKETWARE 1865–1985

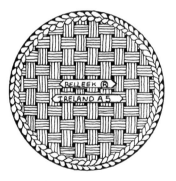

7. "Belleek®/Ireland/[number]" 4-strand, 1985–1989

8. Belleek stamp (gold/brown) 2-strand, 1989–1992

9. Belleek stamp (gold/brown) 3-strand 1989–1992

10. Belleek stamp (gold/brown) 4-strand, 1989–1992

11. Belleek stamp (gold/brown) 3-strand, 1989–1992 Small thistle and carnation baskets only.

12. Belleek stamp (gold/brown) 4-strand, 1989–1992 Small bird's nest basket only.

BELLEEK BASKETWARE 1985–1992 (Illustrations by Marie McGrellis.)

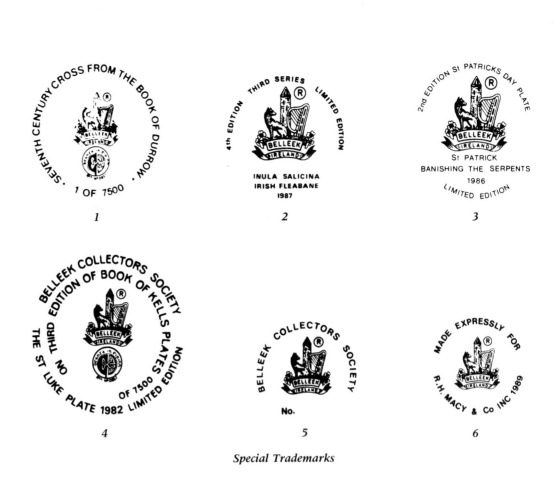

1

2

3

4

5

6

Special Trademarks

Special Marks

The use of trademark designs exclusive to a particular piece, or series, began, in a limited way, with the 1971 Christmas plate. The 1970, 1975, and 1976 Christmas plates are identified solely with the traditional mark of their period of crafting—the Sixth Mark. Designs #1 and #2, above, are examples of the marks used on subsequent editions of Belleek's annual Christmas plates. A special mark, in two colors, denotes the Gaelic Athletic Association (G.A.A.) plate. The Sixth Mark in black is surrounded by orange capital lettering, "ISSUED BY ERNE GAELS G.A.A. CLUB BELLEEK, LIMITED EDITION 1976."

A special mark in red, a color reserved for limited edition pieces exclusively crafted for members of The Belleek Collector's Society, first appeared in 1979. The first offering for the fledgling Society was the St. Matthew Plate. This beautiful plate was later followed by St. Mark, St. Luke, and St. John, as portrayed in the famous *Book of Kells* interpretation of St. Matthew. Examples of two versions of this mark, designs #4 and #5, above, provide space in which is gilted the exclusive number assigned to each individual piece.

Other limited edition and special pieces have been issued in recent years. The St. Patrick's Day Plate, design #3, above, is an example. The practice of dealer identification as a part of the design of the mark, as in example #6, goes back to the First Mark period (see Figure 5-2). It should be noted that this was seldom done.

The Ware

Regardless of the period of creation, all Belleek is quite collectable. Superior examples of the pottery's offerings are representative of each period. Subjects from the First and Second Mark periods, especially the First, which qualify as antique, are the most sought after by advanced collectors. This should not dissuade anyone from collecting pieces of personal fancy, or interest, irrespective of the period crafted. As might be surmised, Belleek of the earlier periods is rather scarce and appropriately expensive. A very satisfactory, meaningful, and enjoyable collection can be assembled restricting acquisitions to the Gold/Brown, or current Blue Mark periods.

The fact remains that Belleek is, as it was, handcrafted. Our mechanized society is appreciative of fine handcraft work and recognizes that it is costly to produce and must be priced accordingly. Generally speaking, fine crafts, especially those which have earned an international reputation, are well worth their price. Belleek definitely qualifies. Today's Parian is every bit as handcrafted as was its predecessors. The very nature of its crafting makes it far from plentiful. It is suggested that the collector become acquainted with the retail price of ware of current vintage. Items of recent crafting have been observed at antique shows and sales at prices considerably above current retail. Auctions and estate sales offer additional opportunities to secure Belleek of all periods. The few antique dealers that specialize in Belleek are versed in the product and the value. Please note I emphasize, the *few* antique dealers who *specialize*! Knowledge leads to a purchase of continuing pleasure.

There is no formal pricing of old Belleek. The market is governed by such traditional benchmarks as period of crafting, rarity, special adornment, and condition of the piece. The value guide inserted in this book should be helpful. Please remember, values of older items may change rapidly. Also, one's ardor for a particular piece is a variable factor that cannot be appraised.

It is believed that the 1904 catalogue was the first illustrated offering of Belleek produced by the pottery. The 1928 catalogue could well have been the 1904 catalogue's first illustrated successor. Though there is some duplication, the differences, additions, and deletions are of such interest that the illustrated sections of both have been reproduced in their entirety. Further, two pages from the 1949 catalogue were deemed to be worthy of inclusion. These references, plus the great find of an old Belleek photographic album (located at the pottery in a most unique and remote location, and found while I was in Belleek doing research for the first edition of this book), combine to provide an exceptional resource.

Let me hasten to say that it is virtually impossible to determine all of the pottery's early offerings. This circumstance does have a bright side. New discoveries of antique Belleek keep the collector alert and the pastime exciting. Discoveries include D1803-I, Irish Squirrel Wall Bracket, (Figure 5-9), or the large Cottage Cheese Dish, approximately 8 inches long, that a customer brought in for me to see while I was appearing on behalf of the pottery in a Tucson, Arizona, store in 1981. I have made a concerted effort to try to find the latter piece again, as I had hoped to include a photograph of this unique item in this book. Perhaps this mention of the piece will aid in its rediscovery. Had the pottery's early records been preserved, there would be no such surprises, only the search for pieces known to have been crafted.

Special orders were accepted during the early periods and were made distinctive, in the majority of instances, by the decorations applied, rather than by a change of mold design. For example, see D763-II, Thorn Tea Ware Dejeuner Set (Figure 5-10), and the front cover of the dust jacket. This service was generally offered without decoration, but as with other services, could be special ordered, (at an increase in price), to suit the color preference of the purchaser. D419-II, Neptune Dejeuner Set (Figure 5-11) was also produced tinted in green or elaborately decorated to meet a particular customer's desire. Porcelain and earthenware with the purchaser's crest emblazoned thereon were specially ordered, and certain patterns were developed to accommodate this touch of individuality.

Principal styles and designs adaptable to a broad range of decoration further en-

Fig. 5-9 D1803-I, Irish Squirrel Wall Bracket, 13⅝" H., 6½" wide. "One of a kind" and "unique." An exceptional, rare piece. (Barbara Bowman Mayer Collection. Robert DeVaul photo.)

hanced the spectrum of ware which was crafted with or without gilt, and with or without overglaze coloring. The combination of gilt and overglaze demanded the most advanced price. Statues, busts, and candelabras dramatically emphasize the extent of the skill of the craftsmen and craftswomen.

Concerning special statues, here is a particularly intriguing reference made by Armstrong in one of his diary entries from March 1863: "My Irish Statuary Porcelain from which the Busts of Mozart, Beethoven, Prince Albert were made." Six various slip recipes were initially tried on these items. In an accompanying memo Armstrong notes: "Result—No. 4 would not cast but all the rest were superb . . . the Prince Albert busts were from No. 2, but the small Beethoven was No. 6." Were these items actually produced for sale? No one knows. In any event, they have escaped the collections of principal museums, and are not pictured in references on Belleek. Perhaps one day they will surface and add their presence to the already known members of the Belleek family.

Belleek's translucent lithophanes are highly prized by collectors. Armstrong's diaries

Fig. 5-10 *D763-II, Thorn Tea Ware Dejeuner Set, painted and gilt. (Richard & Margaret Degenhardt Collection. Mark Jenkins photo.)*

Fig. 5-11 *D419-II, Neptune Tea Ware Dejeuner Set, tinted. An example of ware that could be ordered in a variety of decorated versions. (Marie Bain Collection. Mark Donovan photo.)*

Identification: The Names, the Marks, and the Ware   **81**

dated July 3 and July 12, 1866, give the recipes for trials of these lovely pieces (see, for example, Figure 5-12).

Vases, spills, mugs, tumblers, jugs, candlesticks, centerpieces, paperweights, mirror and picture frames, flowerpots, jardinieres, woven baskets and compotes, even napkin rings, further expand the pottery's porcelain offerings of tea, dinner, and dessert services utilizing a plethora of designs: plant, marine, mythological, and oriental.

Some of the patterns of antique teapots had instructions for their use fired into the underside of the lid. For example, the lid of D515-I, Bamboo Teapot, large size, is marked as follows: "McBirney & Co. Belleek Fermanagh Ireland" appears in concentric circles which surround the trademark and the instructions "Fill with water, blood warm and allow it to stand a few minutes. Empty and use with boiling water" (see Figure 5-13).

The collector should not overlook the better examples of earthenware (Figure 5-14). Earthenware was purchased for daily use; consequently, much of it was broken or chipped over the years. Also, the glaze is crazed on many pieces, probably caused by its repeated use in ovens. Although production was discontinued as recently as 1946, earthenware's share of total pottery output declined considerably prior to that time. Fine examples, difficult to locate in the United States, approach the value of similar Parian pieces in Ireland's antique shops.

Belleek earthenware is noted for the restrained and thoughtful placement of design. Quite a pleasant departure from the more universal motif of Victorian times which called for the pattern used on the rim of the article to be different than the design of the body which it enclosed. The more common treatment of simply decorating the rim surrounding a plain center body was also practiced. It is generally agreed that the pottery employed the same transfer designs from the early years until the latter part of the 1920s. In addition to transfer designs, earthenware was also produced with overglaze and hand-painted decorations. Multicolored circular wall plaques, basically with landscapes or flowers as the design, though rare, are worthy of mention as they are among the most elaborate of the pottery's earthenware offerings. Utilitarian articles of heavy-duty earthenware presenting little or no decoration ranged from telegraph insulators, spittoons, and bedpans, to foot-baths, warming plates, and shaving mugs (Figure 5-15). The pottery's trademarks on earthenware items, though often larger, parallel the use of the basic trademarks on Parian pieces of like periods.

Stoneware, refined material that became vitreous at high temperature, was mass-produced in a wide variety of items—mortar and pestles, natural and colored tiles, kitchen molds, and tableware. The designs were simple, stressing serviceability. Decorations were neither required by customers, nor applied by the pottery. Belleek stoneware was of excellent quality, a salute to Armstrong, who developed and patented a process of compressing dust-dry earth by machine into metal molds. Thus, unskilled workers were employed to mass-produce a tremendous quantity of the ware at predictably low costs, so the ware proved to be highly profitable. Thus stoneware joined with earthenware to provide the base of pottery profit, requisite to the development of porcelain pieces capable of attracting the interest of the world. The crafting of exquisitely artistic Parian pieces achieved the vital appeal to buyers of affluence, so necessary to the development of markets beyond the Emerald Isle, an accomplishment which could never have been realized through the sole production of the less fashionable and luxurious ware.

Beyond question, D1695, United States Bicentennial Plate, Flowered, Figure 5-16, designed by Tommy Campbell and modeled by the charge hand in the Basket and Flowering Shop at the time, Eamon Ferguson, is one of the most prestigious of the modern additions to the pottery's completely new designs. This splendid piece is extremely limited. The official state flowers of the United States' thirteen original colonies, each blossom tediously handcrafted and painted in the same fashion as the floral adornment on Belleek basketware, surround an unfurled early version of the Stars and

Fig. 5-15 Earthenware utilitarian articles. D1055, Telegraph Insulator. D1056, Warming Plate. (Pottery Museum. Allen Markley, LBIPP/Gary Parrott photo.)

Fig. 5-16 D1695, United States Bicentennial Plate, Flowered, painted and gilt, 10" D. Designed by former pottery manager Tommy Campbell. Fewer than thirty of this very limited edition were crafted. (Donald & Victoria Quinn Collection. Chris T. Vleisides photo.)

Fig. 5-17 D1649-VI, Birds on Branch, 5⅞" H. "One-of-a-kind" trial piece. (Jean & Max Norman Collection. Chris T. Vleisides photo.)

Stripes. The names of the colonies are lettered in gold on engraved Parian pads that are applied above the floral sprays. Lettered on Parian pads in silver, the wording "Declaration of Independence" arches above the flag and "1776 Bicentennial 1976" below the flag. The basic plate is similar to handwoven D1254, Cake Plate, except that the entire area enclosed by the rim is plaited. Of particular interest, this plaiting was done in the old three-strand style. At the time, it was the first example of three-strand rod plaiting produced by the pottery in over fifty years.

The parade of innovative and modern Belleek introductions continues—dolls; Christmas ornaments; and electric lamps adapted from vases, biscuit jars, and a marmalade jar, each offered with a shade and brass base. Trinket boxes and a honey pot became music boxes playing beloved Irish tunes. Completely new designs have been created to present the Belleek family of clocks. The vast majority of Belleek's Limited Editions, crafted exclusively for members of the Collector's Society, are entirely new designs.

The mention of limited editions is perhaps the proper time to offer a few definitions. "Limited edition" refers to an item with an assigned number of pieces scheduled to be crafted. Once that limit has been reached, no additional items of that specific piece may be crafted at any future time. "Special edition" pieces are made in a limited number and may be crafted again on one or more future occasions. "One of a kind" is a reference I use to describe a piece that was made as a sample, or as a trial item (for example, see Figure 5-17). More than one example of the item may have been crafted, but the total number at this time is exceedingly restricted. Incidentally, my use of this definition follows its customary use at the pottery. "Unique" describes a piece that is known to exist but whose proper name has been veiled by time.

A listing of Belleek offerings current in 1993, when this book went to press, is offered to serve as a reference to ware being crafted and as a convenient location to record the collector's contemporary collection. It is fitting that this list cannot be finalized, for reasons quite different than that of old Belleek. This very impediment signals the approach of exciting ware awaiting introduction or reintroduction. The latter possibility, representing some of the most honored pieces in Belleek's history, is receiving the pottery's considered attention.

Born of famine to eventually survive wars, depressions, and rumors, Belleek—the pottery, the people, and the village—continues on, enhancing its own traditions and gaining new admirers. All the years that have gone before, the talent, faith, and imagination of those who have perfected the ceramic art form which is Belleek, come together as the legacy of this generation of craftsmen and craftswomen, making possible the improbable thought that the best of the best is yet to be.

During my research, many questions were asked of respected authorities and were answered in a variety of ways. Of all the answers given I would like to relate Kevin McCann's. Kevin, like Tommy Campbell, started at the pottery at age fourteen. Employed as an assistant to a maker of common ware (earthenware) he worked in nearly every department over the years. In 1950 he became responsible for training apprentices, and in 1953 he was appointed warehouse manager. He became sales manager in 1972, a position he held until his retirement in 1981. It gives me particular pleasure to share Kevin's simple direct statement with you: "Belleek has given something to the world beyond a product for market and profit."

PART TWO

BELLEEK

A GALLERY

OF OLD AND

CURRENT WARE

PART TWO begins with a gallery of more than 700 individual Belleek pieces. It illustrates old and rare Belleek from museums and private collections throughout the world, as well as pieces in current production. Each piece, old or current, is individually numbered and named. Collectors will find this to be an especially important chapter of the book.

Following the gallery is a listing of current Belleek parian ware and a listing of old Belleek parian ware and earthenware. Both are numbered and cross-referenced to the pages on which the ware appears.

Using these listings and accompanying illustrations, the collector should have no problem in identifying individual Belleek pieces.

Also included is a reproduction of the illustrated portion of the earliest pictorial catalogue of Belleek known by the pottery and the author to exist, namely the 1904 Catalogue. The 1928 catalogue's illustrated pages have also been included.

The Numbering System

A numbering system is requisite to the identification of both contemporary Belleek ware and Belleek ware that qualifies as antique or is not in current crafting. The Degenhardt numbering system assigns a "D" prefix to the numbers used by the pottery in the 1904 catalogue. Several times in the past, the pottery has reused numbers for different items. Therefore, it was necessary to assign a new "D" prefix number to all ware not featured in the 1904 catalogue. Ware of this description, which I had identified as having been crafted at the time the first edition of *Belleek: The Complete Collector's Guide and Illustrated Reference* was published, was assigned "D" numbers beginning with D1100 and ending with D1575. This second edition continues the system, listing all ware that has subsequently been identified or retired by the pottery during the intervening years. This ware is identified with numbers beginning at D1600 and ending at D2111. Items without a pottery mark are not listed, with the exception of D1721, Queen Victoria Frame, Flowered and D2103, Scent Bottle, Pierced. The mark was on the presentation box of the latter.

For example, "1" refers to the current tall shape, Shamrock Ware Tea Cup, while "3" refers to the Shamrock Ware Tea Saucer. The designation D1 applies to the Figure of Erin; D3 applies to the Prince of Wales Ice Pail. D375 applies to the Shamrock Ware Tea Cup and Saucer, Tall Shape, crafted in a period prior to the Eighth (current) mark.

The periods of crafting are identified by the use of a corresponding Roman numeral. This system applies to pieces marked in the first seven periods of the pottery's history. Thus, D414-II refers to the Neptune Tea Ware Tea Cup and Saucer of the Second Mark period; D414-VI identifies the same set crafted during the Sixth Mark years.

Components of a set are identified by letters: "c" refers to a tea cup, "cc" to a coffee cup, "s" to a saucer, "cr" to a cream, "su" to a sugar and "os" to an open salt. For instance, a Neptune Tea Ware Saucer from the Fourth Mark era, without its companion tea cup, would be referred to as D414-IV-s. The Fifth Mark cream from D243-V, Ribbon Cream and Sugar set, would be designated as D243-V-cr.

The research for this volume was lengthy and painstaking. But, because of Belleek's scant early records, it is likely that pieces not included in this guide may be discovered by sharp-eyed collectors of the future. If you turn out to be a discoverer, please contact the author. The inclusion of newly found ware in possible future literature on Belleek would be of service to collectors everywhere.

D541-II, Lily Tea Ware Dejeuner Set, tinted and gilt. (Robert & Geraldine Moore Collection. Marty Perlman Studio photo.)

D674-I, Finner Tea Ware Dejeuner Set, painted and gilt. (Robert & Geraldine Moore Collection. Marty Perlman Studio photo.)

Sydney Tea Ware, tinted. D611-II, Tray. D607-II, Tea and Saucer. D609-II, Sugar, small size. D610-II, Cream, small size. D608-II, Teapot. (Robert & Geraldine Moore Collection. Marty Perlman Studio photo.)

D488-I, Chinese Tea Ware Dejeuner Set, painted and gilt. (Robert & Geraldine Moore Collection. Marty Perlman Studio photo.)

D804-I, Lace Tea Ware Dejeuner Set, painted silver and gilt. (Robert & Geraldine Moore Collection. Marty Perlman Studio photo.)

D737-I, Grass Tea Ware Dejeuner Set, painted and gilt. (Robert & Geraldine Moore Collection. Marty Perlman Studio photo.)

D371-II, Shamrock Tea Ware Dejeuner Set, painted. (Jean & Charles Weleck Collection. Richard A. Bailey photo.)

D450-II, Erne Tea Ware Dejeuner Set, tinted. (Robert & Geraldine Moore Collection. Marty Perlman Studio photo.)

D529-II, Harp Shamrock Tea Ware Dejeuner Set, painted. (Robert & Geraldine Moore Collection. Marty Perlman Studio photo.)

D437-II, Cone Tea Ware Dejeuner Set, tinted. (Robert & Geraldine Moore Collection. Marty Perlman Studio photo.)

D650-I, Echinus Tea Ware Dejeuner Set, tinted and gilt. (Robert & Geraldine Moore Collection. Marty Perlman Studio photo.)

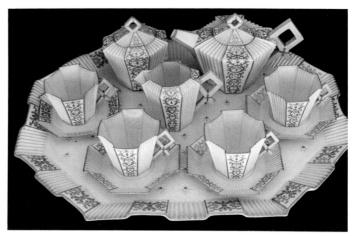

D699-II, Fan Tea Ware Dejeuner Set, tinted and gilt. (Richard & Margaret Degenhardt Collection. Richard Degenhardt photo.)

D396-I & II, Hexagon Tea Ware Dejeuner Set, painted and gilt. Probably a transition set as D-395 tray, 16½" D., is first mark and impressed. All other pieces are second mark. (Donald & Victoria Quinn Collection. Chris T. Vleisides photo.)

Shell Tea Ware, painted. D587-I, Tea and Saucer. D591-I, Tray, 14½" D. D589-I, Sugar. D590-I, Cream. D588-I, Teapot. (Bill & Vicki Houlehan Collection. Chris T. Vleisides photo.)

D784-I, Thistle Tea Ware Dejeuner Set, tinted and gilt. (Berdell L. Dickinson Collection and photo.)

Mask Tea Ware: design embraces smiling face of Bacchus peering through vines heavily laden with grapes. TOP ROW: *D1477. D1488. D1489. D1475. D1491. D1490. D1485.* MIDDLE ROW: *D1480. D1482. D1481. D1492. D1486. D1495.* BOTTOM ROW: *D1548. D1487. D1476. D1478. D1549. D1493. D1494. D1479. D1547. (1949 Belleek Pottery Catalogue. Evan Bracken photo.)*

CLOCKWISE FROM TOP CENTER: *D1159, Root Centre. D80, Erne Basket. D145, Triple Spill, small size. D188, Sunflower Vase. D1205, Double Root Spill. D523, Low Lily Tea Ware Dejeuner Set. D151, Single Root Spill. D133, Coral and Shell Vase. D1206, Double Shell Vase. D172, Triple Flower Holder. (The Belleek Pottery Old Photograph Album. Allen Markley, LBIPP photo.)*

D2069-I, Thorn Tea Ware Stand, painted and gilt, 7" D. (Miriam & Aaron Levine Collection. Mark Donovan photo.)

Harp Collection, formerly named Harp Shamrock. CLOCKWISE FROM TOP: *255, Teapot. 252, Cream. 249, Sugar. D1364-VII, Harp Shamrock Bell. 254, Cereal Bowl. Belleek Pottery. (Allen Markley, LBIPP/Gary Parrott photo.)*

D279-I, Nautilus Cream, tinted. D664-I, Echinus Tea Ware Moustache and Saucer. D295-II, Cleary Salt, tinted and gilt. D2107-III, Spoon, tinted and gilt. (Del E. Domke Collection. Hiroko Saita photo.)

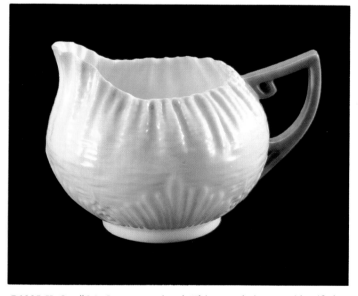

D602-I, Shell Sugar, large size, 4¼″ H. D601-I, Shell Cream, large size, 5″ H. (Richard & Margaret Degenhardt Collection. Evan Bracken photo.)

D1995-II, Set #36, Creamer, painted. This rare design was identified at the pottery only by a set number, and not a name. It may be assumed the pieces to make up a tea set were modeled. It is doubtful the pattern was placed in general crafting. ''Unique.'' (Mrs. Jeanne Dickson Collection. Beach and Barnes Photography.)

D656-I, Echinus Tea Ware Sugar, large size, painted. D795-I, Shell Biscuit Box, 9", painted. D657-I, Echinus Tea Ware Cream, large size, painted. (Josephine & Al Corriveau Collection. Frank Perry photo.)

Grass Tea Ware. D751-I, Kettle, large size, painted. D1405-I, Stand, painted and gilt. D752-I, Covered Muffin Dish, painted. D1402-1, Coffee Pot, large size, painted. (J.N. Lyon Collection. Allen Markley, LBIPP photo.)

Mask Tea Ware. TOP ROW: D1495-VI, Teapot. D1483-VI, Cream, Tall Shape, large size. D1477-VI, Coffee Pot. D1486-VI, Open Sugar, large size. D1485-VI, Milk Jug. BOTTOM ROW: D1476-VI, Coffee Cup. D1478-VI, Coffee Saucer. D1482-VI, Cream, Low Shape, small size. D1480-VI, Covered Sugar, small size. D1493-VI, Tea Cup. D1494-VI, Tea Saucer. (Jean & Max Norman collection. Chris T. Vleisides photo.)

D24-II, Jack-on-Shore Trinket Box; 5¼" H. D176-II, Tobacco Brewer, cob Lustre 8¼" H. (Missing barrel lids). (Del E. Domke Collection. Hiroko Saita photo.)

D1730-VII, Irish Christmas Cottage Music Box, painted. D1729-VII, Enchanted Holly Christmas Music Box, painted. (Del E. Domke Collection. Hiroko Saita photo.)

D111-III, Forget-Me-Not Trinket Box. D1639-I, Harp Brooch, flowered, ''unique.'' (Miriam & Aaron Levine Collection. Mark Donovan photo.)

D1677-II, Forget-Me-Not Flowered Oval Bowl, painted. D111-III, Forget-Me-Not Trinket Box, painted. D1677-II, Forget-Me-Not Flowered Oval Bowl, painted. (Donald & Victoria Quinn Collection. Chris T. Vleisides photo.)

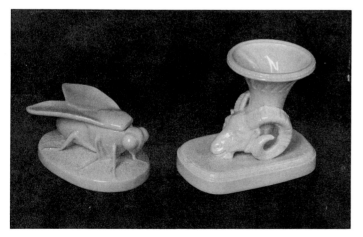

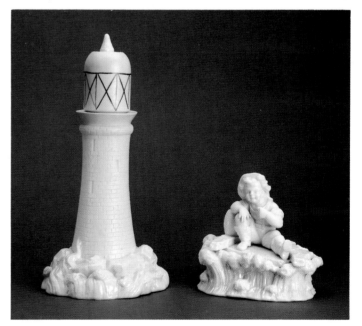

D1505-I, Beetle Fly Matchbox, 2½" H. D1180-I, Ram's Head Flower Holder; 4¼" H. (Del E. Domke Collection. Hiroko Saita photo.)

D346-I, Night Light Holder–Lighthouse, base is original, top is not. D23-I, Jack-at-Sea Trinket Box. (Linda and Larry Beard Collection. David Schilling/Atlanta photo.)

Nine old three-strand baskets, mother of pearl. UPPER ROW: *D114-2, Oval Covered Basket; small size. D113-1, Oval Covered Basket, large size. D124-2, Round Covered Basket, small size.* MIDDLE ROW: *D1269-2, Lily Basket, Flowered. D123-2, Bird's Nest Basket. D120-2, Henshall Basket, large size.* BOTTOM ROW: *D110-1, Shamrock Basket, large size. D109-2, Shamrock Basket, small size. D121-2, Henshall Basket, small size. (Donald & Victoria Quinn Collection. Chris T. Vleisides photo.)*

D1691-1, Round Convolvulus Basket, footed, mother-of-pearl lustre. This lovely basket features the same twisted-rod strand work in the base, sides and edge as D122, crafted prior to 1977. It differs from pre-1977 examples of D122 by having a twisted rod footing. (Charles Belmont Collection.)

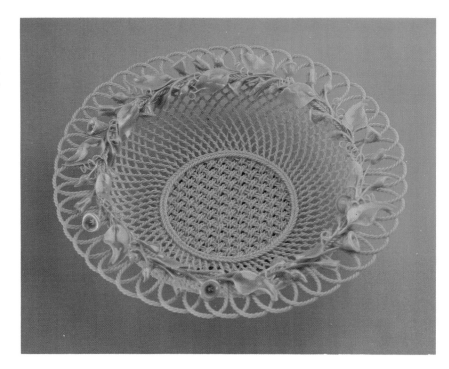

D1686-11, Cosmea Basket, Plaited, painted. 607, Bluebell Basket, painted. 608, Cherry Blossom Basket, painted. (Belleek Pottery. Allen Markley, LBIPP/Gary Parrott photo.)

615, Hawthorne Basket, mother of pearl. 616, Clematis Basket, mother of pearl. 618, Carnation Basket, mother of pearl. (Belleek Pottery. Allen Markley, LBIPP/Gary Parrott photo.)

619, Fuchsia Basket, painted. 621, Wedding Bouquet Basket, painted. 617, Beauty Rose Basket, painted. (Belleek Pottery. Allen Markley, LBIPP/ Gary Parrott photo.)

609, Daisy Basket, painted. D1248-10, Blackberry Basket, painted. 605, Thistle Basket, painted. (Belleek Pottery. Allen Markley, LBIPP/Gary Parrott photo.)

D1687-4, Double Heart Basket, flowered, painted, 9" L., "unique." (Donald & Victoria Quinn Collection. Chris T. Vleisides photo.)

D1274-5, Round Basket, Centre Handled and Flowered. Painted and gilt, 11" D. This special basket was crafted for presentation to the author and his wife on the occasion of their thirtieth wedding anniversary in 1976. Gilted impressed parian pads on the top of the plaited base denote name, years and date. "One of a kind." (Richard & Margaret Degenhardt Collection. Evan Bracken photo.)

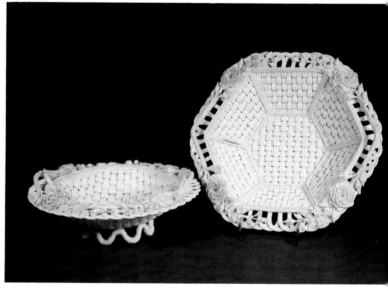

D1314-VI, Vine Tankard Jug, painted, 5½" H. 620, Spring Meadow Basket, painted. (Belleek Pottery. Allen Markley, LBIPP/Gary Parrott photo.)

D115-5, Round Basket No. 8, painted. D1262-5, Hexagon Basket, Plaited and Flowered, painted. (Richard & Margaret Degenhardt Collection. Dale Monaghen photo.)

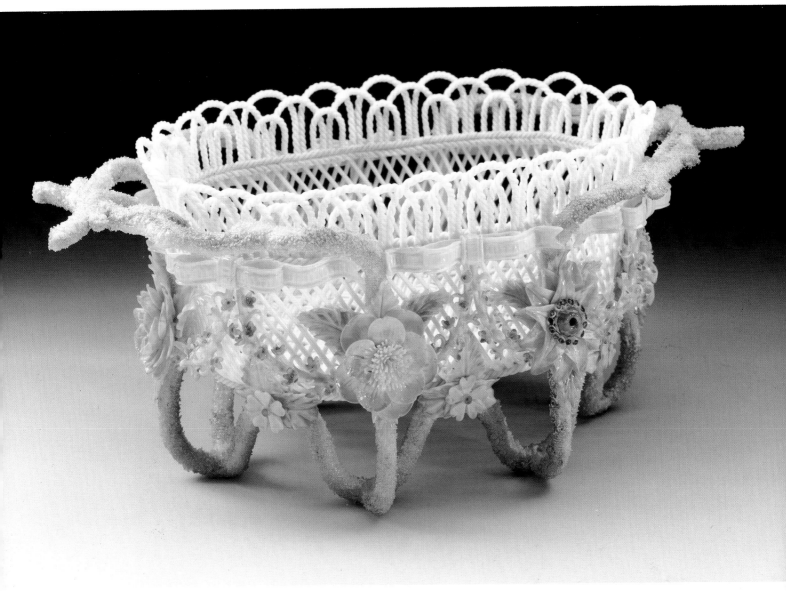

D117-5, Rathmore Oval Basket, painted. (Marie Bain Collection. Mark Donovan photo.)

D1694-4, Tea Rose Scalloped Basket, painted, 8" D, "unique" and "one of a kind." (Josephine & Al Corriveau Collection. Frank Perry photo.)

D1693, Scalloped Basket, flat rod, two strand, 11½" L, 9½" W, "unique." (Miriam & Aaron Levine Collection. Mark Donovan photo.)

D120-10, Henshall Basket, large size, painted mother of pearl. (Richard & Margaret Degenhardt Collection. Evan Bracken photo.)

D1684-3, Boat Shaped Basket, large size, "unique." (McElroy-Clarke Collection. Allen Markley, LBIPP/Gary Parrott photo.)

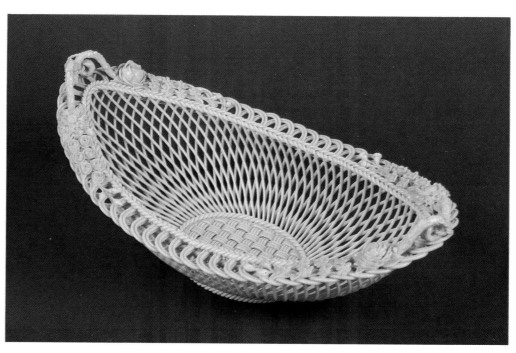

D1682-2, Bird on Round Covered Basket, large size, ''unique.'' (Marie Bain Collection. Mark Donovan photo.)

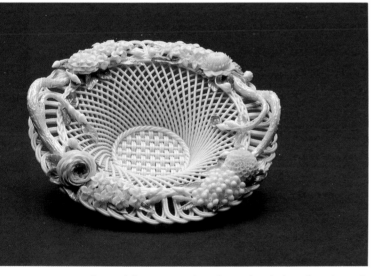

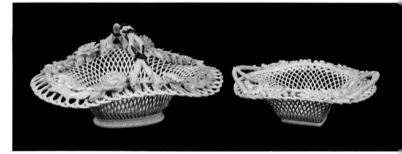

D122-5, Round Convolvulus Basket, painted. D121-5, Henshall Twig Basket, small size; painted. (Richard & Margaret Degenhardt Collection. Dale Monaghen photo.)

D1281-2, Twig Special Two-Strand Basket. Painted; the cob and purple lustre applied to the handles, base margin and some of the leaves are quite unusual. The practice of hand-painting colors on baskets was not introduced until after World War II. The style, plus the fact that it was handpainted in color, provides reason to believe it is ''one of a kind.'' (Liz & Jack Stillwell Collection. Berdell L. Dickinson photo.)

D1268, Italian Flat Twig Basket. D1251, Card Basket. D1247, Basket No. 5, footed. (The Belleek Pottery Old Photograph Album. Allen Markley, LBIPP photo.)

TOP: D1257, Hawthorn Basket, 6" D. D1280, Triple Bird's Nest Basket. D1276, Round Convolvulus Basket, plaited, 6" D. BOTTOM: D1506, Boudoir Candlestick (pair), flowered. D123, Bird's Nest Basket. (The Belleek Pottery Old Photograph Album. Allen Markley, LBIPP photo.)

D1683-4, Boat Shaped Basket, Plaited and Footed, 10¼" L. ''One of a kind'' and unique. (Hart Galleries, Inc.)

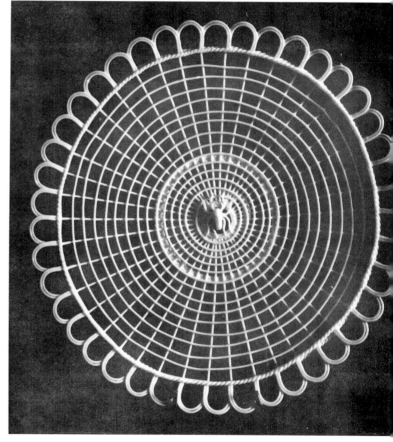

D1279, Spider's Web Cake Plate. (Hart Galleries, Inc.)

D1685-6, Cherry Blossom Plate, Flowered, painted; three strand, 7¼" D.
D1245-4, A.M. Round Basket, round
rod, edged, 8" D. (Jean & Max Norman
Collection. Chris T. Vleisides photo.)

D1250-5, Cake Plate, Round Edge.
D1263-5, Hexagon Cake Plate,
unhandled. (Jean & Max Normal Collection. Chris T. Vleisides photo.)

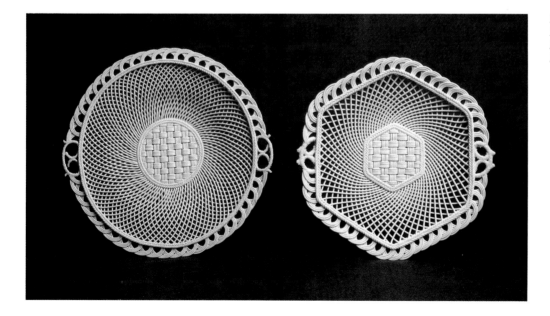

D1282-5 Twig Cake Plate, handled.
D1264-5, Hexagon Twig Cake Plate,
handled. (Jean & Charles Weleck Collection. Richard A. Bailey photo.)

CLOCKWISE FROM TOP: *D1252-3, Covered Round Basket, flat rod, pearl. D1242-3, A.B. Shamrock Basket, flat rod, small size, pearl. D1286-3, Round Basket, flat rod, pearl, 6½" D. 1242-3, A.B. Shamrock Basket, flat rod, small size, pearl. (Donald & Victoria Quinn Collection. Chris T. Vleisides photo.)*

TOP: *D1277-5, Round Covered Baskets, large size; (left) painted; (right) mother of pearl.* BOTTOM: *D124-5, Round Covered Baskets, small size; (left) painted; (right) mother of pearl. (Donald & Victoria Quinn Collection. Chris T. Vleisides photo.)*

D1249-5, Boston Basket, Flowered, mother of pearl. D106-5, Sydenham Twig basket, small size, mother of pearl. D118-5, Oval Basket, large size, painted. (Donald & Victoria Quinn Collection. Chris T. Vleisides photo.)

TOP: *D113-5, Oval Covered Baskets, large size; (left) mother of pearl; (right) painted.* BOTTOM: *D114-5, Oval Covered Baskets, small size; (left) mother of pearl; (right) painted. (Donald & Victoria Quinn Collection. Chris T. Vleisides photo.)*

CLOCKWISE FROM TOP: *D109-6, Shamrock Basket, small size, painted. D1259-6, Heart Basket, small size, painted. D1688-6, Erne Basket, painted. D123-6, Bird's Nest Basket, painted. D1253-6, Forget-Me-Not Basket, painted. (Belleek Pottery. Allen Markley, LBIPP/KR Graphics photo.)*

D1531-I, Harp, Hound and Tower Commemorative Plate, painted and gilt. (Bob & Stella Dierks Collection. Chris T. Vleisides photo.)

D1553-V, Pottery Scenic Celtic Commemorative Plate, painted and gilt. (Kevin McCann Collection. Dale Monaghen photo.)

D1894-VI, United States Bicentennial Plate, George Washington, 1976; tinted, 9" D. D2099-VII, Pottery Scene Plate, 8¼" D. (Jean & Max Norman Collection. Chris P. Vleisides photo.)

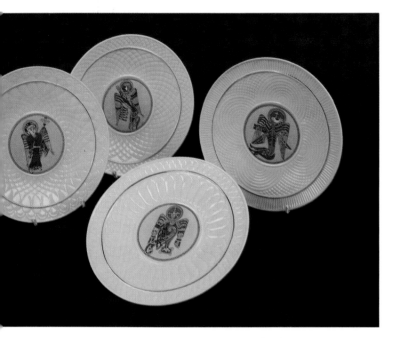

Gospel Plates. Belleek Collectors' Society Limited Editions. D1811-VI, St. Matthew (1979). D1813-VII, St. Mark (1981). D1815-VII, St. Luke (1982). D1817-VII, St. John (1984). Designs from the Book of Kells. The special red Belleek Collectors' Society mark appears on all. (Pottery Museum. Allen Markley, LBIPP/Gary Parrott photo.)

Christmas Plates. CLOCKWISE: D1868-VII, Christmas Eve Homecoming (1988). D1870-VII, Santa Claus Prepares for Journey (1990). D1871-VII, Traveling Home (1991). D1872-VII, Bearing Gifts. 1804, Bell with Candle (1990). Beginning in 1988, the basic design of annual Christmas plates changed. The handpainted rim of the Enchanted Holly pattern encircles a large, colorful decalcomania of a different annual scene. (Belleek Pottery. Allen Markley, LBIPP/Gary Parrott photo.)

Christmas Plates. TOP LEFT: D1850-VI, Castle Caldwell (1970). TOP RIGHT: D1851-VI, Cross from Book of Durrow (1971). LOWER LEFT: D1852-VI, Flight of the Earls (1972). LOWER RIGHT: D1893-VII, Trial Design—Christmas Plate (1978). ''One of a kind.'' The Christmas Mouse bowed to the Leaping Salmon as the center design for the 1978 annual Christmas Plate. (Decalcomania brought a touch of color beginning in 1984.) (Jean & Charles Weleck Collection. Richard A. Bailey photos.)

1904, My Wishes for You Plate. 1902, Irish Blessing Plate. 1907, Marriage Blessing Plate. (Belleek Pottery. Allen Markley, LBIPP/Gary Parrott photo.)

D1881, First Belleek Convention—1993 Limited Edition Collector Plate, painted and gilt, 5¼" D. D799-IV-s, Lace Tea Ware Tea Saucer, gilt, 5¼" D. (Richard & Margaret Degenhardt Collection. Evan Bracken photo.)

D2081-I, "Give Us This Day/Our Daily Bread" tray, 13½" L. (Jim Patton Collection. Allen Markley, LBIPP photo.)

D225-VI, Swan, small size, painted and gilt, 3¼" H. D254-VI, Swan, large size, painted and gilt, 4¼" H. D823-V, Ring Handle Ivory Plate, painted and gilt, 7" D. The swans were actually crafted as creamers—tail as spout and neck as handle. The latter is an example of special order ware with an initial, monogram or crest. (Richard & Margaret Degenhardt Collection. Evan Bracken photo.)

Kilkenny Collection. TOP ROW: D1970-VII, Dinner Plate. D1974-VII, Side Plate. D1973-VII, Serving Plate. BOTTOM ROW: D1977-VII, Tea Cup. D1978-VII, Tea Saucer. D1969-VII, Creamer. D1976-VII, Sugar. (Belleek Pottery. Belleek Pottery photo.)

Seashell Collection, gilt. BACK ROW: 1702, Vase, Large. 1708, Round Plate. 1703, Bud Vase. 1709, Centrepiece/Bowl. FRONT ROW: 1704, Toy Spill. 1705, Bon Bon Dish. 1706, Trinket Box. 1707, Candlestick. (Belleek Pottery. Allen Markley, LBIPP/Gary Parrott photo.)

Shamrock Ware. TOP ROW: 26, Coffee Pot. D1327-VI, Milk Jug, round, small size. D1325-VI, Marmalade Jar. D531-VI, Biscuit Jar. 46, Mug, large size. D1326-VI, Milk Jug, flat, small size. D390-VI, Milk Jug. CENTER ROW: D386-VI, Kettle, large size. 20, Cream, large size. 19, Sugar, covered, large size. D530-VI, Honey Pot On Stand. 8, Bread Plate, D389-VI, Egg Cup. D2009-VI, Honey Pot. D368-VI, Sugar, open, small size. D369-VI, Cream, small size. 16, Teapot, large size. BOTTOM ROW: D2018-VI, T.V. Set. 27, Gaelic Coffee Cup. D2008-VI, Gaelic Coffee Saucer. D1323-VI, Cup Marmalade. 47, Name Mug. 5, Side Plate. 41, Berry Dish. 7, Salad Plate. D372-VI-c, Coffee Cup. D372-VI-s, Coffee Saucer. D366-VI-c, Tea Cup, low shape. 3, Tea Saucer. 36, Dinner Plate. 1, Tea Cup, tall shape. 3, Tea Saucer. 37, Bowl. 12, Butter Plate. D2006-VI, Flower Pot, pierced. (Belleek Pottery. Reginald Preedy photo.)

D258-I, Cardium on Coral, size 2. D1515-I, Chinese Ring Peg. D688-II, Oval Plate, size 1, tinted. D681-II, Worcester Plate, size 1. D261-I, Cardium on Shell, size 2. A first mark in red is placed at the top of the shell swirl near the back edge of this piece. (Liz & Jack Stillwell Collection. Berdell L. Dickinson photo.)

D1552-I, Papal Tiara Cheese Cover and Stand. (National Museum of Ireland, Dublin.)

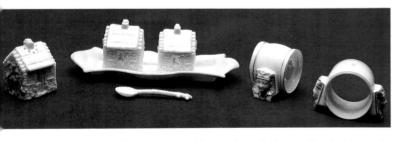

D2089-III, Irish Cottage Condiment Set, cob lustre. (Set includes salt, pepper, mustard, tray and spoon.) D1551-I, Napkin Ring, Sphinx, gilt (pair). (Liz & Jack Stillwell Collection. Berdell L. Dickinson photo.)

FAR LEFT: *D2108-I, Stilton Cheese Dish and Stand, 11" H. (Jean & Charles Weleck Collection. Richard A. Bailey photo.)*

LEFT: *D1362, Belleek Easter Egg (1972) (Richard & Margaret Degenhardt Collection. Richard Degenhardt photo.)*

FAR LEFT: *D1291-II, Ampanida Open Cream. (Brian J. Graham Collection.)*

LEFT: *D251-II-cr, Dairy Cream. This example was made expressly for "The Belgravia Dairy Company Limited." This copy circles the ribbon around the cow. The lower ribbon proclaims, "Fresh Cream." (Brian J. Graham Collection.)*

TOP: *D244, Lotus Cream. D236, Rathmore Cream. D1293, Bearded Mask Cream, middle size. D306, Scale Cream. D250, Toy Shell Cream.* CENTER: *D1294, Bearded Mask Cream, small size. D1313, Typha Cream. D234, Shamrock Cream. D249, Cleary Cream. D1309, Ribbed Toy Cream. D1303, Harp Cream. D1302, Fluted Cream.* BOTTOM: *D1570, Terrier Dog on Cushion Paperweight, 3" H. D1291, Ampanida Open Cream. D1292, Bearded Mask Cream, large size. D94, Typha Jug Spill. D305, Undine Cream. D1290, Ampanida Covered Cream. D1555, Prince Charles Dog on Cushion Paperweight, 3" H. (The Belleek Pottery Old Photograph Album. Allen Markley, LBIPP photo.)*

D1291-II, Ampanida Open Cream. D1154-V, Achilles Vase. D1179-III, Pierced Spill, flowered, small size, 2¼" H. D1225-III, Shannon Vase, flowered. D469-II, Tridacna Tea Ware Slop, large size, gilt. (Jean & Charles Weleck Collection. Richard A. Bailey photo.)

Dragonfly Collection, painted. D1915-VII, Vase. D1910-VII, Creamer. D1913-VII, Sugar. D1914-VII, Trinket Box. D1911-VII, Preserve Jar. (Belleek Pottery. Allen Markley, LBIPP/Gary Parrott photo.)

D1310-I, Rope Handled Jug, painted gilt. 5½" H. D798-I, Oblong Shell Jelly, painted. D831-I, Ring Handle Ivory Jug, painted and gilt. (Jim Patton Collection. Allen Markley, LBIPP photo.)

D168-VI, Flying Fish Spill. D1567-VII, Shell Muffineer Shaker. D138-VI, Imperial Shell. D535-VI, Triple Shell Menu. D256-VI, Cardium On Coral. (Marie Bain Collection. Mark Donovan photo.)

Spiral Shell Collection. TOP ROW: *D2028-VII, Creamer. D2025-VII, Biscuit Jar. D2029-VII, Preserve Jar.* BOTTOM ROW: *D2026-VII, Butter Dish. D2027-VII, Candlestick. (Belleek Pottery. Allen Markley, LBIPP/Gary Parrott photo.)*

D1512-III, Celtic Fruit Dish, 9⅝" L. (Bob & Stella Dierks Collection. Chris T. Vleisides photo.)

TOP ROW: *1943, Baby Cereal Bowl. 1955, Piggy Bank, tinted.* BOTTOM ROW: *1941, Baby Spoon. 1942, Baby Egg Cup. 1940, Baby Mug. (Belleek Pottery. Allen Markley, LBIPP/Gary Parrott photo.)*

D795-I, Shell Biscuit Box, painted, 9" L, 6" H. (Donald & Victoria Quinn Collection. Chris T. Vleisides photo.)

D604-VII, Shamrock Trinket Box. 929, Round Tower Vase, painted. 902, Shamrock Scent Spill. (Belleek Pottery. Allen Markley, LBIPP/Gary Parrott photo.)

51, Shamrock Pepper. 50, Shamrock Salt. 521, Kylemore Vase. 518, Trunk Stump Vase. D2000-VII, Shamrock Beer Stein. D2076-VII, Belleek Cottage. (Belleek Pottery. Allen Markley, LBIPP/Gary Parrott photo.)

Summer Briar Collection, painted. BACK ROW: 1351, Vase. 1358, planter. 1352, Spill. D2053-VII, Preserve Jar. FRONT ROW: D2054-VII, Trinket Box. D2052-VII, Honey Pot. (Belleek Pottery. Allen Markley, LBIPP/Gary Parrott photo.)

1025, Donegal Vase. 515, Harp, large size. 514, Harp, small size. D2001-VII, Shamrock Bell. 1830, Napkin Ring, Shamrock. (Belleek Pottery. Allen Markley, LBIPP/Gary Parrott photo.)

TOP ROW: 1834, Kylemore Bell Ornament, painted. 1843, Cottage Candleholder. 1846, Snowman Ornament. SECOND ROW: 1825, Turtle Dove Ornament. 1801, Bell with Star Ornament, gilt. 1814, Votive Candleholder, painted. 1832, Baby's First Christmas, "1992," painted. THIRD ROW: 1804, Christmas Bell with Candle, painted. D1643-VII, Shamrock Brooch, Flowered, painted. 1826, Kylemore Ornament, 1840, Woven Shamrock Pendant, painted. FOURTH ROW: D2068-VII, Thorn Napkin Ring, painted. 1924, Rathmore Brooch, painted. 1810, Shamrock Ornament. 1845, Christmas Stocking Ornament, gilt. BOTTOM ROW: 1923, Forget-Me-Not Brooch, painted. (Belleek Pottery. Allen Markley, LBIPP/Gary Parrott photo.)

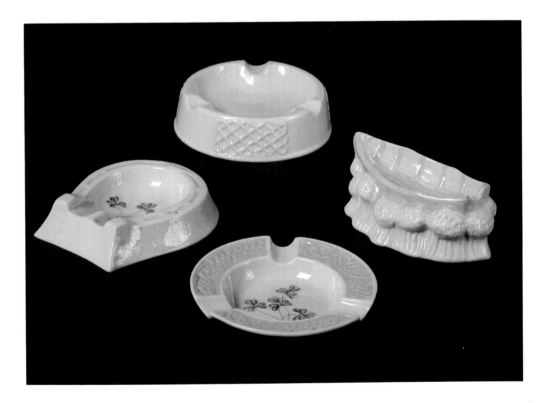

CLOCKWISE FROM TOP: D2092-III, Lattice Ashtray. D292-VI, Boat Salt. D1559-III, Shamrock Ashtray. D2087-IV, Horseshoe Ashtray. (Del E. Domke Collection. Hiroko Saita photo.)

119

Butterfly Collection. TOP ROW: *D1905-VII, Photo Frame. 1601, Vase, small, 1602, Bud Vase. 1614, Vase, wide mouth. 1603, Flower Pot, large. 1608, Vase, large.* MIDDLE ROW: *D1906-VII, Preserve Jar. 1611, Salad Bowl. 1609, Flower Pot, small. 1612, Butter Dish.* BOTTOM ROW: *1604, Candlestick. 1606, Trinket Box. 1607, Toy Spill. 1610, Bell. (Belleek Pottery. Allen Markley, LBIPP/Gary Parrott photo.)*

527, Shamrock Spill. 1221, Liffey Vase. 529, Shamrock Photo Frame. 1213, Shamrock Candlestick Holder. (Belleek Pottery. Allen Markley, LBIPP/Gary Parrott photo.)

D2075-VII, Beer Tankard, gilt. 1225, Trophy. D1765-VII, G.A.A. Vase. D1763-VII, Foyle Vase, painted. D1625-VII, Hexagon Pill Box. (Belleek Pottery. Allen Markley, LBIPP/Gary Parrott photo.)

D1623-VII, Egg Shape Covered Box. D209-V, Nickel Flower Pot.
D270-VII, Appleleaf Candlestick. D1786-V, Tree Trunk Vase. D1534-VII,
Individual Egg Holder. (Jean & Charles Weleck Collection. Richard A.
Bailey photo.)

D83-III, Erne Vase. D1567-VI-salt, Shell Muffineer Shaker. D252-II, Shell
Bowl. D1567-VI-pepper, Shell Muffineer Shaker. D1978-VI, Kilkenny
Spill. (Jean & Charles Weleck Collection. Richard A. Bailey photo.)

Selection of Belleek Collectors' Society Limited Editions. TOP ROW:
D1822-VII, Wild Irish Rose Vase, painted (1987). D1810-VI, Charter
Member Trademark Plaque, painted and gilt (1979). D1823-VII, The
Irish Wolfhound (1987). BOTTOM ROW: D1818-VII, Wild Irish Rose Bell,
painted (1984). D1812-VII, Bonbonniere, flowered, painted and gilt
(1980). D1814-VII-su, Institute Sugar, gilt (1982). D1824-VII, Celtic Bowl
of Roses, flowered, painted (1989). D1824-VII, Society Brooch (1987).
D1814-VII-cr, Institute Cream, gilt (1982). D1816-VII, Wild Irish Rose
Candlestick, painted (1983). D1821-VII, Blarney Demitasse Cup and
Saucer, tinted (1986). The special red Belleek Collectors' Society mark
appears on all of these pieces except the Trademark Plaque. (Jean &
Charles Weleck Collection. Richard A. Bailey photo.)

D268-II, Flowered Crate. D1674-II, Double Shell Flower Pot, flowered.
D2097-I, Pocket Watch Stand. (Jean & Charles Weleck Collection. Richard
A. Bailey photo.)

D275-II, Flowered Menu Holder, pair. ''Unique'' hand-painted earthenware teapot. D1685-I, Elephant and Riders, 'unique.'' (Jim Patton Collection. Allen Markley, LBIPP photo.)

Killarney Collection, painted. TOP ROW: D1981-VII, Biscuit Jar. D1984-VII, Flower Bowl. D1985-VII, Sugar. D1983-VII, Creamer. BOTTOM ROW: D1982-VII, Candlestick. D1986-VII, Spill. D1980-VII, Bell. D1987-VII, Vase. (Belleek Pottery photo.)

D207-VI, Irish Pot, size 2, painted and gilt. D1640-VII, Irish Harp, large size, painted and gilt with handmade and applied shamrocks. D1142-VI, Leprechaun, painted and gilt. (Richard & Margaret Degenhardt Collection. Evan Bracken photo.)

D275-II, Flowered Menu Holder, pair, 2½" H. D2090-II, Irish Independent Tray, earthenware. Features ad for ''Battersby & Co. House and Estate Agents, Auctioneers, Valuers, Dublin. (Del E. Domke Collection. Hiroko Saita photo.) Also note accompanying Copper Engraving from Belleek Pottery Museum (photographed by Allen Markley, LBIPP) which was used to print transfer pattern for this piece.

TOP ROW: D84. D85. D86. D1181. D1359. D1775. D1209. D1326. D1525. D1327. SECOND ROW: D219. D220. D223. D224. D1323. D1561. D225. D1172. D220. D221. D246. D247. THIRD ROW: D305. D229. D26. D301. D130. D231. D230. D500. D249-su. D249-cr. D1284. D481. D605. D389. BOTTOM ROW: D1334. D1336. D1559. D1563. D306. D604. D1356. D1316. (1949 Catalogue. Evan Bracken photo.)

1809, Visitors' Centre Mug, gilt. 1237, Visitors' Centre Spill, gilt. Available only at The Belleek Pottery Visitors Centre. (Belleek Pottery. Allen Markley, LBIPP/Gary Parrott photo.)

D1638-VI, Grand Piano with Flowers, painted, "unqiue." (Donald & Victoria Quinn Collection. Chris T. Vleisides photo.)

D2082-I, Gladstone Chamber Pot, 4" H. The fact that English Prime Minister William Ewart Gladstone was not held in universal esteem in the 1870s is made evident by his likeness on the usable inner surface. (Linda & Larry Beard Collection. David Schilling/Atlanta photo.)

D2096-II, Memorial Monument, World War I, Flowered, 8⅜" H, "unique," "MCMXIV" and "THE GLORIOUS DEAD" embossed on end panels. (Anne & Tom Quilter Collection. Richard Degenhardt photo.)

Earthenware. TOP: *D951, Eldon Ewer. D950, Eldon Basin. D953, Etruscan Ewer. D950, Etruscan Basin. D1033, Italian Ewer. D950, Italian Basin.* CENTER: *D1034, Rathmore Ewer. D950, Rathmore Basin. D939, Bearded Mask Ewer. D934, Bearded Mask Basin. D1035, Minton Shop Ewer. D1036, Minton Shop Basin.* BOTTOM: *D925, Globe No. 1 Ewer. D922, Globe No. 1 Basin. D925, Globe No. 2 Ewer. D922, Globe No. 2 Basin. D925, Globe No. 3 Ewer. D922, Globe No. 3 Basin. (The Belleek Pottery Old Photograph Album. Allen Markley, LBIPP photo.)*

D1744-I, Cross Pendant, flowered, 3" H, 1⅓" W. "Unique." (Joan McNicholas Collection. John Storey photo.)

D1523-I, Flask, painted and gilt, 6" H. (May have been crafted for sale by a Jewish organization in Dublin to raise funds to build a synagogue.) (Jim Patton Collection. Allen Markley, LBIPP photo.)

D1112, Cross Font. D1212, Hamilton Vase. D1207, Dragon Spill. (The Belleek Pottery Old Photograph Album. Allen Markley, LBIPP photo.)

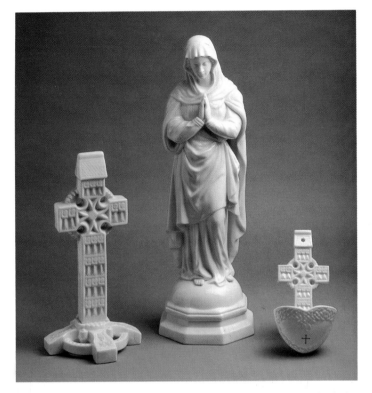

D1746-VI, Celtic Cross, large size, cob lustre. D1105-IV, Blessed Virgin Mary, large size. D1108-VI, Celtic Font No. 6, painted. (Richard & Margaret Degenhardt Collection. Evan Bracken photo.)

681, Cherub Trinket Box, gilt. 1952, Ware Carrier. 492, Cherub Font, small size. 1951, Basket Maker. 480, Blessed Virgin Mary, small size, pearl. (Belleek Pottery. Allen Markley, LBIPP/Gary Parrott photo.)

D1745-VII, Statue of St. Patrick, 18" H, "One of a kind." The other known example was made exclusively for presentation, by the people of Belleek, to Pope John Paul II during his visit to Ireland in 1979. The presentation piece was decorated in gilt and created from original designs that have been at the pottery for over 100 years. (Belleek Pottery Museum. Allen Markley, LBIPP/Gary Parrott photo.)

D1658-I, Gypsy Bather, 14¾″ H, "unique." Unusual first mark, as it is orange. (Donald & Victoria Quinn Collection. Chris T. Vleisides photo.)

D1134-I, Figure of Bather Looking Over Her Left Shoulder, 12⅛″ H. D7-I, Figure of Bather, 12¼″ H. (Del E. Domke Collection. Hiroko Saita photo.)

128

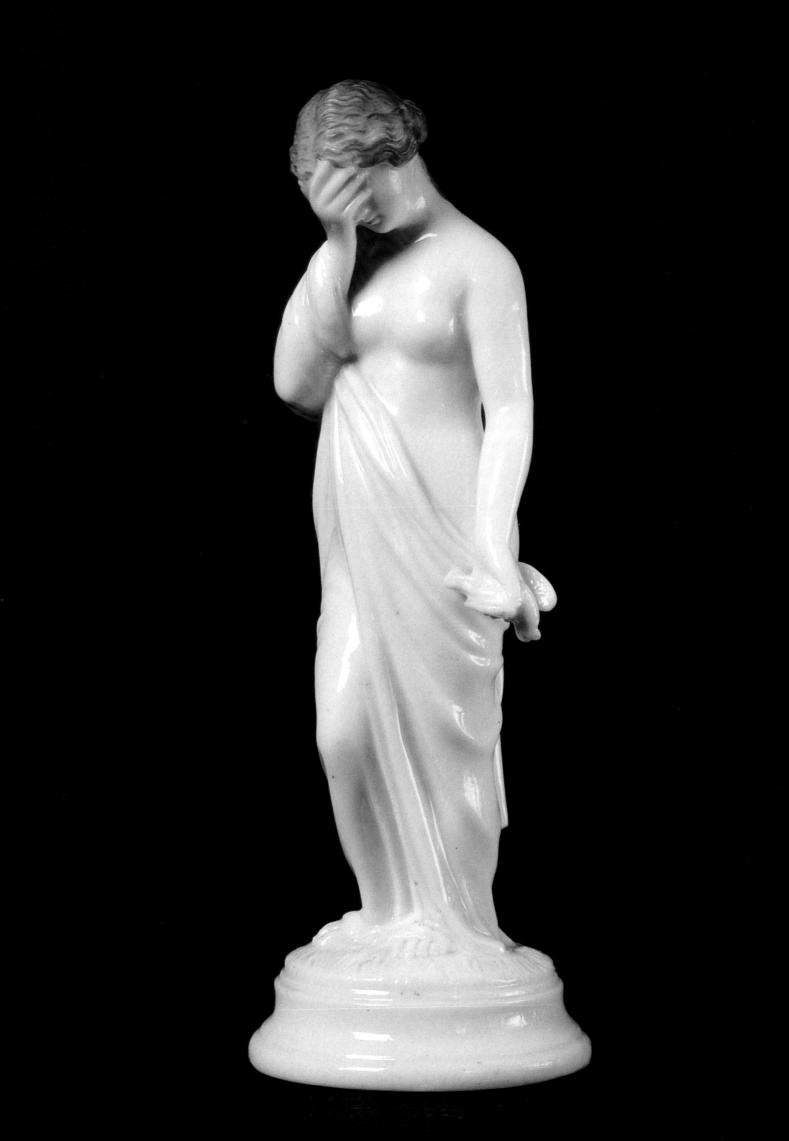

D1132-VII, Bust of Sorrow. D14-VI, Bust of Clytie. D1129-V, Bust of Joy. (Belleek Pottery Museum. Allen Markley, LBIPP photo.)

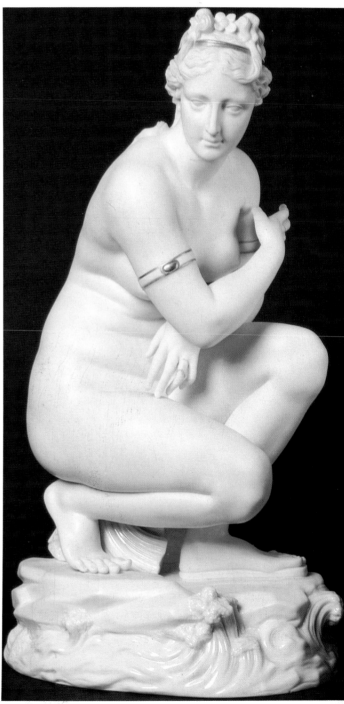

D16-I, Crouching Venus, gilt. (Del E. Domke Collection. Hiroko Saita photo.)

D1130-I, Bust of Queen of the Hops, 11½" H. (Del E. Domke Collection. Hiroko Saita photo.)

D1651-I, Bust of Lesbie, Flowered, painted, 9" H. (Del E. Domke Collection. Hiroko Saita photo.)

D1128-I, Bust of Lord James Butler, 11" H. (J.N. Lyon Collection. Allen Markley, LBIPP photo.)

D1133-VI, Bust of Wesley. The head block mold #23 among the earliest in the pottery's history as it is dated June, 1865. (Belleek Pottery Museum. Allen Markley, LBIPP/Gary Parrott photo.)

FAR LEFT: *D1141-I, Italian Grape Gatherer. (The Belleek Pottery Old Photograph Album. Allen Markley, LBIPP photo.)*

LEFT: *D1125, Basket Flower Carrier, another version of D1141 with a handwoven basket (artificial flowers). (The Belleek Pottery Old Photograph Album. Allen Markley, LBIPP photo.)*

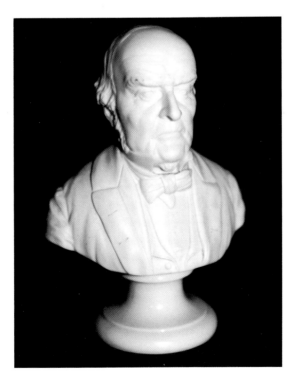

FAR LEFT: *D1136, Figure of Round-head. (The Belleek Pottery Old Photograph Album. Allen Markley, LBIPP photo.)*

LEFT: *D1650-II, Bust of Gladstone, 8¾" H, "unique." (Anne & Tom Quilter Collection. Richard Degenhardt photo.)*

D1143-II, Man with Cat and Puppies, painted, 7¼" H. Considered to be a figural piece, it is worth noting that the tree stump behind the man could be used as a small vase. (Donald & Victoria Quinn Collection. Chris T. Vleisides photo.)

D1648-I, Belgian Hawker Carrying Firewood, female, painted, 6½" H. "Unique." (Bob & Stella Dierks Collection. Chris T. Vleisides photo.)

1960, Aran Doll. 1961, Irish Dancing Doll. 1848, Elizabeth Anne Doll (limited edition of 300). (Belleek Pottery. Allen Markley, LBIPP/Gary Parrott photo.)

D10-I, Minstrel with Cymbals Paperweight. D1144-I, Minstrel with Horn Paperweight. D1146-I, Minstrel with Lute Paperweight. (Miriam & Aaron Levine Collection. Aaron Levine photo.)

D21-I, Belgian Hawker, male, 6¹/₂" H, painted. D15-I, Belgian Hawker, female, 6¹/₂" H, painted. (Miriam & Aaron Levine Collection. Mark Donovan photo.)

D94-I, Typha Jug Spill (pair). D176-I, Tobacco Brewer, painted. (Dr. & Mrs. Steinberg Collection. Berdell L. Dickinson photo.)

D9-I, Single Boy and Shell (pair), painted, 9" H. (Bill & Vicki Houlehan Collection. Chris T. Vleisides photo.)

D11-I, Double Boy and Shell, painted and gilt, 11¹/₂" H. (Donald & Victoria Quinn Collection. Chris T. Vleisides photo.)

D1526-VI, Frog Lily Pad Paperweight, painted. D137-II, Dolphin and Shell, tinted, 7" H. D1526-I, Frog Lily Pad Paperweight, painted. (Del E. Domke Collection. Hiroko Saita photo.)

D1139-III, Horse and Snake, 17" H. (Del E. Domke Collection. Hiroko Saita photo.)

TOP ROW: 1906, Belleek Kitten. D1138-VII, Greyhound, single, female. D1238-VII, Owl Spill. 910, Owl Figure. 1999, Belleek Cat. 423, Terrier. FRONT ROW: D255-VII, Swan, small size, painted and gilt. 456, Pig, large size. 425, Rabbit, tinted. (Belleek Pottery. Allen Markley, LBIPP/Gary Parrott photo.)

D1654-VII, Eagle On Crag with Prey, 21½" H, "one of a kind." (Belleek Pottery Museum. Allen Markley, LBIPP/Gary Parrott photo.)

551, Polar Bear Resting, tinted and gilt. 933, Harsbell Vase, painted. 550, Polar Bear Standing, tinted and gilt. (Belleek Pottery. Allen Markley, LBIPP/Gary Parrott photo.)

D1570-VI, Terrier Dog on Cushion Paperweight. D1138-VI, Greyhound, single, male. D1555-VI, Prince Charles Dog (Spaniel) on Cushion Paperweight. (Jean & Max Norman Collection. Chris T. Vleisides photo.)

D12, Group of Greyhounds, 8" H. (Ulster Museum, Belfast.)

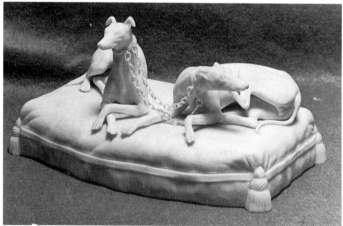

D1657-I, Greyhound Pair on Cushion. (Miriam & Aaron Levine Collection. Aaron Levine photo.)

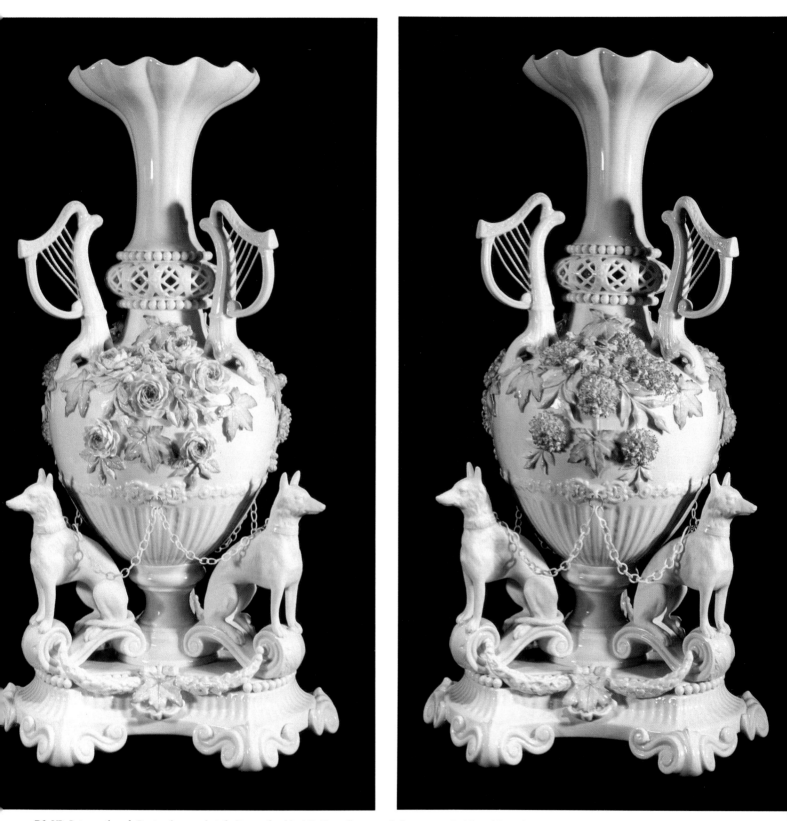

D2-VI, International Centrepiece, painted, "one-of-a-kind." Canadian maple leaves are fashioned into the three distinct flowered panels (two shown here). Commissioned by Breslauer and Warren Jewelers, Winnipeg, and presented to the Citizens of Manitoba to commemorate Canada's Centennial year, 1867–1967. (Manitoba Centennial Centre, Winnipeg, MB, Canada.)

D34-I, *Prince of Wales Centre. (Adrienne & Charles Oster Collection. Berdell L. Dickinson photo.)*

D1160-I, *Tazza on Flowered Pedestal Centre, painted and gilt. (Donald & Victoria Quinn Collection. Chris T. Vleisides photo.)*

D1165-I, *Tri Dolphin Comport, tinted, 7½" H. (Linda and Larry Beard Collection. David Schilling/Altanta photo.)*

D4-I, Minstrel Comport, gilt. (Charles Gardiner Collection. Allen Markley, LBIPP photo.)

D1610, Hippiritus Centre. (The Belleek Pottery Old Photograph Album. Allen Markley, LBIPP photo.)

D1158, Greek Table Centre, three levels with revolving trays. (The Belleek Pottery Old Photograph Album. Allen Markley, LBIPP photo.)

D1521, Echinus Footed Bowl, 7⅞" H. D1613, Tri Dolphin Comport, 5" H. (The Belleek Pottery Old Photograph Album. Allen Markley, LBIPP photo.)

CLOCKWISE FROM LEFT: *Imperial Centre, 10" H. D25, Belleek Fruit Basket. D95, Marine Vase, large size, 11" H. D258, Cardium on Coral, size 2. D805, Lace Tea Ware Coffee and Saucer. D259, Cardium on Coral, size 1. (The Belleek Pottery Old Photograph Album. Allen Markley, LBIPP photo.)*

D5, Minstrel Centre. (The Belleek Pottery Old Photograph Album. Allen Markley, LBIPP photo.)

D1162, Triboy Comport, large size. (The Belleek Pottery Old Photograph Album. Allen Markley, LBIPP photo.)

D1164, Triboy Comport, small size. (The Belleek Pottery Old Photograph Album. Allen Markley, LBIPP photo.)

D1163, Triboy Comport, middle size. (The Belleek Pottery Old Photograph Album. Allen Markley, LBIPP photo.)

143

D6-II, Bittern Comport, gilt, 12" H. (Ulster Museum, Belfast.)

D33-I, Boy on Swan Comport, gilt, 10" H. (Richard and Margaret Degenhardt Collection.)

D1166-I, Vine Comport, pierced, painted and gilt. D345-I, Boy and Vine Candlestick, painted and gilt. (Charles Belmont Collection.)

D1616-II, Victoria Triple Shell Centre, tinted, 10" H, "unique." (Mc-Elroy–Clarke Collection. Allen Markley, LBIPP/Gary Parrott photo.)

D25-II, Belleek Fruit Basket, 14" H, 14½" D. This magnificent and rare piece combines the skills of flower making, casting and pierced work with the firing techniques of a master. (Bob & Stella Dierks Collection. Chris T. Vleisides photo.)

D1510-VI, *Celtic Bowl of Roses, painted. (Marie Bain Collection. Mark Donovan photo.)*

D28-I & II, *Greek Comport, painted and gilt, 4½" H. This is an example of a transition piece between the First and Second Mark periods in pottery history. In this case, the First Mark is impressed and the Second Mark is in black. The date of crafting would be 1890–1891. (Linda and Larry Beard Collection. David Schilling/Atlanta photo.)*

FAR RIGHT: D1227-III, *Special Covered Vase, flowered, painted and gilt, "unique." (Ulster Museum, Belfast.)*

RIGHT: D3-V, *Prince of Wales Ice Pail, mother of pearl. (Marie Bain Collection. Mark Donovan photo.)*

D1571-I, Thorn Bowl, flowered. (J.N. Lyon Collection. Allen Markley, LBIPP photo.)

D1230-I, Triboy Vase, 15" H. (Donald & Victoria Quinn Collection. Chris T. Vleisides photo.)

D93-I, Tulip Vase, large size. (Berdell L. Dickinson Collection and photo.)

147

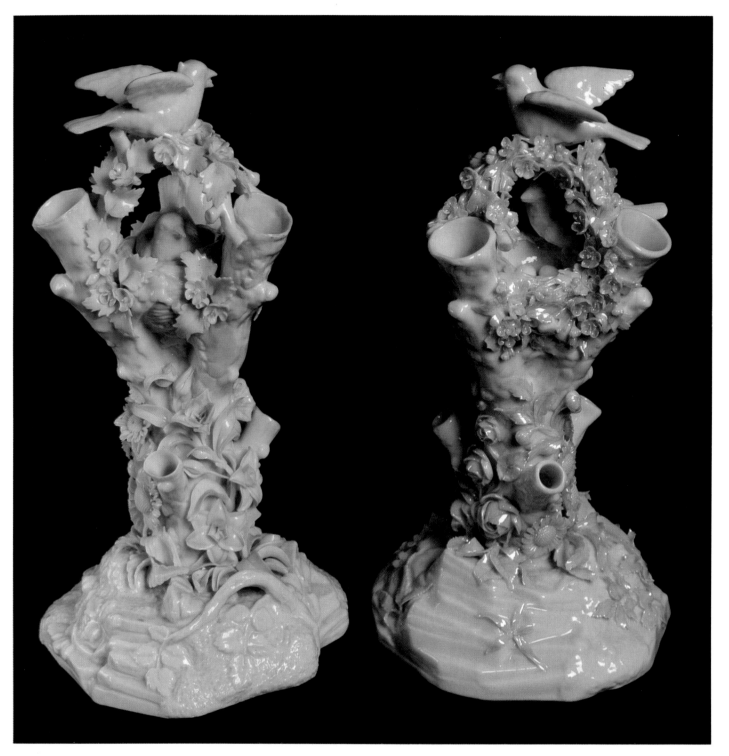

D57-I, Bird Nest Stump Vase. D57-II, Bird Nest Stump Vase. Unusual version with female perched on side of nest in which there are eggs. ''One-of-a-kind.'' (Del E. Domke Collection. Hiroko Saita photo.)

D1170-I, Angel Flower Pot, footed. (Don & Betty Clinton Collection. Berdell L. Dickinson Photo.)

D51-II, Belleek Flower Pot, footed, 10½" H. (Richard & Margaret Degenhardt Collection. Evan Bracken photo.)

D1676-I, Footed Bowl, flowered, 6¾" H, 9" D, "unique." (Ron and Pat Ring Collection. Hiroko Saita photo.)

D43-II, Rathmore Flower Pot. (Del E. Domke Collection. Hiroko Saita photo.)

D74-II, Mask Jug Vase. (Jean & Charles Weleck Collection. Richard A. Bailey photo.)

D1209-III, Finner Vase. D132-II, Covered Vase. (Jean & Charles Weleck Collection. Richard A. Bailey photo.)

D54-III, Bird Vase, 10" H. D1285, Round Flat Rod Basket, 8" D. D54-III, Bird Vase, 10" H. (Linda & Larry Beard Collection. David Schilling/Atlanta photo.)

D70-VI, Aberdeen Vase, large size, painted and gilt, 9¼" H. D1756-VI, Erin Vase, flowered, painted, 6¼" H. D70-VI, Aberdeen Vase, large size, painted and gilt, 9¼" H. (Richard & Margaret Degenhardt Collection. Evan Bracken photo.)

D60-VI, Princess Vase, flowered, painted, 9" H. D1222-VI, Rose Isle Vase, flowered, painted, 13" H. D56-V, Table Centre, flowered, painted, 11³/₈" H. (Richard & Margaret Degenhardt Collection. Evan Bracken photo.)

D1770-II, Lily-of-the-Valley Vase, 13³/₈" H. (pair). (Donald & Victoria Quinn Collection. Chris T. Vleisides photo.)

D1218-IV, Prince Arthur Vase, flowered. D1758-IV, Feather Vase, flowered, large size, painted. D1759-IV, Feather Vase, flowered, small size, painted. D1758-IV, Feather Vase, flowered, large size, painted. D1218-IV, Prince Arthur Vase, flowered. (Donald & Victoria Quinn Collection. Chris T. Vleisides photo.)

D1671-I, Basket in Hand, painted, "unique." (Don & Betty Clinton Collection. Berdell L. Dickinson photo.)

D129-I, Seahorse and Shell. D1183-I, Swan Flower Holder. D130-I, Seahorse Flower Holder. (Miriam & Aaron Levine Collection. Mark Donovan photo.)

D1226-II, Double Shell Spill. D149-I, Amphora Vase, middle size, gilt. D1749-I, Acanthus Vase, ''unique.'' (Linda & Larry Beard Collection. David Schilling/Atlanta photo.)

D127-IV, Leinster Flower Holder. D1761-V, Fluted Scroll Spill, 5" H. D127-IV, Leinster Flower Holder. (Josephine & Al Corriveau Collection. Frank Perry photo.)

D68-VI, Diana Vase (pierced). D2101-II, Rope Handled Bowl, flowered, 3" H, ''unique.'' D68-VI, Diana Vase, pierced. (Josephine & Al Corriveau Collection. Frank Perry photo.)

D156-I, Onion Spill, large size, painted (pair). D755-I, Grass Tea Ware Honey Pot on Stand, painted. (Jim Patton Collection. Allen Markley, LBIPP photo.)

D1235-II, Water Lily Vase On Rocks, painted. D151-II, Single Root Spill, painted. (Liz & Jack Stillwell Collection. Berdell L. Dickinson photo.)

D1234, Water Lily Vase. (The Belleek Pottery Old Photograph Album. Allen Markley, LBIPP photo.)

D1637-II, Dahlia, tinted. 5½" D, "unique." (Miriam & Aaron Levine Collection. Aaron Levine photo.)

D174-I, Lily Basket, painted. (Bob & Stella Dierks Collection. Chris T. Vleisides photo.)

D1635-I, Carnation Floral, painted, "unique." (National Museum of Ireland, Dublin.)

D1769-III, Iris Vase, painted, 6½" H. (Liz & Jack Stillwell Collection. Berdell L. Dickinson photo.)

D1778-II, Scalloped Shell Vase, 7¼" H, "unique" and "one of a kind." (Uric & DeLores Henehan Collection.)

D131-II, Nautilus on Coral, tinted, 9½" H. D1185-I, Violet Holder, tinted, 4½" H. D133-II, Coral and Shell Vase, tinted, 8½" H. (Richard & Margaret Degenhardt Collection. Dale Monaghen photo.)

D1232, Triple Hippiritus, 7" H. D146, Single Hippiritus, 7" H. (The Belleek Pottery Old Photograph Album. Allen Markley, LBIPP photo.)

D1180, Ram's Head Flower Holder. D1184, Triple Flower Holder, entwined handles. D195, Snake Spill. D1507, Cadawite Candle Extinguisher and Stand. (The Belleek Pottery Old Photograph Album. Allen Markley, LBIPP photo.)

D160-II, Hand and Shell Vase, tinted. D2103, Scent Bottle, pierced, painted and gilt, ''unique'' (missing stopper). Note: This piece was not marked. The mark appeared on the accompanying presentation box. D160-II, Hand and Shell Vase, tinted. (Linda & Larry Beard Collection. David Schilling/Atlanta photo.)

D128-VI, Victoria Shell, tinted and gilt. D1568-I, Single Dolphin and Wink, painted. (Berdell L. Dickinson Collection and photo.)

D76-I, Triple Dolphin and Wink. (Pickerill Collection.)

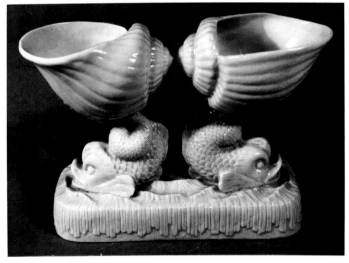

D1520-I, Double Dolphin and Wink. (National Museum of Ireland, Dublin.)

D1754-II, Diamond Vase with Handle, tinted, 9⅝" H. (Bob & Stella Dierks Collection. Chris T. Vleisides photo.)

D140-I, Clam Shell and Griffin. D1215-I, Lizard Vase. 8½" H. (Del E. Domke Collection. Hiroko Saita photo.)

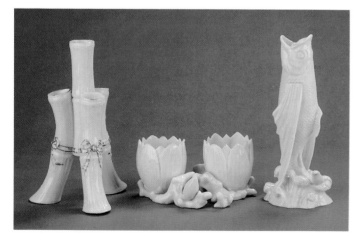

D167-I, Cane Spill, small size, gilt. D1205-II, Double Root Spill. D184-I, Fish Spill. (Miriam & Aaron Levine Collection. Mark Donovan photo.)

D184-I, Fish Spill, tinted (pair), 7" H. D8-I, Boy and Fish Spill, tinted, 8½" H. (Linda & Larry Beard Collection. David Schilling/Atlanta photo.)

D1788-I, Triple Fish and Water Lily Vase, 10″ H, ''unique.'' (Mulhern Collection. Bill Swartz/BBS Images photo.)

CLOCKWISE FROM LEFT: 435, Bird's Nest Tree Stump Vase, painted. 663, Princess Vase, painted. 646, Triple Fish Vase, painted. 661, Thistle Vase, painted. (Belleek Pottery. Allen Markley, LBIPP/KR Graphics photo.)

D1204-I, Double Fish Vase, painted, 11⅞″ H. D1231-I, Triple Fish Vase, painted and gilt, 16¼″ H. (Linda and Larry Beard Collection. David Schilling/Atlanta photo.)

159

D89-II, Triple Shell Spill, tinted (pair), 4" H.
D1550-I, Menu Tablet. (Linda and Larry Beard
Collection. David Schilling/Atlanta photo.)

D1768-I, Greyhound Vase, tinted, 7" H. (Charles Belmont Collection.)

D1972-VI, Kilkenny Round Candlestick,
4³/₄" H. D1521-VI, Echinus Footed
Bowl, painted and gilt. 7⁷/₈" H.
D1762-VI, Footed Vase, 6⁵/₈" H. (Jean &
Max Norman Collection. Chris T.
Vleisides photo.)

D179-II, Flat Fish Vase, 8" H. (Anne &
Tom Quilter Collection. Richard K. Degenhardt photo.)

D152-I, Quiver Vase. (Miriam & Aaron Levine Collection. Mark Donovan photo.)

D184, Fish Spill. D1203, Dolphin Vase. (The
Belleek Pottery Old Photograph Album. Allen
Markley, LBIPP photo.)

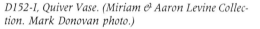

D1773-II, Michael Collins Vase, painted, 4⅛" H, (pair). "Unique." Irish patriot of the early 1900s. Another version, D1201, Collins-Griffith Vase was made with rounded sides curving out from the footed base and then back in as they reached the mouth. The profile of another Irish patriot of the time, Arthur Griffith, is on the reverse side. The same likeness of Collins as D1773 is on the obverse side. Both versions have the same Celtic design on the end panels. (Kevin & Veronica Gilmartin Collection. Allen Markley, LBIPP/Gary Parrott photo.)

D1784-VII, Thorn Vase, small size, painted, 4½" H. D85-VI, Nile Vase, middle size. D305-VII, Undine Cream. (John & Mary Ruth Steen Collection. David Schilling/Atlanta photo.)

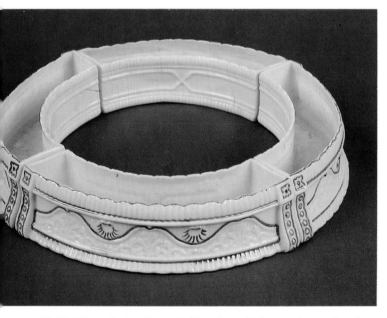

D1678-I, Four Section Flower Holder, gilt, 11¹/₁₆" D, "unique." (McElroy-Clarke Collection. Allen Markley, LBIPP/Gary Parrott photo.)

D171-I, Cactus Spill, painted, 5" H. D-181-I, Frog Vase, large size, 5½" H. (J.N. Lyon Collection. Allen Markley, LBIPP photo.)

BACK ROW: *D636-VII, Heart Plate, size 3. 676, Lagan Planter, gilt. 1077, Lagan Vase, gilt.* FRONT ROW: *D634-VII, Heart Plate, size 1. 355, Miniature Heart Dish. D635-VII, Heart Plate, size 2. 451, Undine Cream, gilt. 432, Cardium Shell, No. 3. (Belleek Pottery. Allen Markley, LBIPP/Gary Parrott photo.)*

D189-II, Dolphin Spill, tinted, 6½" H. D-343-VI, Dolphin Candlestick, painted and gilt, 7½" H. D139-VI, Fermanagh Vase, tinted and gilt, 5" H. (Richard & Margaret Degenhardt Collection. Evan Bracken photo.)

D1755-VI, Elm Vase, painted. D87-IV, Moore Vase, cob lustre. D1781-VII, Sheerin Vase, painted, 8¼" H. (Special edition—Year of the Disabled Person, 1981.) This piece, with the special mark, was sold only in Ireland. Named in honor of Eugene Sheerin. D1238-VII, Owl Spill, cob lustre. D1771-VI, Melvin Vase, painted and gilt. (Berdell L. Dickinson Collection. Berdell L. Dickinson photo.)

D1760-VII, Fluted Flower Spill. D188-V, Sunflower Vase. D1785-VI, Toy Panel Vase, gilt. D1753-VI, Diamond Vase. D618-VI-churn, Churn, gilt. D1752-VI, Celtic Vase. D1757-VI, Erne Spill. D1219-VI, Rathmore Vase. D193-VI, Cleary Spill, large size. (Jean & Charles Weleck Collection. Richard A. Bailey photo.)

977, Scroll Flower Vase, pink, tinted. D1782-VII, Thistle Top Vase, flowered, painted. 533, Cherry Blossom Vase, tinted and gilt. 536, Cherry Blossom Vase, small, tinted and gilt. (Belleek Pottery. Allen Markley, LBIPP/Gary Parrott photo.)

FROM LEFT: 674, Ribbon Spill, painted. D1220-VII, Ribbon Vase, flowered, painted. 662, Belleek Flower Pot, flowered, small size, painted. 624, Belleek Flower Pot, flowered, large size, painted. 623, Belleek Flower Pot, flowered, middle size, painted. (Belleek Pottery. Allen Markley, LBIPP/Gary Parrott photo.)

975, Shell Vase, tinted and gilt. 538, Fermanagh Vase, tinted and gilt. 532, Mourne Vase, gilt. 1222, Coral Vase, tinted and gilt. D1779-VII, Scroll Vase, tinted and gilt. FRONT CENTER: 672, Typha Spill, tinted and gilt. (Belleek Pottery. Allen Markley, LBIPP/Gary Parrott photo.)

BACK ROW: D1796-VII, Wicklow Vase, tinted. D87-VII, Moore Vase. 1074, Lotus Blossom Vase, tinted and gilt. 1230, Lotus Blossom Spill, tinted and gilt. FRONT ROW: 1012, Shell Mint Tray, tinted. 234, New Shell Plateaux, pink, tinted. (Belleek Pottery. Allen Markley, LBIPP/Gary Parrott photo.)

D2086-VII, Honey Pot, flowered, painted. D1791-VII; Tyrone Vase, tinted and gilt. D1634-VII, Canadian-Irish Stick Pin, painted. D142-VI, Honeysuckle Vase. (Stick Pin from the Pickerill Collection. Other items, Richard & Margaret Degenhardt Collection. Evan Bracken photo.)

D226-II, Double Shell Flower Pot, tinted. D2084-VI, HB Dairy Ice Cream Bowl, flowered, painted (Echinus Pattern). D2105-II, Shamrock Wedding Cup, painted. (Berdell L. Dickinson Collection and photo.)

D98-II, Shamrock Flower Pot, 8" H. (Ron & Pat Ring Collection. Hiroko Saita photo.)

513, Galway Vase. 911, Colleen Spill. 512, Sligo Vase. (Belleek Pottery. Allen Markley, LBIPP/Gary Parrott photo.)

468, Sperrin Vase. 469, Corrib Vase. 1212, Shamrock Bud Vase. 1210, Caldwell Vase. (Belleek Pottery. Allen Markley, LBIPP/Gary Parrott photo.)

FROM LEFT: 530, Leitrim Vase. D2011-VII, Shamrock Letter Opener. D2014-VII, Shamrock Pie Server. D2002-VII, Shamrock Cake Knife. 517, Daisy Spill. 1076, Connemara Vase. 544, Island Vase, Shamrocks. (Belleek Pottery. Allen Markley, LBIPP/Gary Parrott photo.)

469, Corrib Vase. 467, Island Vase, small size. 470, Setanta Vase. 468, Sperrin Vase. (Belleek Pottery. Allen Markley, LBIPP/Gary Parrott photo.)

FROM LEFT: 524, Typha Jug Spill. 513, Galway Vase. D1217-VII, Pierced Shamrock Vase. 30, Open Salt, Shamrock. D1231-VII, Harp Vase. D159-VII, Panel Vase, small size. (Belleek Pottery. Allen Markley, LBIPP/Gary Parrott photo.)

D1530-I, Gothic Candlestick (pair), 9³⁄₈″ H. D813-I, Florence Jug, gilt. (Jim Patton Collection. Allen Markley, LBIPP photo.)

D347-I, Piano Candlestick, painted and gilt, pair. (Photo courtesy of Porcelain Gallery.)

D1506-I, Boudoir Candlestick, flowered. D45-II, Flowered Spill, large size. D271-II, Woven Flowered Jewel Stand, cast base. (Del E. Domke Collection. Hiroko Saita photo.)

RIGHT: *D1604-II, Stag's Head Candelabrum, painted and gilt, 16¹⁄₃″ H, 12¹⁄₂″ W., "unique" and "one of a kind." Dr. Patrick F. Doran, writing about this rare piece (Vol. XX 1978, North Muster Antiquarian Journal) advised it "Was commissioned by a County Donegal family and does not seem to have gone into general production." (Courtesy of The Hunt Museum, Limerick, Ireland.)*

D1603-I, Shepherd and Dog Candle Holder, painted and gilt, 7" D, "unique." May well be "one of a kind." (Del E. Domke Collection. Hiroko Saita photo.)

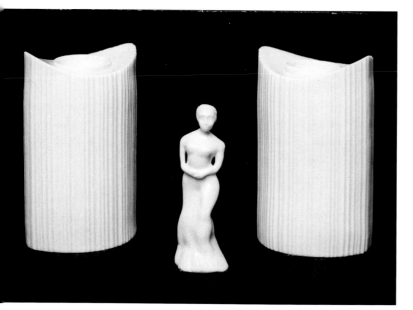

D1971-VI, Kilkenny Oval Candlestick, pair. D1660-VI, Opera Singer, 4" H, "one of a kind." Only a few of these were crafted as part of a ceramic students' project. (Pickerill Collection.)

D1126-I, Boy Candlestick, pierced. D1137-I, Girl Candlestick, pierced. (Miriam & Aaron Levine Collection. Aaron Levine Photo.)

D1602, Raised Hand Candle Extinguisher, "unique." D1600, Lady with Tall Hat Candle Extinguisher, "unique." D1356, Harp Shamrock Tea Ware Butter Plate, painted. (Ulster Museum, Belfast.)

645, Cherub Candelabra, mother of pearl, 15" H. (Belleek Pottery. Allen Markley, LBIPP/Gary Parrott photo.)

D1474-VII, Mask Hurricane Lamp. 1410, Snowflake Candleholder. (Belleek Pottery. Allen Markley, LBIPP/Gary Parrott photo.)

169

D1502-I, Amphora Lamp, painted. The body, feet and base of D148, Amphora Vase, were used to craft this piece. (Sean O'Loughlin Collection. Allen Markley, LBIPP photo.)

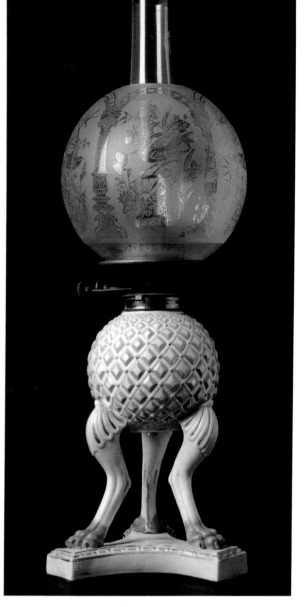

D1529-I, Globe Amphora Lamp, painted and gilt, 22" H. Base is similar to D1210, Globe Amphora Vase. (Del E. Domke Collection. Hiroko Saita photo.)

D1601-I, Papal Candle Lamp, painted and gilt, 5¾ " H, 12⅞" L. (Donald & Victoria Quinn Collection. Chris T. Vleisides photo.)

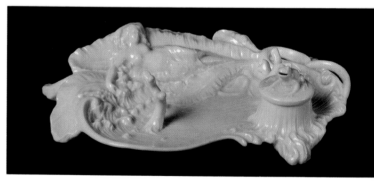

D274-II, Mermaid Inkstand; 9½" L. (Del E. Domke Collection. Hiroko Saita photo.)

641, Girl Basket Bearer. 54, Cherub Mantle Clock, gilt. 640, Boy Basket Bearer. (Belleek Pottery. Allen Markley, LBIPP/Gary Parrott photo.)

911, Colleen Spill. 1075, Blarney Vase. 53, Glenveigh Mantle Clock. 1211, Limerick Spill. (Belleek Pottery. Allen Markley, LBIPP/Gary Parrott photo.)

D1131-VII, Bust of Shakespeare, 8½" H. 58, Desk Set with Clock. 1919, Mantel Clock. (Belleek Pottery. Allen Markley, LBIPP/Gary Parrott photo.)

TOP: 90, Cashel Clock. LOWER ROW: 1929, Florentine Clock, gilt. 1931, Oranmore Clock. 1927, Killarney Clock. 1930, Celtic Clock. (Belleek Pottery. Allen Markley, LBIPP/Gary Parrott photo.)

D1721, Queen Victoria Mirror Frame, Flowered, 30" H, 22" W, un-marked. "One of a kind" and "Unique." The unmistakably Belleek figures of the Irish Harp, Round Tower and Wolfhound aptly identify this mirror as Belleek. (Hart Galleries, Inc.)

D1524-II, Flowered Frame, footed, 22" H. (Belleek Pottery Museum. Allen Markley, LBIPP photo.)

D1535, Lily of the Valley Frame, large size. D67, Flowered Frame, middle size. D62, Flowered Frame, small size. (The Belleek Pottery Old Photograph Album. Allen Markley, LBIPP photo.)

D1722-I, Ribbon Flowered Frame, 12³⁄4" H, "unique." (Anne & Tom Quilter Collection. Richard Degenhardt photo.)

D63-II, Flowered Mirror Frame, large size, painted mother of pearl.
(Richard & Margaret Degenhardt Collection. Mark Donovan photo.)

D1720-I, Lily of the Valley Frame, small size. D1503-II, Armorial Souvenir Item, City Arms of Belfast, ''Pro Tonto Quid Retribuamus.'' D1503-II, Armorial Souvenir Item, City Arms of Dublin, ''Obedientia Civium Urbis Felicitas.'' (Jim Patton Collection. Allen Markley, LBIPP photo.)

1946, Paros Vase, tinted and gilt. 1939, Oval Coral Frame, tinted. 1953, Maritime Desk Set, gilt. 1954, Maritime Paper Knife, gilt. 1938, Oval Shamrock Frame. (Belleek Pottery. Allen Markley, LBIPP/Gary Parrott photo.)

D1557-I, Round Wall Plaque, hand painted, ''Ballynahinch, Connemara.'' Dated 8-9-1880 and signed ''E. Sheerin,'' Crown/Harp, earthenware. D1557-I, Round Wall Plaque, hand painted, ''Rydal Water.'' Signed ''E. Sherrin,'' Crown/Harp, earthenware. (Jim Patton Collection. Allen Markley, LBIPP photo.)

D1533-IV, Hunter's Wall Plaque, painted and gilt, 13³/4″ H, 11¹/8″ W. (Donald & Victoria Quinn Collection. Chris T. Vleisides photo.)

D1804-II, Melon Vine Wall Bracket, painted, 14" H. (Linda & Larry Beard Collection. David Schilling/Atlanta photo.)

D1801-I, Bird and Nest Wall Bracket, 11" H. (Del E. Domke Collection. Hiroko Saita photo.)

D1800-5, Basket Woven Wall Bracket, flowered, painted, "unique," 13" H, 5" W. (Josephine & Al Corriveau Collection. Frank Perry photo.)

D1806-I, Thistle Flowered Wall Bracket. (Miriam & Aaron Levine Collection. Aaron Levine photo.)

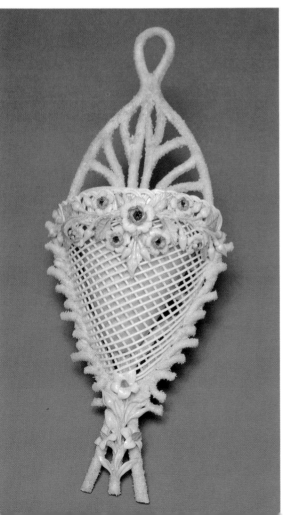

D1546-I, Lyre Wall Bracket, gilt, 8³/₄" H. (Bob & Stella Dierks Collection. Chris T. Vleisides photo.)

D1518-VI, Coral and Shell Wall Bracket, painted, 8¹/₄" H. (Richard & Margaret Degenhardt Collection. Evan Bracken photo.)

D1808-I, Wall Plaque, "Praise Ye the Lord," painted, earthenware. The copy above the angel blowing the trumpet reads, "In thee O Lord do I put my trust: let me never be confounded. Psa XXXI. Ver. 1." 8" × 9¹/₄", "unique." (Lauresa A. Stillwell Collection. Berdell L. Dickinson photo.)

D1528-I, Girl Wall Bracket, 10¹/₂" H. (Charles Belmont Collection.)

D1543, Lithophane, Ladies with Fan. (Belleek Pottery Museum. Allen Markley, LBIPP photo.)

D1542, Lithophane, Ladies with Pigeon. (Belleek Pottery Museum. Allen Markley, LBIPP photo.)

D1539, Lithophane, Child Looking in Mirror. (Belleek Pottery Museum. Allen Markley, LBIPP photo.)

D1540, Lithophane, Lovers at Table. (Belleek Pottery Museum. Allen Markley, LBIPP photo.)

177

D1537, Lithophane, Farm Girl with Goat. (Tommy Campbell Collection. Richard K. Degenhardt photo.)

D2094, Lithophane, The Alms Giver. (Bob & Stella Dierks Collection. Chris T. Vleisides photo.)

D1541, Lithophane, Child and Old Man With Harp. (J.N. Lyon Collection. Allen Markley, LBIPP photo.)

D1545, Lithophane, Priest and Altar Boy Crossing Stream. (J.N. Lyon Collection. Allen Markley, LBIPP photo.)

THE 1904 CATALOGUE

The 1904 catalogue is the earliest known visual record of The Belleek Pottery. Although earlier catalogues may have been published, there is no evidence or indication in pottery records to substantiate such a claim. The 1904 catalogue is, in fact, very collectible in its own right. Only a handful are known to exist. The one used to reproduce the photographs in this chapter came from the public library in Enniskillen, County Fermanagh, about 25 miles from the pottery.

The importance of the 1904 catalogue to collectors lies in the fact that its photos are the best point of reference for early Belleek. It is the most complete record of the pottery's work of the Nineteenth Century even though it is obvious that many early pieces were dropped from production and therefore do not appear in this catalogue.

Even if an earlier catalogue is someday found, it will still not include everything ever made by The Belleek Pottery because of the sheer volume and frequent changes in style and decoration. Thus, the catalogue is best used as a general reference. Determining the date of a specific piece still depends upon the markings.

Figures, etc.

Nos.	DESCRIPTION.		Height	Cob or Pearl.		Tinted any Colour.		Tinted and Gold.	
			Inches	s	d	s	d	s	d
1	Figure of Erin	... each	17½	63	0	...		...	
2	International Centre ...	„	36	400	0	...		...	
3	Prince of Wales Ice Pail	„	...	90	0	...		...	

Figures, etc.

Nos.	DESCRIPTION.		Height	Cob or Pearl.		Tinted any Colour.		Tinted and Gold.	
			Inches	s	d	s	d	s	d
4	Minstrel Comport	... each	12	90	0	...		...	
5	Minstrel Centre	... „	20	189	0	...		...	
6	Bittern Comport	... „	12	45	0	...		...	

D3

D1

D2

D4

D5

D6

180

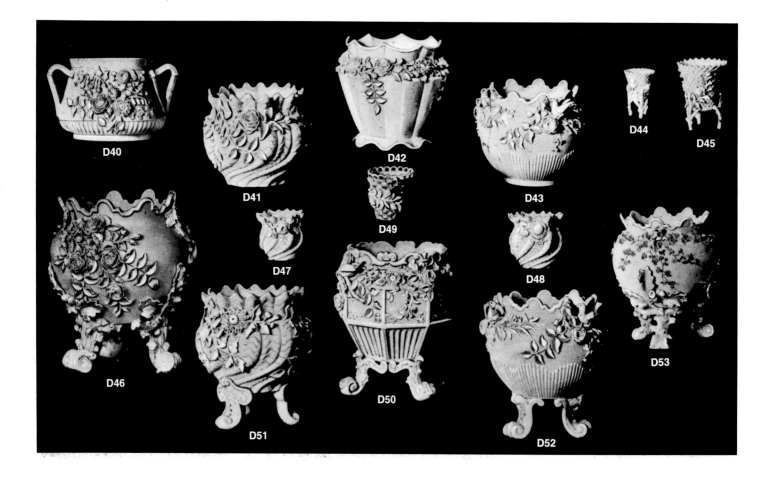

D40   D41   D42   D43   D44   D45   D46   D47   D48   D49   D50   D51   D52   D53

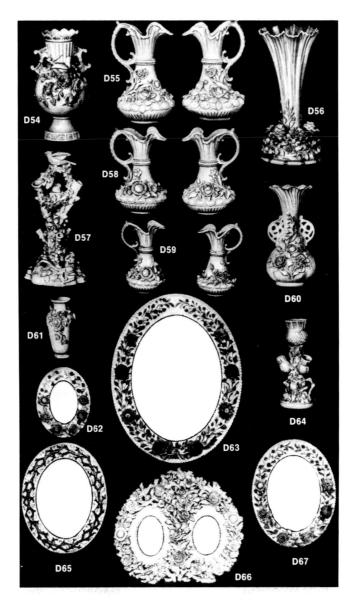

D54   D55   D56   D57   D58   D59   D60   D61   D62   D63   D64   D65   D66   D67

D68 D69 D70 D71 D72 D73 D74
D75 D76 D77 D79 D78 D80 D81
D82 D83 D85 D84 D86 D87 D88 D89

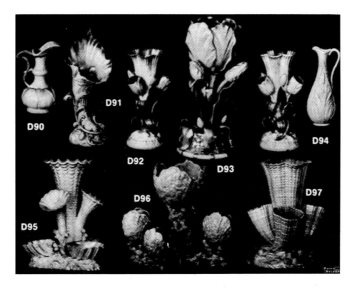

D90 D91 D92 D93 D94 D95 D96 D97

D98 D99 D101 D105 D100 D102 D103 D104

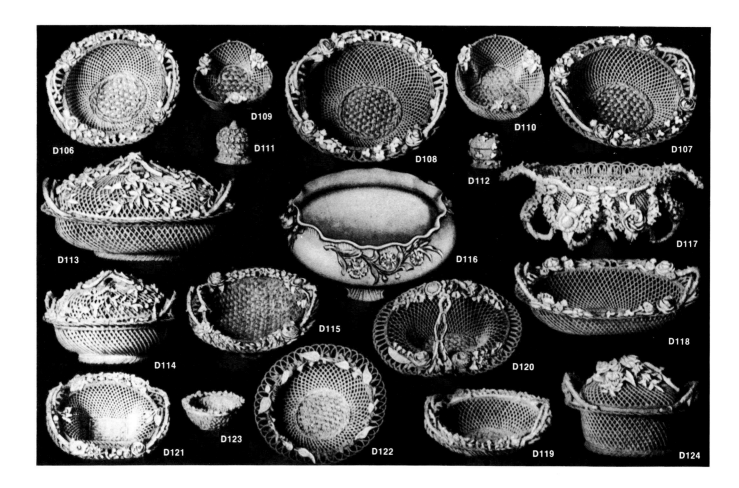

D106
D109
D111
D108
D110
D107
D113
D116
D117
D114
D115
D120
D118
D121
D123
D122
D119
D124

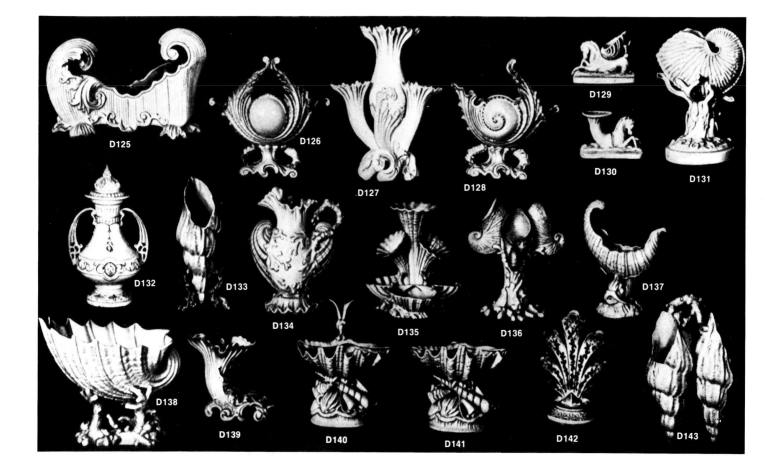

D125
D126
D127
D128
D129
D130
D131
D132
D133
D134
D135
D136
D137
D138
D139
D140
D141
D142
D143

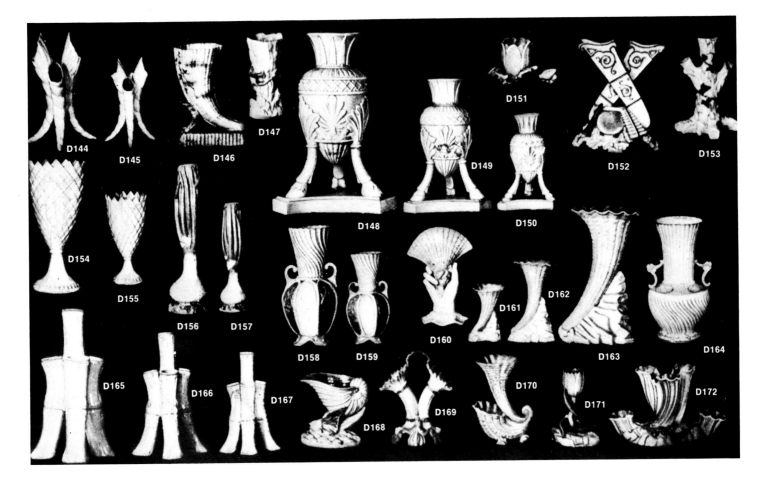

D144   D145   D146   D147   D151   D152   D153

D148   D149   D150

D154   D155   D156   D157

D158   D159   D160   D161   D162   D163   D164

D165   D166   D167   D168   D169   D170   D171   D172

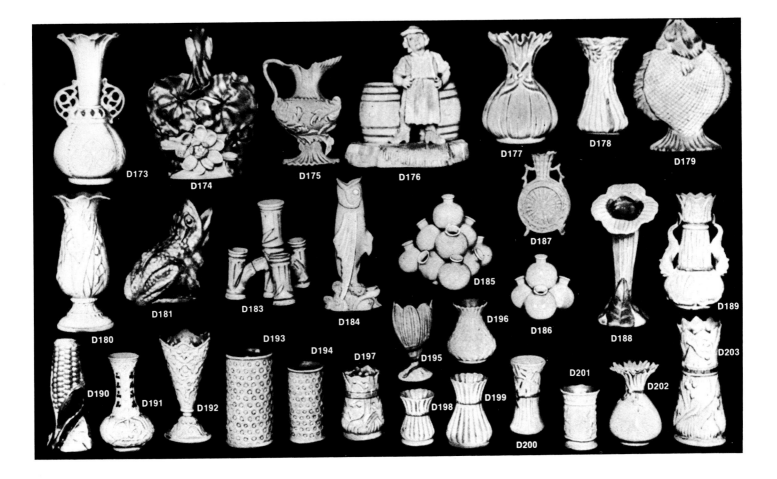

D173   D174   D175   D176   D177   D178   D179

D180   D181   D183   D184   D185   D187   D186   D188   D189

D190   D191   D192   D193   D194   D196   D195   D197   D198   D199   D200   D201   D202   D203

D204 D205 D206 D207 D208 D209
D210 D211 D212 D213 D214 D215 D216 D217 D218
D219 D220 D221 D222 D223 D224 D225
D226 D227 D228 D229 D230 D231

D232 D233 D234 D235 D236
D237 D238 D239 D240 D241 D242
D243 D244 D245 D246 D247 D248
D249
D250 D251 D252 D253 D254 D255

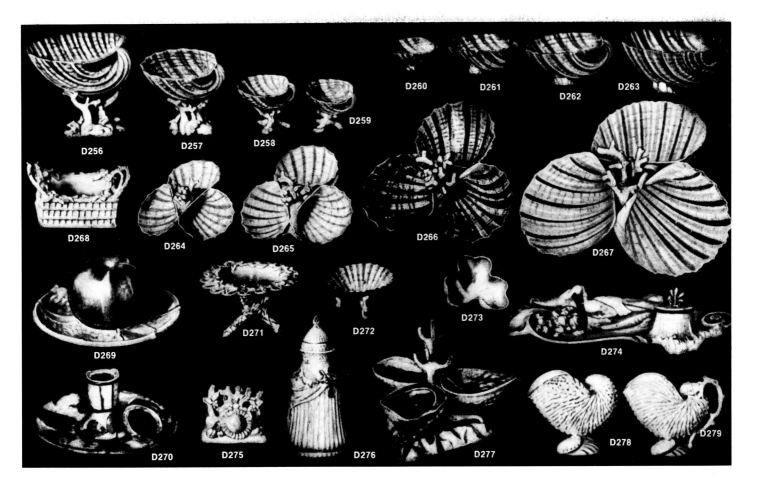

D256 D257 D258 D259 D260 D261 D262 D263 D264 D265 D266 D267 D268 D269 D270 D271 D272 D273 D274 D275 D276 D277 D278 D279

D280 D281 D282 D283 D284 D285 D286 D287 D288 D289 D290 D291 D292 D293 D294 D295 D297 D298 D299 D300 D301 D302 D303 D305 D308 D309 D310 D311 D312 D313 D314 D315

D317   D325   D333

D318   D327   D326   D334   D335   D342   D341

D319   D320   D321   D328   D329   D336   D337

D322   D323   D330   D331   D338   D339

D344   D345   D346   D347   D348   D343

D349

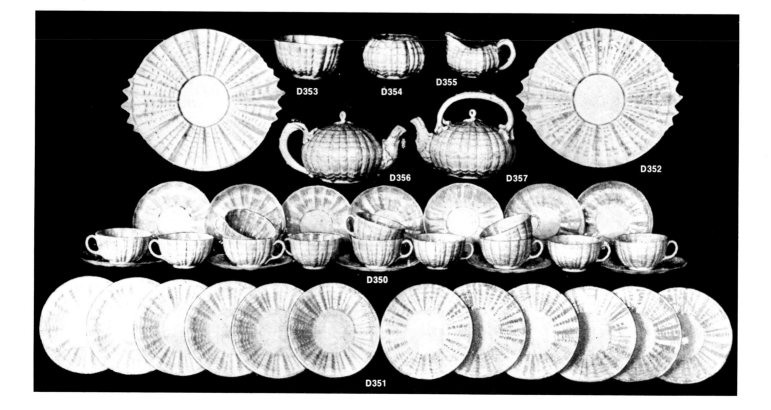

D353   D354   D355   D352

D356   D357

D350

D351

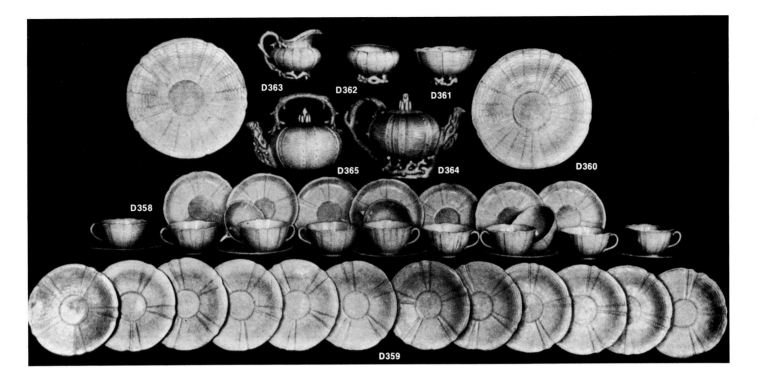

D363   D362   D361

D365   D364   D360

D358

D359

D384   D379   D372   D386

D375

D373   D376   D382   D374

D383   D389

D388   D368   D367   D369

D380   D366   D370   D371   D390

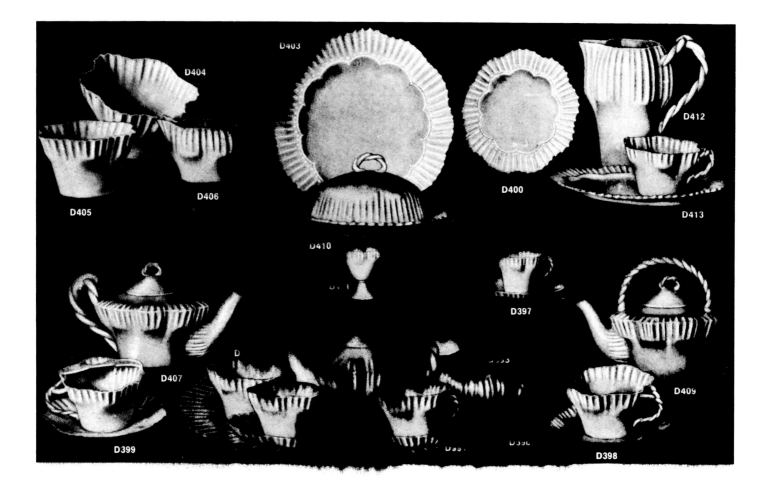

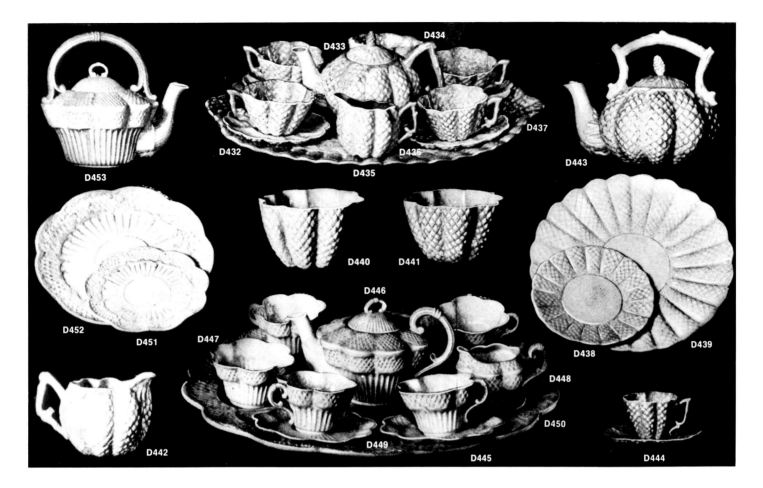

D453 · D433 · D434 · D432 · D435 · D436 · D437 · D443 · D452 · D451 · D440 · D441 · D438 · D439 · D447 · D446 · D448 · D450 · D442 · D449 · D445 · D444

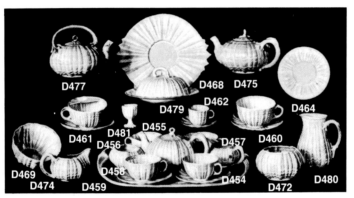

D477 · D468 · D475 · D479 · D462 · D464 · D461 · D481 · D455 · D457 · D460 · D469 · D456 · D458 · D454 · D472 · D480 · D474 · D459

D482

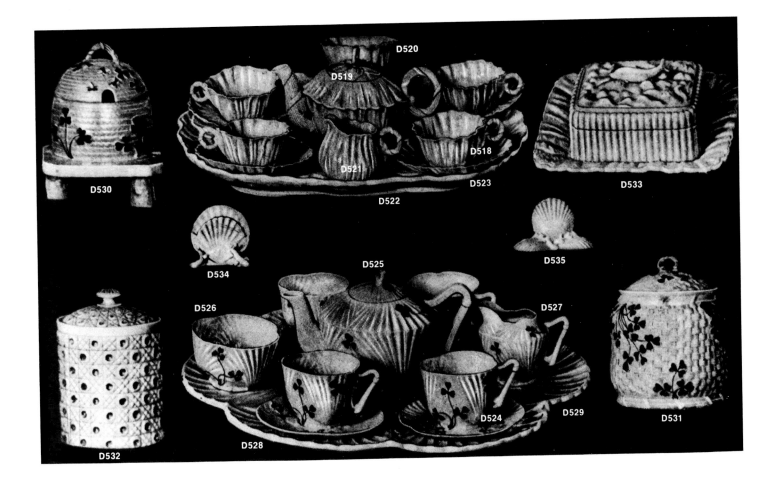

D530 D519 D520 D518 D523 D522 D521 D533
D534 D525 D535
D526 D527 D531
D532 D528 D524 D529

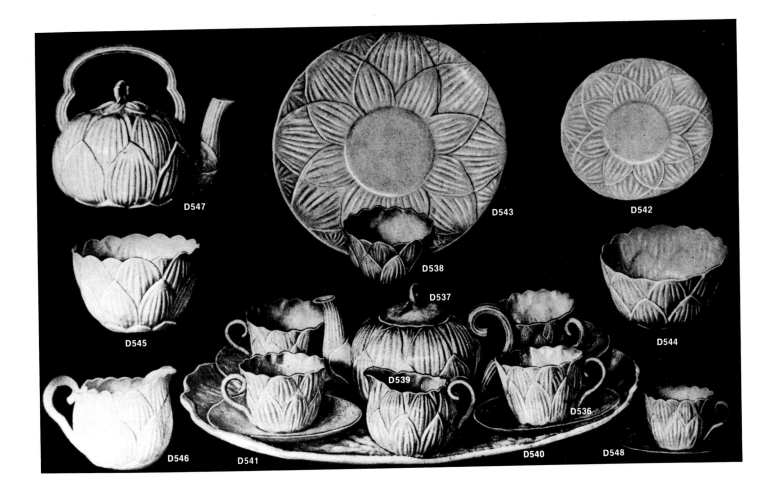

D547 D543 D542
D538
D545 D537
D539 D544
D546 D541 D540 D536 D548

193

D562 · D558 · D563 · D564 · D560 · D551 · D550 · D552 · D555 · D561 · D549 · D553 · D554 · D559 · D557 · D556

D599 · D603 · D588 · D587 · D591 · D589 · D590 · D592 · D600 · D601 · D604 · D602 · D595 · D594 · D596 · D605 · D598 · D597 · D593 · D606

D586 · D585 · D584 · D583 · D582 · D575 · D579 · D581 · D573 · D568 · D574 · D577 · D580 · D570 · D569 · D576 · D572 · D571 · D567 · D1392

D616 · D618 · D619 · D615 · D621 · D617 · D614 · D608 · D620 · D610 · D609 · D613 · D611 · D612 · D607

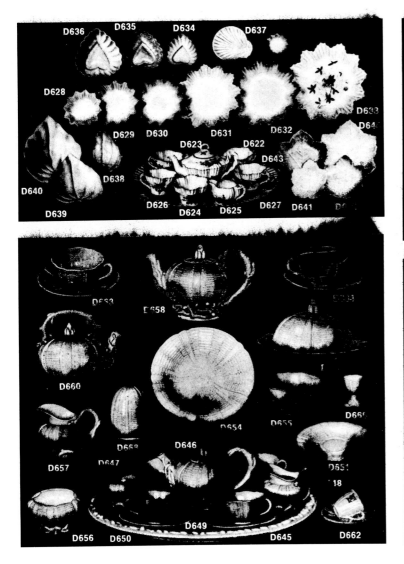

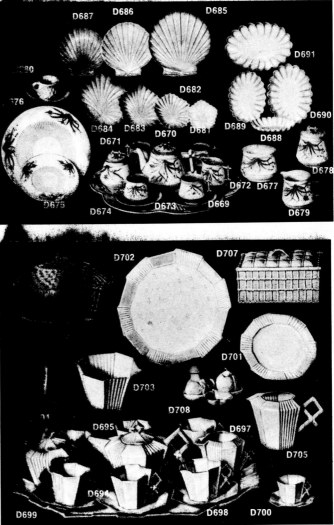

195

D716

D721

D715

D717

D723

D724

D727

D726

D730

D728

D729

D718

D719

D710

D711

D712

D709

D714

D722

D720

D713

D755

D751

D753

D756

D739

D744

D745

D754

D733

D747

D743

D752

D735

D732

D734

D736

D737

D740

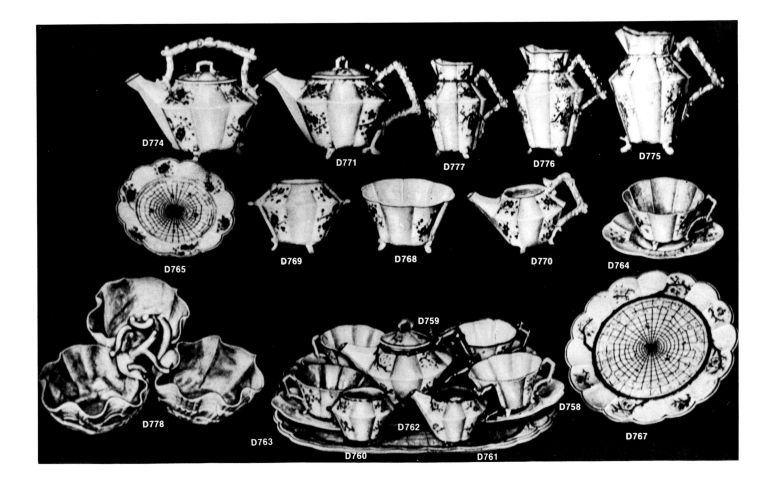

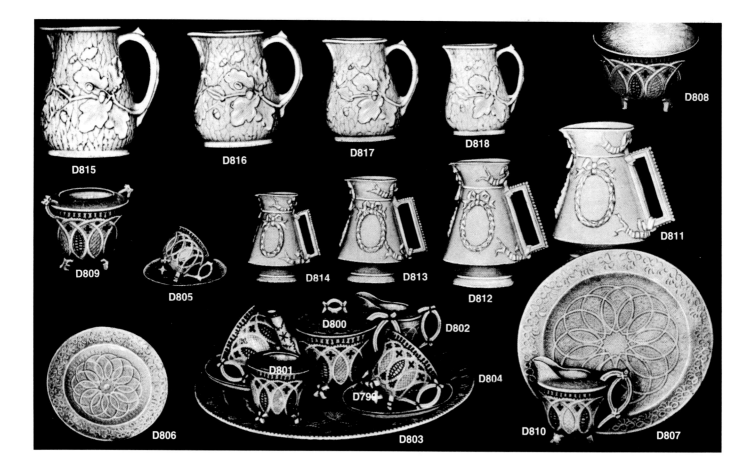

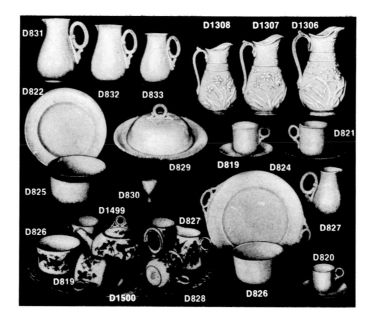

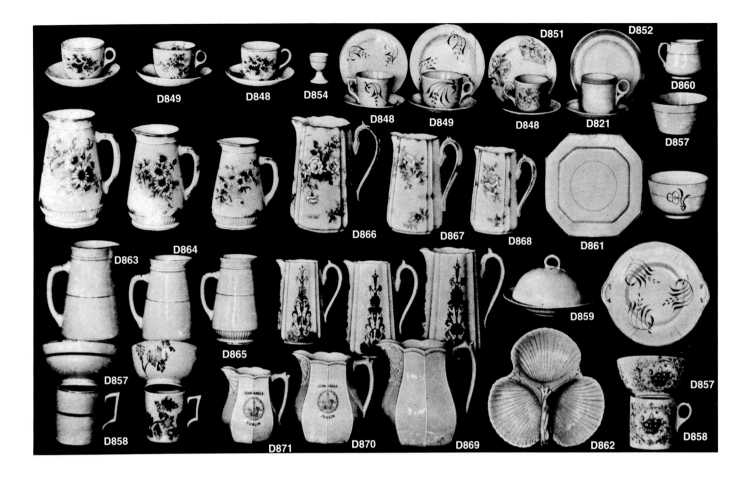

D851 D852

D849 D848 D854 D848 D849 D848 D821 D860

D857

D866 D867 D868 D861

D863 D864 D865 D859

D857

D857

D858 D871 D870 D869 D862 D858

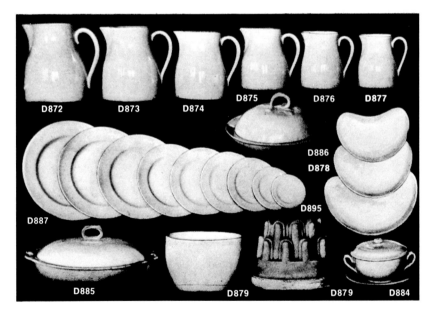

D872 D873 D874 D875 D876 D877

D886
D878

D895

D887

D885 D879 D879 D884

D915 D912

D900 D914

D897 D890

D908

D887 D892

199

D908

D915

D912

D915

D900

D890

D892

D887

D914

D887

D915

D915

D915

D915

D932

D928

D925

D929

D932

D922

D931

D925

D928

D925

D925

D932

D928

D933

D931

D922

D939

D939

D939

D934

D934

D939

D934

D934

D939

D939

D939

D934

D953

D950

D950

D953

D948

D951

D952

D953

D960

D959

D950

D949

201

D998　D991　D983　D999

D973　D961

D1021　D1018

D1027

D1026　D1028　D1029　D1022　D1025　D1024

D1013　D1015　D1014　D1008

202

THE 1928 CATALOGUE

The 1928 catalogue has also become a collector's item, as it is believed to be the first illustrated catalogue to follow the 1904 catalogue. As with the earlier catalogue, only a few are known to exist. I am indebted to Clinton O'Rourke, a former chairman of the board of the Belleek Pottery Limited, for allowing me to reproduce his personal copy in this book.

D558

D1372

D564

D1370

D559

D552

D565

D551

D272

D555

D549

D562

D466

D468

D1346

D480

D470

D477

D475

D456

D457

D1345

D462

D454

D1350

D1349

D1348

D1435 D1425

D1436 D1439 D1429 D1433 D1434

D1427

D1437

D1428

D1430 D1431 D1426 D1432 D1438

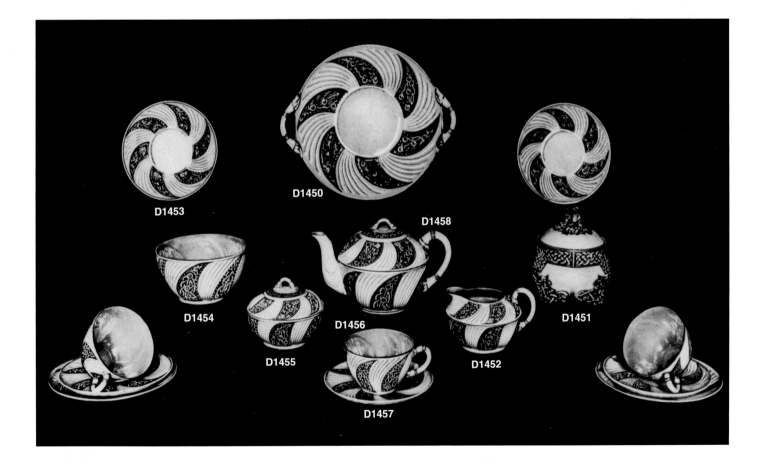

D1453 D1450 D1458

D1454 D1456 D1451

D1455 D1452

D1457

205

D1413 D1410 D1465 D1468

D1414 D1415 D1417 D1472 D1469

D1470

D1411 D1416 D1412 D1467 D1471 D1466

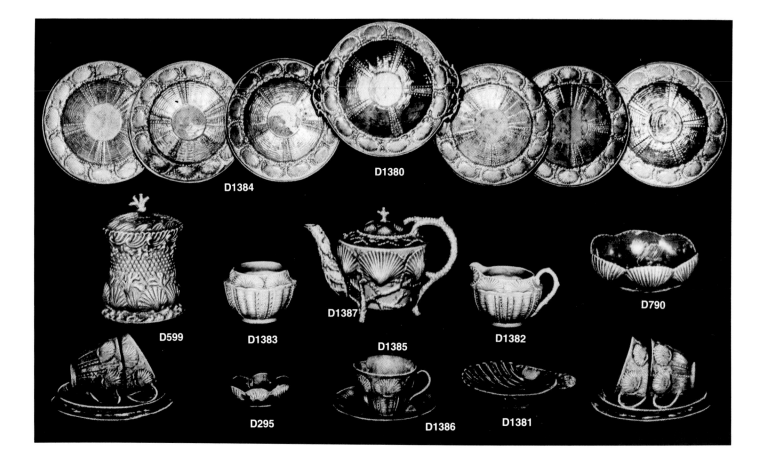

D1384 D1380

D599 D1383 D1387 D1385 D1382 D790

D295 D1386 D1381

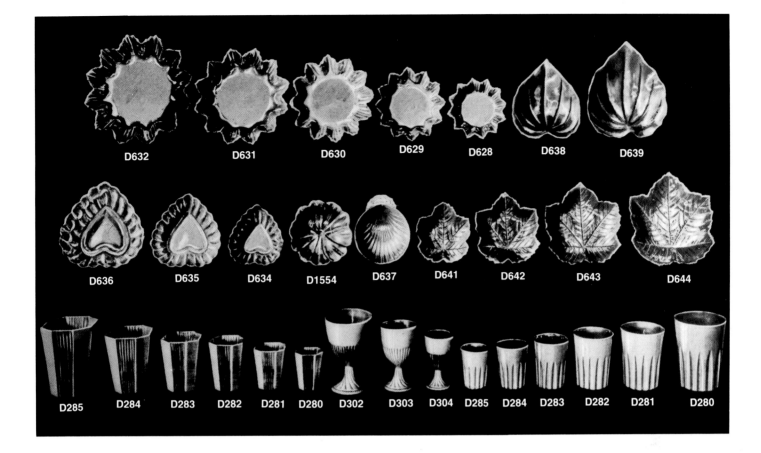

D632   D631   D630   D629   D628   D638   D639

D636   D635   D634   D1554   D637   D641   D642   D643   D644

D285   D284   D283   D282   D281   D280   D302   D303   D304   D285   D284   D283   D282   D281   D280

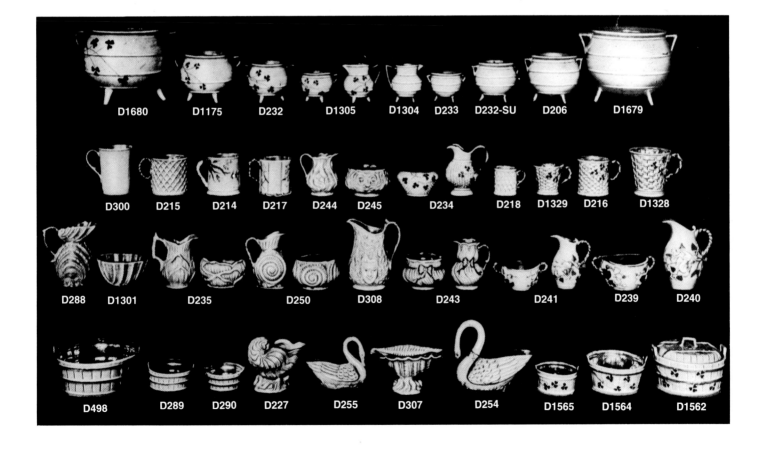

D1680   D1175   D232   D1305   D1304   D233   D232-SU   D206   D1679

D300   D215   D214   D217   D244   D245   D234   D218   D1329   D216   D1328

D288   D1301   D235   D250   D308   D243   D241   D239   D240

D498   D289   D290   D227   D255   D307   D254   D1565   D1564   D1562

207

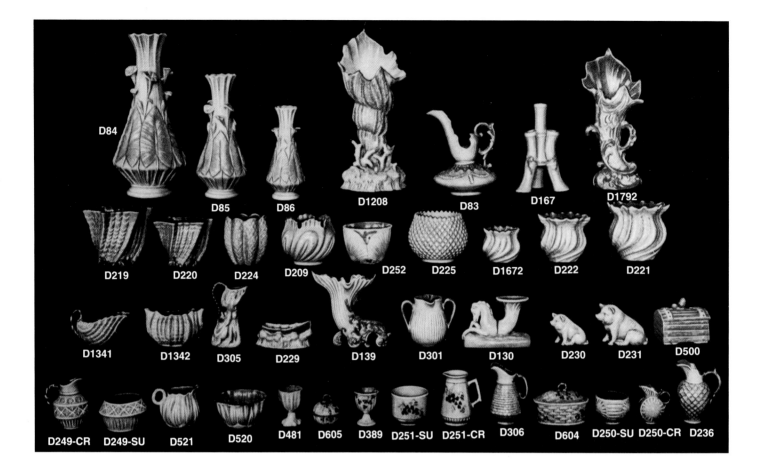

D84
D85
D86
D1208
D83
D167
D1792

D219
D220
D224
D209
D252
D225
D1672
D222
D221

D1341
D1342
D305
D229
D139
D301
D130
D230
D231
D500

D249-CR
D249-SU
D521
D520
D481
D605
D389
D251-SU
D251-CR
D306
D604
D250-SU
D250-CR
D236

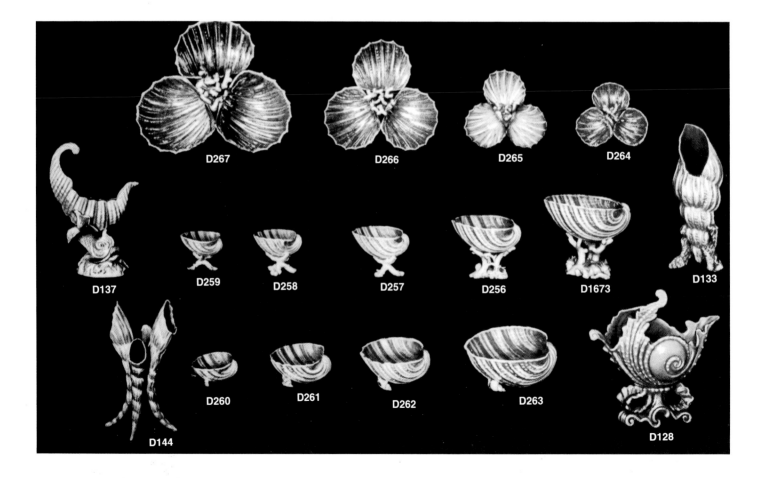

D267
D266
D265
D264

D137
D259
D258
D257
D256
D1673
D133

D144
D260
D261
D262
D263
D128

D1198

D1189   D1198   D1200   D1153   D1200   D1198   D1189

D1202   D1512   D1197   D1199   D1202

D1192   D1199   D1197   D1192

D1190   D1297   D1299   D1513   D1296   D1295   D1190

D1191   D1195   D1193   D1194   D1298   D1142   D1300   D1196   D1509   D1223   D1191

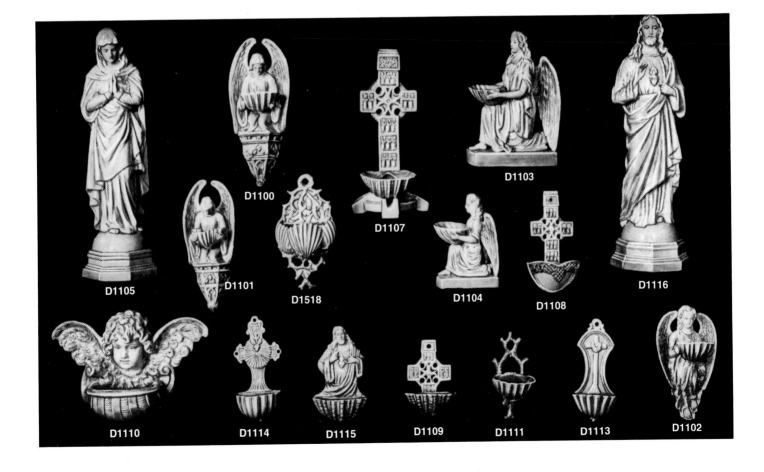

D1105   D1100   D1107   D1103   D1116

D1101   D1518   D1104   D1108

D1110   D1114   D1115   D1109   D1111   D1113   D1102

D188   D1790   D78   D77   D1213   D178   D1224   D159   D158   D88   D1217

D155   D154   D135   D95   D163   D162   D161

D43   D203   D87   D189   D191   D40

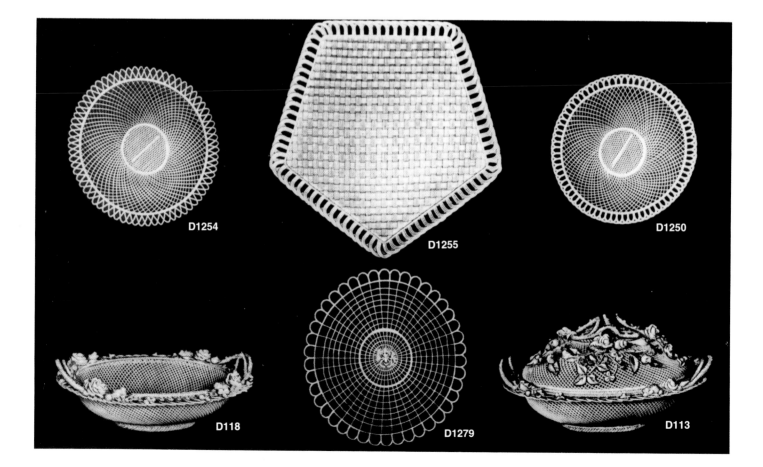

D1254   D1255   D1250

D118   D1279   D113

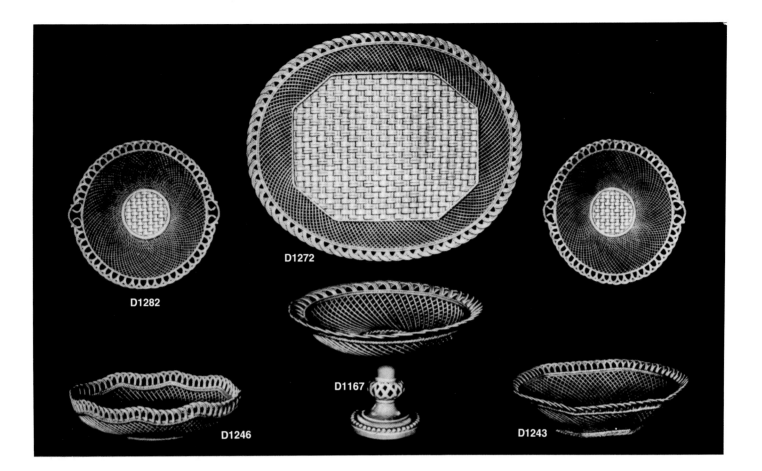

D1282

D1272

D1167

D1246

D1243

D1218

D64

D56

D60

D58

D1220

D66

D55

D59

D61

D45

D44

D62

D1179

D49

D1782

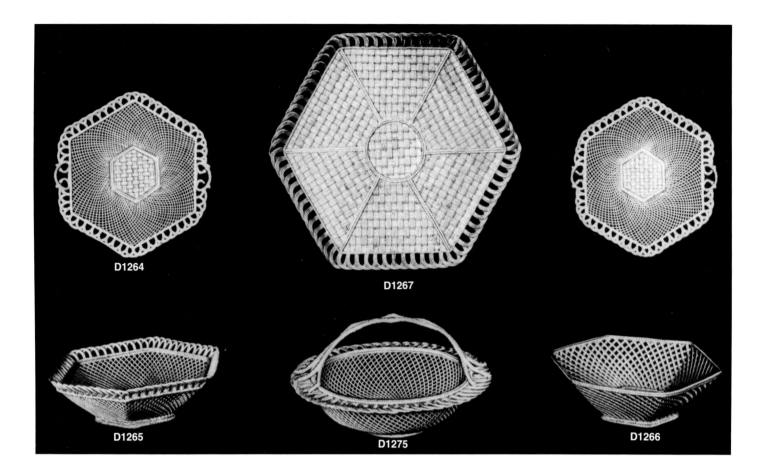

D1264

D1267

D1265

D1275

D1266

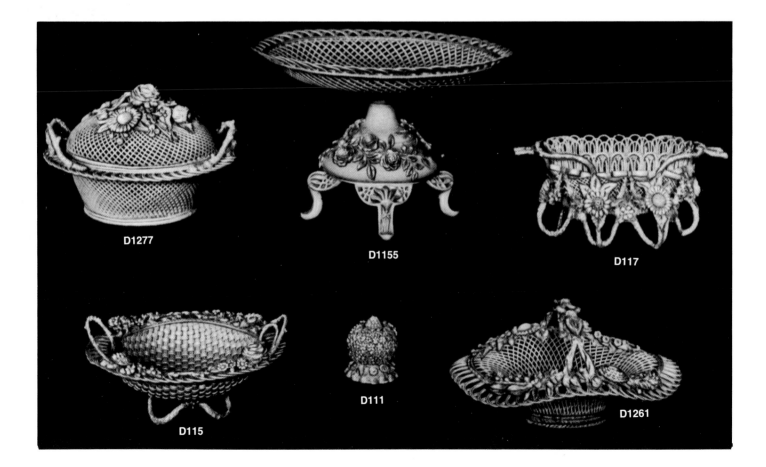

D1277

D1155

D117

D115

D111

D1261

D52

D1244

D57

D1245

D53

D48

D120

D1262

D47 D211 D212 D112 D14 D271 D1242 D20

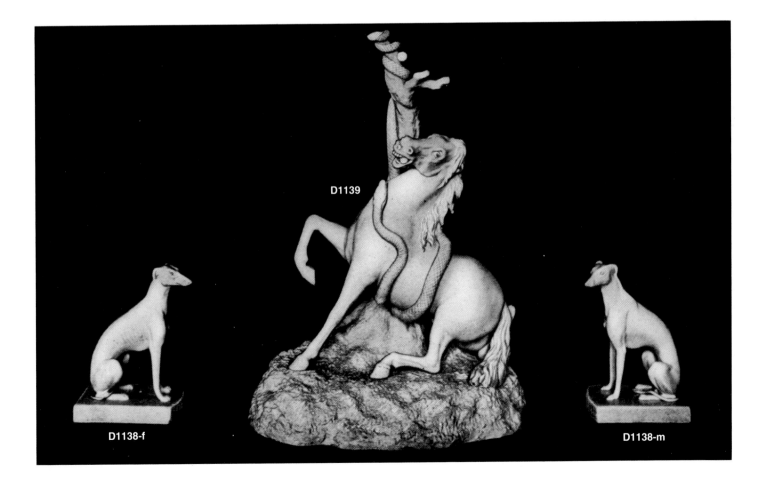

D1139

D1138-f

D1138-m

213

BIBLIOGRAPHY

Newspapers and Periodicals

Dublin Telegraph, February 21, 1883.

Ireland's Gazette, Loyal and National, 1884.

Landed Estates Court Title, Fermanagh Times, February 28, 1884.

The Belleek Potteries—Meeting to Prevent the Closing of the Works, The Donegal Independent, May 3, 1884.

Belleek Pottery Company, The Donegal Independent, May 10, 1884.

Application For Shares, The Donegal Independent, May 24, 1884.

The Belleek Potteries Company, The Donegal Independent, November 15, 1884.

Healy, Cahir, *Belleek Pottery, World-Famed Products*, Irish Independent, Dublin, October 7, 1919.

The Belleek Pottery, Sir Charles Cameron's Discovery, Fermanagh Herald, October 18, 1919.

Peripatetic Pressman's Notes, The Donegal Independent, January 17, 1920.

Belleek Pottery Sold to Irish Syndicate, Fermanagh Herald, January 24, 1920.

Belleek, Fermanagh Herald, January 31, 1920.

Belleek Pottery Shareholders Confirm Sale, Fermanagh Herald, February 21, 1920.

Belleek Pottery Sale Confirmed, The New Company, Fermanagh Herald, March 13, 1920.

Belleek China, Fermanagh Herald, March 20, 1920.

Belleek Ware—Development of the Pottery, Irish Times, 1927.

Belleek, Irish Press, 1932.

Whittaker, Andrew, *Quiet Success Story of Belleek China*, The Irish Times, Dublin, July 30, 1974.

MacGoris, Mary, *The Art of Greening the Shamrock*, Irish Independent, Dublin, May 14, 1975.

Hickey, Helen, *The Master of White Island*, Ireland of the Welcomes, Vol. 26, No. 1, Limerick, Ireland, January–February, 1977.

Nicassio, Susan, *Belleek*, Ireland of the Welcomes, Vol. 26, No. 5, Limerick, Ireland, September-October, 1977.

Doran, Patrick F., *The Hunt Museum*, The North Munster Antiquarian Journal, Vol. XIV 1978.

Reynolds, Mairead, *Eugene Sheerin*, The Clogher Record, 1980.

Reynolds, Mairead, *Early Belleek Designs*, Irish Arts Review, Vol. 1, No. 3, Autumn 1984.

Pamphlets

Seigler, Ralph H., *An Illustrated Guide to Irish Belleek Parian China*, E. Jay Lease & Associates, Los Angeles, California, 1969.

McCrum, S., *The Belleek Pottery*, Ulster Museum, Botanic Gardens, Belfast, c. 1969.

Reynolds, Mairead, *Early Belleek Wares*, National Museum of Ireland, 1978.

Reference Books

Armstrong, Robert Williams, Diaries, Museum of Applied Arts and Sciences, Broadway, 2007, Australia, 1862–1881.

Jewitt, Llewellynn, F.S.A., *The Ceramic Art of Great Britain*, Virtue & Co. Ltd., London, 1883.

Litchfield, *Pottery & Porcelain*, M. Barrows & Co., N.Y., 1950.

Eberlein & Ramsdell, *The Practical Book of Chinaware*, J.B. Lippincott, 1948.

Kovel, Ralph M. and Terry H., *Dictionary of Marks—Pottery and Porcelain*, Crown Publishers, Inc., New York, 1953.

Cushion & Honey, *Handbook of Pottery & Porcelain Marks*, Faber & Faber Ltd., London, 1955.

Manowitz & Haggar, *English Pottery & Porcelain (Encyl. of)*, Ambre Deutsch Ltd., London, 1957.

Ormsbee, Thomas. H., *English China & Its Marks*, Hearthside Press, London, 1957.

Kovel, Ralph and Terry, *Know Your Antiques*, Crown Publishers, Inc., New York, 1967.

Cox, Warren E., *The Book of Pottery & Porcelain*, Crown Publications, 1968.

Boger, Louise Ade, *The Dictionary of World Pottery & Porcelain*, Charles Scribner's Sons, New York, 1971.

Cunningham, John B., *The Story of Belleek*, St. Davog's Press, Belleek, 1992.

O'Loughlin, Joe, Charlie Ward, and Ann Monaghan, *The Church Upon the Hill*, Donegal Democrat, Ballyshannon, 1992.

CURRENT BELLEEK PARIAN WARE

Decorating Code

A—Plain (Glazed Only)   E—Painted Shamrocks   J—Mother of Pearl
B—Cob Lustre   F—Gilted   K—Painted and Gilted
C—Tinted   G—Tinted and Gilted   L—Bisque and Plain
D—Painted   H—Painted Shamrocks and Gilted   M—Decalcomania

(All decoration, with the exception of "M" [Decalcomania], is done by hand.)

Measurements

The measurements of ware are approximate and may vary slightly from piece to piece.

Height (H) is measured to the tallest point of the piece.

Diameter (D) is measured at the point of greatest span, excluding handles, spouts, etc.

Length (L) is a measurement of the greatest length of the piece, including handles, spouts, etc. when they appear.

NOTES: Items are introduced, reintroduced and retired from current offerings periodically.

"NS" means the item is not shown.

« » means there was a change of pattern or interruption in its production.

Pottery No.	Item	Code	Measurement in Inches	Page	Pottery No.	Item	Code	Measurement in Inches	Page
	SHAMROCK WARE				26	Coffee Pot			114
1	Tea Cup, Tall Shape	E/H	2⅝H	114	27	Gaelic Coffee Cup	E/H	4H	114
3	Tea Saucer	E/H	6⅛D	114	30	Salt, Open	E/H	3¼L	165
5	Plate, 5	E/H	5⅜D	114	36	Dinner Plate	E/H	10½D	114
7	Plate, 7	E/H	7⅜D	114	37	Cereal Bowl	E/H	2¾H	114
8	Bread Plate	E/H	11L	114	41	Berry Dish	E/H	6½D	114
12	Butter Plate	E/H	5½L	114	46	Mug, large size	E/H	3⅜H	114
16	Teapot, large size	E/H	10⅛L	114	47	Name Mug	E/H	2¾H	114
19	Sugar, Covered, large size	E/H	4¼D	114	50	Tower Salt	E/H	2½H	118
20	Cream, large size	E/H	5¼L	114	51	Tower Pepper	E/H	2½H	118

HARP TEA WARE
(Formerly designated "Harp Shamrock Tea Ware")

Pottery No.	Item	Code	Measurement in Inches	Page
240	Tea Cup	E	2¼H	NS
241	Tea Saucer	E	5⅜D	NS
245	Side Plate	E	5⅞D	NS
248	Bread Plate	E	9¼D	NS
249	Sugar	E	2½H	97
252	Cream	E	3¾H	97
253	Butter Plate	E	6¾L	NS
254	Cereal Bowl	E	5D	97
255	Teapot	E	4¾H	97

BUTTERFLY COLLECTION

Pottery No.	Item	Code	Measurement in Inches	Page
1601	Vase, small size	F	6½H	120
1602	Bud Vase (spill)	F	8H	120
1603	Pot, large size	F	5⅝H	120
1604	Candlestick	F	6H	120
1606	Trinket Box	F	2⅝H	120
1607	Toy Spill	F	3¾H	120
1608	Vase, large size	F	8H	120
1609	Pot, small size	F	3½H	120
1610	Bell	F	5¼H	120
1611	Salad Bowl	F	2¾H	120
1612	Butter Dish	F	5⅛L	120
1614	Vase, wide mouth	F	11½H	120

SEASHELL COLLECTION

Pottery No.	Item	Code	Measurement in Inches	Page
1701	Photo Frame	F	9½L	NS
1702	Vase, large size	F	9½H	113
1703	Bud Vase	F	6¼H	113
1704	Toy Spill	F	3¾H	113
1705	Bon Bon Dish	F	2¼H	113
1706	Trinket Box	F	3¼H	113
1707	Candlestick	F	2½H	113
1708	Round Plate			113
1709	Centrepiece	F	4¾H	113

SUMMER BRIAR COLLECTION

Pottery No.	Item	Code	Measurement in Inches	Page
1351	Vase	D	7H	118
1352	Spill	D	5H	118
1358	Planter	D	5H	118
1403	Vase, 40th Anniversary	F	7H	NS

STATUES AND HOLY WATER FONTS

Pottery No.	Item	Code	Measurement in Inches	Page
480	Blessed Virgin Mary, small size	A	12¼H	127
492	Cherub Font, small size	A	2¾H	127
499	Sacred Heart Font	A/D	6¼H	NS

FIGURES, ETC.

Pottery No.	Item	Code	Measurement in Inches	Page
423	Terrier	A	3½H	136
425	Rabbit	C	5¼L	136
456	Pig, large size	A	2⅞H	136
550	Polar Bear, standing	G	3H	137
551	Polar Bear, reclining	G	2¼H	137
626	Meditation	A	14⅝H	NS
627	Affection	A	14⅝H	NS
640	Boy Basket Bearer	A	8¾H	171
641	Girl Basket Bearer	A	8¾H	171
645	Cherub Candelabra	L	14H	169
647	Prince of Wales Ice Pail	L	18½H	NS
648	Crouching Venus	L	17H	NS
910	Owl Figurine	A	5¼H	136
919	Belgian Hawker, Woman	A	6⅝H	NS
920	Belgian Hawker, Man	A	6⅝H	NS
933	Harsbell Vase			137
1906	Kitten	A	4⅛H	136
1951	Basket Maker	A	5¼H	127
1952	Ware Carrier	A	6H	127

Pottery No.	Item	Code	Measurement in Inches	Page
1955	Piggy Bank	C	2½H	117
1973	Piggy Bank	E	2½H	NS
1999	Belleek Cat	A	4½H	136
2002	Baby Jesus in Crib Figurine	A	3L	NS
2003	Mary Figurine	A	5½H	NS
2004	Joseph Figurine	A	7½H	NS

FLOWER HOLDERS AND POTS

Pottery No.	Item	Code	Measurement in Inches	Page
458	Belleek Pot, small size	G	2¾H	NS
459	Belleek Pot, middle size	G	2⅞H	NS
460	Belleek Pot, large size	G	4H	NS
522	Kylemore Planter	E	5⅜H	NS
622	Belleek Flower Pot, small size	D/J	2¾H	163
623	Belleek Flower Pot, middle size	D/J	2¾H	163
624	Belleek Flower Pot, large size	D/J	4H	163
676	Lagan Planter	F	5H	162
948	Lily Plateaux, green & gilt	G	2½H	NS
1220	Colonial Pot	G	5¾H	NS

VASES AND SPILLS

Pottery No.	Item	Code	Measurement in Inches	Page
435	Bird Nest Stump Vase	D	12¼H	159
467	Island Vase, small size	E	7H	165
468	Sperrin Vase	E	8¾H	165
469	Corrib Vase	E	9H	165
470	Setanta Vase	E	7¼H	165
512	Sligo Vase	E	5½H	164
513	Galway Vase (Toy Spill)	E	4¼H	164, 165
517	Daisy Spill	E	5¾H	165
518	Trunk Stump Vase	E	6¼H	118
521	Kylemore Vase	E	8H	118
524	Typha Jug Spill	E	7H	165
527	Shamrock Spill	E	5H	120
530	Leitrim Vase	E	4¾H	165
532	Mourne Vase	F	7½H	163
533	Cherry Blossom Vase	D	8⅜H	163
534	Lismore Vase	F	6⅞H	NS
536	Cherry Blossom Vase, small size	G	7H	163
538	Fermanagh Vase	G	5½H	163
544	Island Vase	E	8¼H	165
646	Triple Fish Vase	D	18⅞H	159
661	Thistle Vase	D/J	8¼H	159
663	Princess Vase	D/J	9⅛H	159
664	Aberdeen Vase, small size, left	D/J	5⅞H	NS
665	Aberdeen Vase, small size, right	D/J	5⅞H	NS
666	Aberdeen Vase, middle size, left	D/J	7½H	NS
667	Aberdeen Vase, middle size, right	D/J	7½H	NS
668	Aberdeen Vase, large size, left	D/J	9⅛H	NS
669	Aberdeen Vase, large size, right	D/J	9⅛H	NS
672	Typha Spill, pink & gilt	G	3¾H	163
674	Ribbon Spill, Flowered	D	6½H	163
680	Vine Vase	D	6⅞H	NS
686	Typha Spill, green & gilt	G	3¾H	NS
901	Toy Panel Vase, pink & gilt	G	3½H	NS
902	Shamrock Scent Spill	E	4H	118
903	Toy Panel Vase, blue & gilt	G	3½H	NS
904	Toy Panel Vase, green & gilt	G	3½H	NS
908	Allingham Spill, pink	D	2½H	NS
909	Allingham Spill, yellow	D	2½H	NS
911	Colleen Vase	E	5½H	164, 171
929	Round Tower	D/E	8¼H	50, 118
975	Shell Vase			163
977	Scroll Flower Vase, pink	C	7⅛H	163
1025	Donegal Vase	E	6H	118
1074	Lotus Blossom Vase	G	8H	163
1075	Blarney Bud Vase	E	6⅞H	171
1076	Connemara Vase	E	5⅞H	165
1077	Lagan Vase	F	8H	162
1210	Caldwell Vase	E	7½H	165

Pottery No.	Item	Code	Measurement in Inches	Page
1211	Limerick Bud Vase	E	7H	171
1212	Shamrock Bud Vase	E	6½H	165
1219	Colonial Vase	G	6H	NS
1221	Liffey Vase	E	6H	120
1222	Coral Vase	G	6½H	163
1224	Giants Causeway Spill	F	8½H	NS
1228	Shannon Vase	A	5½H	NS
1230	Lotus Blossom Spill	G	6½H	163
1237	Visitors Centre Spill	F	4⅛H	124
1304	Fermanagh Vase, green & gilt	G	5½H	NS
1380	Lakeland Vase	A	6⅞H	NS
1390	Avalon Vase	A	9H	NS
1395	Rossmore Vase, 25th	G	8¾H	NS
1396	Lotus Blossom Spill, 25th	G	6½H	NS
1398	Lotus Blossom Vase, 50th	G	8H	NS
1399	Lotus Blossom Vase, 25th	G	8H	NS
1401	Lotus Blossom Spill, 50th	G	6½H	NS
1402	Lotus Blossom Spill, 21st	G	6½H	NS
1404	Lotus Blossom Vase, 30th	G	8H	NS
1408	Lotus Blossom Vase, 40th	G	8H	NS
1918	Rossmore Vase	G	8¾H	NS
1932	Daisy Vase, tall	E	10½H	NS
1933	Daisy Vase, large	E	9H	NS
1934	Daisy Toy Spill	E	3¼H	NS
1946	Paros Vase, pink	G	11H	174
1947	Paros Vase, blue	G	11H	NS

BASKETWARE

Pottery No.	Item	Code	Measurement in Inches	Page
560	Heart Basket, No. 1	D/J	5L	NS
562	Heart Basket, No. 3	D/J	6⅜L	NS
569	Oval Covered Basket, small size	D/J	9L	NS
572	Henshall Basket, small size	D/J	8L	NS
575	Shamrock Basket, small size	D/J	5¼L	NS
580	Forget-Me-Not Basket	D/J	5⅞L	NS
587	Rathmore Oval Basket	D/J	11L	NS
588	Oval Covered Basket, large size	D/J	12⅜L	NS
602	Erne Basket	D/J	6½L	NS
603	Birds Nest Basket	D/J	4⅛D	NS
605	Thistle Basket	D/J	5¼D	101
607	Bluebell Basket	D/J	8⅝D	101
608	Cherry Blossom Basket	D/J	6D	101
609	Daisy Basket	D/J	4¾D	101
615	Hawthorne Basket	D/J	7¾L	101
616	Clematis Basket	D/J	8D	101
617	Beauty Rose Basket	D/J	5¾D	101
618	Carnation Basket	D/J	5¼D	101
619	Fushia Basket	D/J	8L	101
620	Spring Meadow Basket	D/J	8½D	102
621	Wedding Bouquet Basket	D/J	8¼D	101

SUGARS AND CREAMS

Pottery No.	Item	Code	Measurement in Inches	Page
390	Lotus Cream	F	3⅛H	NS
391	Lotus Sugar	F	2⅛H	NS
394	Toy Shamrock Cream	E	3⅜H	NS
395	Toy Shamrock Sugar	E	2H	NS
451	Undine Cream	A	4½H	162

ASSORTED WARE

Pottery No.	Item	Code	Measurement in Inches	Page
67	Limpet Salad Plate	A	8⅛D	NS
355	Miniature Heart Dish	A	4¾L	162
360	Claddagh Heart, medium	F	5⅜L	NS
361	Claddagh Heart, medium	G	5⅜L	NS
363	Claddagh Heart, large	F	6¼L	NS
364	Claddagh Heart, large	G	6¼L	NS
420	Cottage Cheese Set	D	4⅝H	NS
426	Irish Violet Pourri	G	4⅛D	NS
427	Wild Irish Rose Pourri	G	5⅛L	NS
428	Irish Bouquet Pourri	E	4½D	NS

Pottery No.	Item	Code	Measurement in Inches	Page
429	Shamrock Pourri	E	5½D	NS
432	Cardium Shell No. 3	A	3⅝L	162
461	Shamrock Ashtray	E	4⅜D	NS
514	Harp, small size	E	6⅛H	118
515	Harp, large size	E	8⅜H	118
529	Shamrock Photo Frame	E	9½L	120
681	Cherub Trinket Box	F	5L	127
965	Christening Mug, Boy	G	2⅛H	NS
966	Christening Mug, Girl	G	2⅛H	NS
1012	Mint Tray	C	8¾D	163
1031	Shamrock Thimble	E	¾D	NS
1213	Shamrock Candlestick Holder	E	2¾H	120
1214	Christmas Shamrock Bell	E	2⅛H	NS
1225	Trophy	F	12⅛H	120
1410	Snowflake Candleholder	A	5½H	169
1809	Visitors Centre Mug	F	3½H	124
1814	Votive Candleholder	A	2H	119
1824	Snow Scene Candleholder	A	3¼H	NS
1828	Shamrock Wine Coaster	E	4⅛D	NS
1830	Shamrock Napkin Ring	E	1⅝D	118
1840	Woven Shamrock Pendant	E	2L	119
1841	Cast Pendant	E	2⅞L	NS
1843	Cottage Candleholder	A	3¼H	119
1844	Decanter Label	F	2½L	NS
1902	Irish Blessing Plate	E/M	11D	112
1903	Irish Blessing Plate	E/M	7D	NS
1904	My Wishes For You Plate	E/M	8D	112
1905	Clogher Plate	E/M	9¼D	NS
1907	Marriage Blessing Plate	E/M	8½D	112
1912	Name Brooch	K	1⅞L	NS
1923	Forget-Me-Not Brooch	D	1½D	119
1924	Rathmore Brooch	D	1½D	119
1925	Erne Brooch	A	1½D	NS
1926	Ardagh Chalice	F	7H	NS
1936	Daisy Trinket Box	E	2½H	NS
1938	Oval Shamrock Frame	E	6¼H	174
1939	Oval Coral Frame	C	6¼H	174
1940	Baby Mug	F	2½H	117
1941	Baby Spoon	F	4¾L	117
1942	Baby Egg Cup	F	2H	117
1943	Baby Cereal Bowl	F	2¼H	117
1953	Maritime Desk Set	F	7¼D	174
1954	Maritime Paper Knife	F	9½L	174
1975	Baby Spoon	E	4¾L	NS
1976	Baby Egg Cup	E	2H	NS
1977	Baby Mug	E	2½H	NS
1978	Baby Cereal Bowl	E	2¼H	NS

BELLEEK COLLECTORS' SOCIETY EXCLUSIVE LIMITED EDITION

Pottery No.	Item	Code	Measurement in Inches	Page
1945	The Papillion Vase, 1993	F/K	8½H	NS

CHRISTMAS ORNAMENTS AND PLATES

Pottery No.	Item	Code	Measurement in Inches	Page
848	Christmas Plate, 1992	D/M	8⅜D	NS
849	Christmas Plate, 1993	D/M	8⅜D	NS
1227	Shillelagh	A	5L	NS
1231	Round Tower Christmas Bell	E	2¾H	NS
1235	Cottage Christmas Ornament	E	2¾H	NS
1238	Shillelagh	E	5¼L	NS
1800	Christmas Tree Ornament	E	4½H	NS
1801	Bell with Star	F	2⅛H	119
1804	Bell with Candle	D	2⅛H	111, 119
1806	Dove Ornament	E	2⅛H	NS
1807	Leprechaun Bell	E	3H	NS
1810	Shamrock Ornament	E	2½H	119
1811	Christmas Snowflake	A	3H	NS
1813	Celtic Cross	E	4½H	NS

Pottery No.	Item	Code	Measurement in Inches	Page
	CHRISTMAS ORNAMENTS AND PLATES (*continued*)			
1815	Christmas Tree Star	H	7½H	NS
1816	Church Ornament	E	2¾H	NS
1818	Partridge in a Pear Tree	F	2½H	NS
1819	Christmas Harp Ornament	E	3H	NS
1823	Cottage Bell	E	2H	NS
1825	Two Turtle Doves Bell	F	2½H	119
1826	Kylemore Ornament	E	2¾H	119
1827	Claddagh Trivet Ornament	E	6H	NS
1829	Claddagh Ornament	F	2⅞L	NS
1832	Baby's First Christmas, 1992			119
1834	Kylemore Bell	E	3H	119
1836	Christmas Cross	G	2½D	NS
1842	Wreath (Holly & Shamrock)	F	3D	NS
1845	Christmas Stocking Ornament	F	5H	119
1846	Snowman Ornament	F	3¼H	119
1956	O'Brien's Pub Bell	E	2H	NS
1957	Christmas Tree Ornament	E		NS
1959	Baby's First Christmas, 1993	D	3H	NS
1979	Garland Ornament	F	3H	NS
1980	Gospel Bell	F	2½H	NS
1981	Cherub Ornament	A	3H	NS
	CLOCKS			
53	Glenveigh Mantel Clock	H	9½H	171
54	Cherub Mantel Clock	F	9½H	171
56	Vine Clock	F	7½H	NS
57	Glenveigh Clock, small size	H	7½H	NS

Pottery No.	Item	Code	Measurement in Inches	Page
58	Desk Set Clock	F	11D	171
59	Blarney Shamrock Clock	H	4H	NS
90	Cashel Clock	H	7½H	171
1919	Mantel Clock	F	8½H	171
1927	Killarney Clock	H	3¼H	171
1929	Florentine Clock	F	4¼H	171
1930	Celtic Clock	A	3¼H	171
1931	Oranmore Clock	E	4¼H	171
	DOLLS			
1848	Elizabeth Anne Doll	D	19"H	134
1960	Aran Doll	D	12½H	134
1961	Irish Dancing Doll	D	12½H	134
*	Colleen	D	14"H	NS
	(Limited Edition Offering of the New England Collectors Society).			
	LAMPS, ELECTRIC			
546	Rose Isle Lamp	D	10H	56
547	Rose Isle Lamp	J	10H	NS
548	Lotus Blossom Lamp, pink	C	5¾H	NS
549	Lotus Blossom Lamp, blue	C	5¾H	NS
552	Lotus Blossom Lamp, pink-UL	C	5¾H	NS
553	Rose Isle Lamp, UL	J	10H	NS
1248	Kylemore Lamp	E	10H	NS
1249	Kylemore Lamp, UL	E	10H	NS
1935	Daisy Lamp	E	10H	NS
1937	Daisy Lamp, UL	E	10H	NS
1950	Cherub Lamp	K	10½H	NS

OLD BELLEEK PARIAN WARE AND EARTHENWARE

TRINKET SETS, ETC. (*continued*)

Degenhardt No.	Item	Measurement in Inches	Page
D323	Low Box, Fan		188
D324	Set complete, 9 pieces		NS
D325	Brush Tray, Neptune		188
D326	Pin Tray, Neptune		188
D327	Scent Bottle, Neptune		188
D328	Ring Peg, Neptune		188
D329	Lip Salve, Neptune		188
D330	Tall Box, Neptune		188
D331	Low Box, Neptune		188
D332	Set complete, 9 pieces		NS
D333	Brush Tray, Thorn		188
D334	Pin Tray, Thorn		188
D335	Scent Bottle, Thorn		188
D336	Ring Peg, Thorn		188
D337	Lip Salve, Thorn		188
D338	Tall Box, Thorn		188
D339	Low Box, Thorn		188
D340	Set complete, 9 pieces		NS
D341	Cherub Candelabra	15H	188
D342	Single Boy and Shell		188
D343	Dolphin Candlestick	8H	162, 172, 188
D344	Thorn Candlestick	7H	188
D345	Boy and Vine Candlestick	9H	144, 188
D346	Night Light Holder, Lighthouse	11H	99, 188
D347	Piano Candlestick	9H	166, 188
D348	Allingham Candlestick	3H	188
D349	Anchorite Candlestick	3½H	188

EGG SHELL TRIDACNA TEA WARE

Degenhardt No.	Item	Measurement in Inches	Page
D350	Cup and Saucer		188
D351	Plate, 5		188
D352	Bread Plate		188
D353	Slop, large size		188
D354	Sugar, large size		188
D355	Cream, large size		188
D356	Teapot		188
D357	Kettle		188

ECHINUS EGG SHELL TEA WARE

Degenhardt No.	Item	Measurement in Inches	Page
D358	Cup and Saucer		72, 189
D359	Plate	5D	189
D360	Bread Plate		189
D361	Slop, large size		189
D362	Sugar, large size		189
D363	Cream, large size		189
D364	Teapot, large size		189
D365	Kettle, large size		189

SHAMROCK TEA WARE

Degenhardt No.	Item	Measurement in Inches	Page
D366	Tea and Saucer, Low Shape		114, 189
D367	Teapot, middle size		189
D368	Sugar, small size		114, 189
D369	Cream, small size		114, 189
D370	Tray		189
D371	Set complete		93, 189
D372	Coffee and Saucer		114, 189, 203
D373	Breakfast and Saucer		189
D374	Moustache and Saucer		189
D375	Tea and Saucer		189
D376	Plate	5D	189
D377	Plate	7D	NS
D378	Plate	8D	203
D379	Bread Plate		189
D380	Slop, large size		189
D381	Slop, middle size		NS
D382	Cream, large size		189

Degenhardt No.	Item	Measurement in Inches	Page
D383	Sugar, large size		189
D384	Teapot, large size		189
D385	Teapot, small size		NS
D386	Kettle, large size		114, 189
D387	Kettle, small size		NS
D388	Covered Muffin Dish		189
D389	Egg Cup		114, 123, 189, 208
D390	Milk Jug		114, 189

HEXAGON TEA WARE

Degenhardt No.	Item	Measurement in Inches	Page
D391	Tea and Saucer		190
D392	Teapot, middle size		190
D393	Cream, small size		190
D394	Sugar, small size		190
D395	Tray	16½D	95, 190
D396	Set complete		95, 190
D397	Coffee and Saucer		190
D398	Breakfast and Saucer		190
D399	Moustache and Saucer		190
D400	Plate	5D	190
D401	Plate	6D	NS
D402	Plate	7D	NS
D403	Bread Plate		190
D404	Slop, large size		190
D405	Sugar, large size		190
D406	Cream, large size		190
D407	Teapot, large size		190
D408	Teapot, small size		NS
D409	Kettle, large size		190
D410	Covered Muffin Dish		190
D411	Egg Cup		190
D412	Milk Jug		190
D413	Cup and Tray		190

NEPTUNE TEA WARE

Degenhardt No.	Item	Measurement in Inches	Page
D414	Tea and Saucer		190
D415	Teapot, middle size		190
D416	Sugar, small size		190
D417	Cream, small size		190
D418	Tray		190
D419	Set complete		81, 90, 190
D420	Coffee and Saucer		190
D421	Plate	5D	190
D422	Plate	6D	NS
D423	Plate	7D	NS
D424	Plate	8D	NS
D425	Bread Plate		190
D426	Slop, large size		190
D427	Sugar, large size		190
D428	Cream, large size		190
D429	Teapot, large size		190
D430	Teapot, small size		NS
D431	Kettle, large size		190

CONE TEA WARE

Degenhardt No.	Item	Measurement in Inches	Page
D432	Tea and Saucer		191
D433	Teapot		191
D434	Sugar, small size		191
D435	Cream, small size		191
D436	Tray		191
D437	Set complete		94, 191
D438	Plate	5D	191
D439	Bread Plate		191
D440	Slop, large size		191
D441	Sugar, large size		191
D442	Cream, large size		191

Degenhardt No.	Item	Measurement in Inches	Page
D671	Sugar		195
D672	Cream		195
D673	Tray		195
D674	Set complete		91, 195
D675	Plate	5D	195
D676	Bread Plate		195
D677	Slop, large size		195
D678	Sugar, large size		195
D679	Cream, large size		195
	« »		
D680	Custard Cup and Saucer		195
D681	Worcester Plate, size 1		114, 195
D682	Worcester Plate, size 2		195
D683	Worcester Plate, size 3		195
D684	Worcester Plate, size 4		195
D685	Shell Plate, large size		195
D686	Shell Plate, middle size		195
D687	Shell Plate, small size		195
D688	Oval Plate, size 1		114, 195
D689	Oval Plate, size 2		195
D690	Oval Plate, size 3		195
D691	Oval Plate, size 4		195
D692	Oval Plate, size 5		NS
D693	Oval Plate, size 6		NS

FAN TEA WARE

Degenhardt No.	Item	Measurement in Inches	Page
D694	Tea and Saucer		195
D695	Teapot		195
D696	Sugar		195
D697	Cream		195
D698	Tray		195
D699	Set complete		94, 195
D700	Coffee and Saucer		195
D701	Plate	5D	195
D702	Bread Plate		195
D703	Slop, large size		195
D704	Sugar, large size		195
D705	Cream, large size		195
	« »		
D706	Basket Biscuit Box		195
D707	Crate Biscuit Box		195
D708	Shamrock Cruet		195

ARTICHOKE TEA WARE

Degenhardt No.	Item	Measurement in Inches	Page
D709	Tea and Saucer		196
D710	Teapot		196
D711	Sugar Box		196
D712	Cream		196
D713	Tray		196
D714	Set complete		196
D715	Plate	5D	196
D716	Bread Plate		196
D717	Slop		196
D718	Sugar		196
D719	Cream		196
D720	Covered Muffin Dish		196
D721	Egg Cup		196

INSTITUTE TEA WARE

(Originally crafted for the Queen's Institute, Dublin)

Degenhardt No.	Item	Measurement in Inches	Page
D722	Tea and Saucer		196
D723	Breakfast and Saucer		196
D724	Plate	6D	196
D725	Plate	7D	NS
D726	Bread Plate		196
D727	Slop		196
D728	Sugar Box		196

Degenhardt No.	Item	Measurement in Inches	Page
D729	Cream		196
D730	Egg Cup		196
D731	Covered Muffin		NS

GRASS TEA WARE

Degenhardt No.	Item	Measurement in Inches	Page
D732	Tea and Saucer		196
D733	Teapot, middle size		196
D734	Sugar Box, small size		196
D735	Cream, small size		196
D736	Tray		196
D737	Set complete		92, 196
D738	Breakfast and Saucer		NS
D739	Moustache and Saucer		196
D740	Plate	5D	196
D741	Plate	6D	NS
D742	Plate	7D	NS
D743	Bread Plate		196
D744	Slop, large size		196
D745	Sugar Box, large size		196
D746	Sugar Box, middle size		NS
D747	Cream, large size		196
D748	Cream, middle size		NS
D749	Teapot, large size		NS
D750	Teapot, small size		NS
D751	Kettle, large size		98, 196
D752	Covered Muffin Dish		98, 196
D753	Milk Jug		196
D754	Egg Cup		196
D755	Honey Pot		153, 196
	« »		
D756	Erne Leaf Plate, No. 1, Painted		196
D757	Erne Leaf Plate, No. 2, Painted		NS

THORN TEA WARE

Degenhardt No.	Item	Measurement in Inches	Page
D758	Tea and Saucer	2H	197
D759	Teapot	7L	197
D760	Sugar, small size	3¼D	197
D761	Cream, small size	3¼D	197
D762	Tray	14¾L	197
D763	Set complete		81, 197
D764	Breakfast and Saucer		197
D765	Plate	5D	197
D766	Plate	6D	NS
D767	Bread Plate		197
D768	Slop, large size		197
D769	Sugar, large size		197
D770	Cream, large size		197
D771	Teapot, large size		197
D772	Teapot, middle size		NS
D773	Teapot, small size		NS
D774	Kettle, large size		197
D775	Jug, large size		197
D776	Jug, middle size		197
D777	Jug, small size		197
	« »		
D778	Triple Bucket, large size		197

THISTLE TEA WARE

Degenhardt No.	Item	Measurement in Inches	Page
D779	Tea and Saucer		197
D780	Teapot		197
D781	Sugar		197
D782	Cream		197
D783	Tray		197
D784	Set complete		95, 197
D785	Plate	6D	197
D786	Bread Plate		197
D787	Slop, large size		197
D788	Sugar, large size		197

Degen-hardt No.	Item	Measurement in Inches	Page
	THISTLE TEA WARE (*continued*)		
D789	Cream, large size		197
	« »		
D790	Shell Plateaux	4½D	197, 206
D791	Shell Plateaux	7D	197
D792	Shell Plateaux	9D	197
D793	Shell Biscuit Box	4½D	NS
D794	Shell Biscuit Box	7D	197
D795	Shell Biscuit Box	9D	98, 117, 197
D796	Oval Shell Jelly		197
D797	Square Shell Jelly		197
D798	Oblong Shell Jelly		116, 197
	LACE TEA WARE		
D799	Tea and Saucer		112, 198
D800	Teapot		198
D801	Sugar		198
D802	Cream		198
D803	Tray		198
D804	Set complete		92, 198
D805	Coffee and Saucer		142, 198
D806	Plate	6D	198
D807	Bread Plate		198
D808	Slop, large size		198
D809	Sugar, large size		198
D810	Cream, large size		198
	« »		
D811	Florence Jug, 12s		198
D812	Florence Jug, 24s		198
D813	Florence Jug, 30s		166, 198
D814	Florence Jug, 36s		198
D815	Acorn Jug, 12s		198
D816	Acorn Jug, 24s		198
D817	Acorn Jug, 30s		198
D818	Acorn Jug, 36s		198
	RING HANDLE IVORY		
	(*Beginning with the 1928 catalogue, this pattern was referred to as "Belleek Shape"*)		
D819	Tea and Saucer		198
D820	Coffee and Saucer		198
D821	Breakfast and Saucer		198, 199
D822	Plate	5D	198
D823	Plate	7½D	113
D824	Bread Plate		198
D825	Slop		198
D826	Sugar		198
D827	Cream		198
D828	Afternoon Set complete		198
D829	Covered Muffin Dish		198
D830	Egg Cup		198
	« »		
D831	Jug, 24s, Stoneware		116, 198
D832	Jug, 30s, Stoneware		198
D833	Jug, 36s, Stoneware		198
	EARTHENWARE		
	Tea Ware, etc.		
D834	Evening or London Teas		NS
D835	Irish size Teas		198
D836	Muffin Plate		NS
D837	Muffin Plate		198
D838	Muffin Plate		NS
D839	Muffin Plate		NS
D840	Egg Plate		NS
D841	Egg Plate		NS

Degen-hardt No.	Item	Measurement in Inches	Page
D842	Bowls, 24s, 30s, 36s		198
D843	Creams		198
D844	Bread Plate		198
D845	Teapots, 18s		198
D846	Teapots, 24s		198
D847	Teapots, oval		198
D848	Evening or London Teas		199
D849	Breakfast or Irish size		199
D850	Muffin Plate		NS
D851	Muffin Plate		199
D852	Muffin Plate		199
D853	Muffin Plate		NS
D854	Egg Cup		199
D855	Egg Plate		NS
D856	Egg Plate		NS
D857	Bowls, 24s, 30s, 36s		199
D858	Mugs, 24s, 30s, 36s		199
D859	Covered Muffin Dish		199
D860	Creams		199
D861	Bread Plate		199
D862	Triple Bread and Cheese Tray		199
D863	Plain Jug, 12s		199
D864	Plain Jug, 24s		199
D865	Plain Jug, 30s		199
D866	Fluted Jugs, 12s		199
D867	Fluted Jugs, 24s		199
D868	Fluted Jugs, 30s		199
D869	Octagon Jugs, 12s		199
D870	Octagon Jugs, 24s		199
D871	Octagon Jugs, 30s		199
	Dinner Ware		
D872	Ship Jugs, 6s		199
D873	Ship Jugs, 12s		199
D874	Ship Jugs, 24s		199
D875	Ship Jugs, 30s		199
D876	Ship Jugs, 36s		199
D877	Ship Jugs, 42s		199
D878	Salad Plates, large size, middle size, small size		199
D879	Jelly Moulds		199
D880	Jelly Moulds		NS
D881	Jelly Moulds		NS
D882	Jelly Moulds		NS
D883	Jelly Moulds		NS
D884	Broth Bowl and Stand, 24s		199
D885	Hot Water Cover Dish		199
D886	Hot Water Plate		199
D887	Plate		14, 199, 200
D888	Soup Plate		199
D889	Plate		199
D890	Plate		199, 200
D891	Plate		199
D892	Plate		199, 200
D893	Plate		199
D894	Plate		199
D895	Plate		199
D896	Plate		NS
D897	Flat Dish		199
D898	Flat Dish		NS
D899	Flat Dish		NS
D900	Flat Dish		199, 200
D901	Flat Dish		NS
D902	Flat Dish		NS
D903	Flat Dish		NS
D904	Gravy Dish		NS
D905	Gravy Dish		NS
D906	Gravy Dish		NS

Degen-hardt No.	Item	Measurement in Inches	Page
D907	Gravy Dish		NS
D908	Soup Tureen and Stand		199, 200
D909	Soup Tureen and Stand		NS
D910	Soup Ladle		NS
D911	Soup Ladle		NS
D912	Sauce Tureen and Stand		199, 200
D913	Sauce Ladle		NS
D914	Sauce Boat		199, 200
D915	Cover Dish		14, 199, 200
D916	Cover Dish		NS
D917	Cover Dishes, 2 compartments		NS
D918	Cover Dishes, 3 compartments		NS

Toilet Ware

D922	Basin, 12s		125, 200
D923	Basin, 9s		NS
D924	Basin, 6s		NS
D925	Ewer, 12s		125, 200
D926	Ewer, 9s		NS
D927	Ewer, 6s		NS
D928	Chamber, 12s		200
D929	Chamber, 9s		200
D930	Chamber, 6s		NS
D931	Covered Soap Box, 6s		200
D932	Covered Brush Tray, 6s		200
D933	Slop Jar		200
D934	Basin, 12s		125, 201
D935	Basin, 9s		NS
D936	Basin, 6s		NS
D937	Ewers, 12s		NS
D938	Ewers, 9s		125
D939	Basin, 6s		125, 201
D940	Chambers, 12s	5¾H	15
D941	Chambers, 9s		NS
D942	Chambers, 6s		NS
D943	Uncovered Soap		NS
D944	Uncovered Brush		NS
D945	Sponge Bowl		NS
D946	Slop Jar, Cane Handle		NS
D947	Unhandled Chambers, 9s		NS
D948	Basin, 12s		201
D949	Basin, 9s		201
D950	Basin, 6s	15½D	15, 125, 201
D951	Ewer, 12s		125, 201
D952	Ewer, 9s		201
D953	Ewer, 6s	13⅛H	83, 125, 201
D954	Chamber, 12s		NS
D955	Chamber, 9s		NS
D956	Chamber, 6s		NS
D957	Covered Soap Box, 6s		NS
D958	Covered Brush Tray, 6s		NS
D959	Sponge Bowl		201

Assorted Ware

D960	Slop Pail & Cane Handle		201
D961	K Pans, Lettered		202
D962	K Pans, Lettered		202
D963	K Pans, Lettered		202
D964	K Pans, Lettered		202
D965	K Pans, Lettered		202
D966	K Pans, Lettered		202
D967	K Pans, Lettered		202
D968	K Pans, Lettered		202
D969	K Pans, Lettered		202
D970	K Pans, Lettered		202
D971	K Pans, Lettered		NS
D972	K Pans, Lettered		NS
D973	Milk Pans		202

Degen-hardt No.	Item	Measurement in Inches	Page
D974	Milk Pans		202
D975	Milk Pans		202
D976	Milk Pans		202
D977	Milk Pans		202
D978	Milk Pans		202
D979	Milk Pans		202
D980	Milk Pans		202
D981	Milk Pans		202
D982	Milk Pans		202
D983	Milk Bowls, Lipped, 2s		202
D984	Milk Bowls, Lipped, 3s		202
D985	Milk Bowls, Lipped, 4s		202
D986	Milk Bowls, Lipped, 6s		202
D987	Milk Bowls, Lipped, 9s		202
D988	Milk Bowls, Lipped, 12s		202
D989	Milk Bowls, Lipped, 18s		202
D990	Milk Bowls, Lipped, 24s		202
D991	Plain Milk Bowls, 2s		202
D992	Plain Milk Bowls, 4s		202
D993	Plain Milk Bowls, 6s		202
D994	Plain Milk Bowls, 9s		202
D995	Plain Milk Bowls, 12s		202
D996	Plain Milk Bowls, 18s		202
D997	Plain Milk Bowls, 24s		202
D998	Pudding Bowls, 2 to 36		202
D999	Baking Dish		202
D1202	Baking Dish		202
D1001	Baking Dish		202
D1002	Baking Dish		202
D1003	Baking Dish		202
D1004	Baking Dish		202
D1005	Baking Dish		202
D1006	Baking Dish		202
D1007	Baking Dish		NS
D1008	Chair Pans		202
D1009	Chair Pans		202
D1010	Chair Pans		202
D1011	Chair Pans		202
D1012	Chair Pans		202
D1013	Round Bed Pan, large size		202
D1014	Round Bed Pan, small size		202
D1015	French Bed Pan		202
D1016	Urinals (Male), Handled		NS
D1017	Urinals (Female), Handled		NS
D1018	Foot Bath, Hooped		202
D1019	Foot Bath, Hooped		NS
D1020	Foot Bath, Hooped		NS
D1021	Foot Bath, best shape		202
D1022	Spitting Mugs, 30s		202
D1023	Spitting Mugs, 36s		NS
D1024	Goblets		202
D1025	Shaving Mug		202
D1026	Salt		202
D1027	Pepper		202
D1028	Mustard		202
D1029	Bedroom Candlestick and Extinguisher		202
D1030	Jelly Cans, all sizes		NS
D1031	Sick Feeders		NS
D1032	Double Ink Well		NS
D1033	Italian Ewer		125
D1034	Rathmore Ewer	13½H	15, 125
D1035	Minton Shop Ewer		125
D1036	Minton Shop Basin		125
D1037	Appletop Jug		NS
D1038	Appletop Slop Jar		NS
D1039	Appletop Foot Bath		NS
D1040	Wash Basin, Slop Bowl and Wooden Stand	32⅝H	8

Degen-hardt No.	Item	Measurement in Inches	Page
SUGARS, CREAMS, AND JUGS (*continued*)			
D1306	Lily Jug, 24's, Stoneware		198
D1307	Lily Jug, 30's, Stoneware		198
D1308	Lily Jug, 36's, Stoneware		198
D1309	Ribbed Toy Cream		115
D1310	Rope Handled Jug	5½H	116
D1311	Rope Handled Jug	4½D	29
D1312	Toy Shell Sugar, small size		NS
D1313	Typha Cream		115
D1314	Vine Tankard Jug	5½H	102
SHAMROCK WARE			
D1315	Berry dish, large size		NS
D1316	Berry dish, small size		123
D1317	Bouillon Cup and Saucer		203
D1318	Butter Plate		NS
D1319	Coffee Pot		NS
D1320	Covered Butter Dish		NS
D1321	Covered Sugar, small size		NS
D1322	Covered Vegetable Dish		203
D1323	Cup Marmalade Jar		114, 123
D1324	Gravy Boat		203
D1325	Marmalade Jar		114
D1326	Milk Jug, Flat, small size		114, 123
D1327	Milk Jug, Round, small size		114, 123
D1328	Mug, large size		207
D1329	Mug, small size		207
D1330	Plate	10D	203
D1331	Platter, large size		203
D1332	Platter, small size		203
D1333	Salt Shaker		NS
D1334	Sandwich Tray		123
D1335	Soup Tureen and Ladle		203
D1336	Tobacco Box		123
TRIDACNA TEA WARE			
D1341	Boat Shaped Cream		208
D1342	Boat Shaped Sugar		208
D1343	Breakfast Tray		NS
D1344	Brush Tray		NS
D1345	Butter Plate		204
D1346	Coffee Pot		204
D1347	Covered Sugar, small size		NS
D1348	Mustard		204
D1349	Open Salt		204
D1350	Pepper Shaker		204
D1351	Salt Shaker		NS
D1352	TV Set		NS
HARP SHAMROCK TEA WARE			
D1355	Bread Plate		NS
D1356	Butter Plate		123, 169
D1357	Coffee Pot		NS
D1358	Cream, large size		NS
D1359	Kettle		123
D1360	Plate	7D	NS
D1361	Slop Bowl		NS
D1362	Sugar, large size		NS
D1363	Teapot, large size		NS
D1364	Bell		97
D1365	Coffee Cup		NS
D1366	Coffee Saucer		NS
D1367	Plate	5D	NS
D1368	Plate	6D	NS
LIMPET TEA WARE			
(*Early ware was coral branch footed*)			
D1370	Coffee Pot		204
D1371	Covered Sugar, small size		NS
D1372	Plate	7D	204
D1373	Teapot, middle size		NS
D1374	Plate	10½D	NS
D1375	TV Set	6¼L	NS
D1376	Two Tier Cake Plate		NS
NEW SHELL TEA WARE			
(*Adaptation of Shell Tea Ware and Echinus Tea Ware designs*)			
D1379	Plate	10D	206
D1380	Bread Plate		206
D1381	Butter Plate		206
D1382	Cream, large size		206
D1383	Open Sugar, large size		206
D1384	Plate	7D	206
D1385	Tea Cup		206
D1386	Tea Saucer		206
D1387	Teapot		206
D1388	Plate	6D	NS
D1389	Two Tier Cake Plate		NS
INSTITUTE TEA WARE			
(*Originally crafted for the Queen's Institute, Dublin*)			
D1390	Butter and Stand		NS
D1391	Butter and Stand, Scalloped		NS
D1392	Honey Pot		194
D1393	Platter	10D	NS
D1394	Steak Dish, 3 Pieces		NS
CHINESE TEA WARE			
D1396	Cream, large size		NS
D1397	Plate	5¾D	NS
D1398	Sugar, large size		NS
D1399	Teapot, large size		NS
GRASS TEA WARE			
D1400	Butter Tub, Covered		NS
D1401	Coffee and Saucer		NS
D1402	Coffee Pot, large size		98
D1403	Coffee Pot, middle size		NS
D1404	Coffee Pot, small size		NS
D1405	Teapot Stand		98
D1406	Footed Platter	12¾L	NS
IVY TEA WARE			
(*Body design similar to Shamrock Tea Ware, but decorated with sprigs of ivy.*)			
D1410	Bread Plate		206
D1411	Covered Sugar		206
D1412	Cream		206
D1413	Plate		206
D1414	Slop Bowl		206
D1415	Tea Cup		206
D1416	Tea Saucer		206
D1417	Teapot		206

Degen-hardt No.	Item	Measure-ment in Inches	Page
	MISCELLANEOUS (*continued*)		
D1527	Gilted Scenic Plate, Hand Painted (various Irish scenes)		37
D1528	Girl Wall Bracket		176
D1529	Globe Amphora Lamp		170
D1530	Gothic Candlestick		166
D1531	Harp, Hound and Tower Commemorative Plate	9¼×9¼	110
D1532	Harp, Hound and Tower Wall Plaque, Hand Painted	9¼D	NS
D1533	Hunter's Wall Plaque, Hand Painted Centre	14⅝L	174
D1534	Individual Egg Holder		121
D1535	Lily of the Valley Frame		172
D1536	Lily of the Valley Salt		NS
D1537	Lithophane—Farm Girl With Goat	8½H	178
D1538	Lithophane—Girl at Wall	8H	NS
D1539	Lithophane—Child Looking In Mirror	5½D	177
D1540	Lithophane—Lovers At Table	6½H	177
D1541	Lithophane—Child and Old Man With Harp		178
D1542	Lithophane—Ladies With Pigeon	6½H	177
D1543	Lithophane—Ladies With Fan		177
D1544	Lithophane—Madonna, Child and Angel		83
D1545	Lithophane—Priest and Altar Boy Crossing Stream		178
D1546	Lyre Wall Bracket	8½H	176
D1547	Mask Ware Powder Bowl, large size		96
D1548	Mask Ware Powder Bowl, small size		96
D1549	Mask Ware Tobacco Box	6½L	96
D1550	Menu Tablet	2¾H	160
D1551	Napkin Ring—Sphinx		114
D1552	Papal Tiara Cheese Cover		114
D1553	Pottery Scene Celtic Commemorative Plate		110
D1554	Primrose Butter Plate	5D	207
D1555	Prince Charles Dog (Spaniel) on Cushion Paperweight	3H	115, 138
D1556	Ribbon Wall Bracket	10¼H	NS
D1557	Round Wall Plaque, Hand Painted (variety of subjects)	14³⁄₁₆D	20, 37, 174
D1558	Scallop Salt		NS
D1559	Shamrock Ashtray	4⅜D	119, 123
D1560	Shamrock Ashtrough		NS
D1561	Shamrock Barrel Marmalade Jar	3⅝H	123
D1562	Shamrock Covered Butter Tub	4¾D	207
D1563	Shamrock Pin Tray	4¾L	123
D1564	Shamrock Salt Tub No. 2, large size	4½D	207
D1565	Shamrock Salt Tub No. 1, small size		207
D1566	Shell Biscuit Box	11L	NS
D1567	Shell Muffineer Shaker		116, 121
D1568	Single Dolphin and Wink		157
D1569	Slender Scent Bottle		NS
D1570	Terrier Dog (Boxer) on Cushion Paperweight	3H	115, 138
D1571	Thorn Flowered Bowl	7H	147
D1572	Triple Bucket, small size		NS
D1573	Wink Salt		NS
D1574	Worcester Plate		NS
D1575	Woven Flowered Jewel Stand, Pedestal Base	2½H	NS
	CANDLE ITEMS		
D1600	Lady with Tall Hat Candle Extinguisher		169
D1601	Papal Candle Lamp	5¾×12⅞	170
D1602	Raised Hand Candle Extinguisher		169
D1603	Shepherd and Dog Candle Holder	7D	168
D1604	Stag's Head Candelabrum	16⅓×12½	166
	CENTRES AND COMPORTS		
D1609	Echinus Comport Variation		73
D1610	Hippiritus Centre		142
D1611	Pierced Reticulated Covered Comport		29
D1612	Triboy Woven Basket Comport, middle size	8⅞H	76
D1613	Tri Dolphin Comport	5H	142
D1614	Triple Root Centre	10H	NS
D1615	Two Cherubs with Shell Sweet		NS
D1616	Victoria Triple Shell Centre	10H	144
	COVERED BOXES AND JARS		
D1621	Cherub Trinket Box		NS
D1622	Devenish Covered Box	4D	NS
D1623	Egg Shape Covered Box		121
D1624	Hexagon Covered Box		NS
D1625	Hexagon Pill Box		120
D1626	Melvin Candy Jar		NS
D1627	Oval Pill Box		NS
D1628	Round Pill Box		NS
D1629	Thorn Covered Box		NS
	DECORATIVE ITEMS		
D1632	Belleek Easter Egg, 1972		NS
D1633	Brooch, Flowered		119
D1634	Canadian-Irish Stick Pin		164
D1635	Carnation Floral		155
D1636	Celtic Bowl of Flowers	3½H	NS
D1637	Dahlia	5½D	154
D1638	Grand Piano with Flowers	8⅛×4⅝	124
D1639	Harp with Brooch, Flowered		99
D1640	Harp with Applied Shamrocks, large size	8⅝H	NS
D1641	Harp with Applied Shamrocks, small size	6½H	NS
D1642	Pendant, Flowered		NS
D1643	Shillelagh	5L	NS
	FIGURES AND BUSTS		
D1648	Belgian Hawker Carrying Firewood (Female)	6½H	134
D1649	Birds on Branch	5⅞H	84
D1650	Bust of Gladstone	8¾H	133
D1651	Bust of Lesbie, Flowered	9H	131
D1652	Collie (Female)	5¼H	75
D1653	Collie (Male)	5½H	75
D1654	Eagle on Crag with Prey	21½H	137
D1655	Elephant and Riders		NS
D1656	Figure of Lesbie	10H	128
D1657	Greyhound Pair on Cushion		138
D1658	Gypsy Bather	14¾H	128
D1659	Irish Setter	5⅛H	75
D1660	Opera Singer	4H	168
D1661	Spaniel	3¾H	75
D1662	Terrier	3½H	NS
D1663	Terrier, small size	2½H	NS

Degen-hardt No.	Item	Measure-ment in Inches	Page
	FLOWER HOLDERS AND POTS		
D1670	Basket Flower Pot, Flowered	3H	NS
D1671	Basket in Hand		152
D1672	Belleek Flower Pot, tiny		208
D1673	Cardium on Coral, size 5		208
D1674	Double Shell Flower Pot, Flowered		121
D1675	Finner Flower Pot with Twig Handles		NS
D1676	Footed Bowl, Flowered	6¾×9	149
D1677	Forget-Me-Not Flowered Oval Bowl		99
D1678	Four Section Flower Holder	11¹/₁₆D	161
D1679	Irish Pot, size 6		207
D1680	Irish Pot, Shamrocks, size 6		207
D1681	Turkey Flower Holder	7H	NS
	HANDWOVEN BASKETS, PLATES AND TRAYS		
D1682	Bird on Round Covered Basket, large size		105
D1683	Boat Shaped Basket, Plaited and Footed	10¼L	106
D1684	Boat Shaped Basket, large size	13L	104
D1685	Cherry Blossom Plate, Three Strand, Flowered	7¼D	107
D1686	Cosmea Basket, Plaited		101
D1687	Double Heart Basket, Flowered		102
D1688	Erne Basket		109
D1689	Henshall Flat Rod Basket, small size	7½L	NS
D1690	Melvin Basket		NS
D1691	Round Convolvulus Basket, Footed		100
D1692	Round Flat Rod Basket	6¾D	150
D1693	Scalloped Basket, Flat Rod, Two Strand	11½L	104
D1694	Tea Rose Scalloped Basket	8½D	103
D1695	United States Bicentennial Plate, Flowered	10D	84
	LAMPS, ELECTRIC		
D1700	Armstrong		70
D1701	Belgian Hawker, Man		NS
D1702	Belgian Hawker, Woman		NS
D1703	Island Shamrock		NS
D1704	Killarney Biscuit Jar		NS
D1705	Marmalade Jar		NS
D1706	Panel Shamrock		NS
D1707	Pierced Shamrock		NS
D1708	Rathmore Barrel		NS
D1709	Ribbon Barrel		NS
D1710	Scale		NS
D1711	Shamrock Barrel		NS
D1712	Shell		NS
D1713	Summer Briar		NS
D1714	Thorn		NS
	MIRROR FRAMES		
D1720	Lily of the Valley Frame, small size		174
D1721	Queen Victoria Frame, Flowered	30H, 22W	172
D1722	Ribbon Flowered Frame	12¾H	172
D1723	Shell Frame, large size	16H, 13½W	NS

Degen-hardt No.	Item	Measure-ment in Inches	Page
	MUSIC BOXES		
D1728	Devenish Honey Pot	4D	NS
D1729	Enchanted Holly	3¼H	99
D1730	Irish Christmas Cottage	4½H	99
D1731	Shamrock Honey Pot	5H	NS
D1732	Shamrock Trinket	3H	NS
	STATUES AND CROSSES		
D1740	Celtic Cross, large size	12H	127
D1741	Celtic Cross, small size	6¼H	NS
D1742	Cherub Font, middle size	9L	NS
D1743	Cherub Font, small size	7⅞L	NS
D1744	Cross Pendant, Flowered	3H	126
D1745	Statue of St. Patrick	18H	127
	SUGARS AND CREAMS		
D1747	Belleek Pot Suagar	2⅞H	NS
D1748	Belleek Pot Cream	3H	NS
	VASES AND SPILLS		
D1749	Acanthus Vase		153
D1750	Allingham Spill	2½H	NS
D1751	Armstrong Vase	11¾H	70
D1752	Celtic Vase	7¾H	162
D1753	Diamond Vase	7⅝H	162
D1754	Diamond Vase with Handle	9⅝H	158
D1755	Elm Vase	3⅝H	162
D1756	Erin Vase, Flowered	6⅜H	150
D1757	Erne Spill	3¼H	162
D1758	Feather Vase, Flowered, large size	8½H	151
D1759	Feather Vase, Flowered, small size	6H	151
D1760	Fluted Flower Spill	5H	162
D1761	Fluted Scroll Spill	5H	153
D1762	Footed Vase	6⅝H	160
D1763	Foyle Vase	5½H	120
D1764	Frederick and Nelson Vase		NS
D1765	G.A.A. Vase		120
D1766	Gaelic Athletic Association Centennial Vase		43
D1767	Garland Vase		NS
D1768	Greyhound Vase	7H	160
D1769	Iris Vase	6½H	155
D1770	Lily-of-the-Valley Vase	13⅜H	151
D1771	Melvin Vase	5⅞H	162
D1772	Michael Collins and Arthur Griffith Vase		161
D1773	Michael Collins Vase	4⅛H	161
D1774	Owl Spill	8¼H	NS
D1775	Rathmore Vase, Flowered	7⅛H	123
D1776	Rose of Tralee Vase	7H	NS
D1777	Round Tower Vase	8¼H	NS
D1778	Scalloped Shell Vase	7¼H	156
D1779	Scroll Vase	7H	163
D1780	Shamrock Scent Spill	4H	NS
D1781	Sheerin Vase	8¼H	162
D1782	Thistle Top Vase, Flowered	5⅛H	163, 211
D1783	Thorn Vase, large size	7½H	NS
D1784	Thorn Vase, small size	4½H	161
D1785	Toy Panel Vase	3½H	162
D1786	Tree Trunk Vase	6½H	121
D1787	Tree Trunk Vase, Flowered	6½H	NS
D1788	Triple Fish and Water Lily Vase	10H	159
D1789	Twig Urn Vase, Flowered	15H	NS
D1790	Typha Jug Spill, Shamrocks	7H	210
D1791	Tyrone Vase	8⅛H	164
D1792	Ulster Vase		208
D1793	Vase with Bird, Flowered	5H	NS

Degenhardt No.	Item	Measurement in Inches	Page
D1927	Creamer	2½H	NS
D1928	Dinner Plate	10¼D	NS
D1929	Salad Plate	8¼D	NS
D1930	Salt and Pepper Shakers	2¾H	NS
D1931	Serving Plate	10½D	NS
D1932	Sugar Bowl	2½H	NS
D1933	Tea Cup	2½H	NS
D1934	Tea Saucer	6¼D	NS
D1935	Pie Server	11½L	NS

FIVE O'CLOCK TEA WARE

(The commonly referred to name for this pattern is "Five O'Clock." A close look at the handles on the cream, tea cup and teapot reveals a "5", an "O" and a "C". There is some evidence that the pattern was designed by a pottery craftsman named Harris and was called "Harris Tea Ware" at the pottery.)

Degenhardt No.	Item	Measurement in Inches	Page
D1940	Creamer		98
D1941	Sugar		98
D1942	Tea Cup		98
D1943	Teapot		98
D1944	Tea Saucer		98
D1945	Tray		NS
D1946	Set, complete		NS

HOLLY WARE

(The pattern features individual holly leaves and berries painted on a plain background.)

Degenhardt No.	Item	Measurement in Inches	Page
D1950	Ashtray		NS
D1951	Bell	6H	NS
D1952	Napkin Holder		NS
D1953	Candlestick	2⅝H	NS
D1954	Coffee Cup		NS
D1955	Coffee Mug	3⅝H	NS
D1956	Coffee Saucer		NS
D1957	Cream		NS
D1958	Dinner Plate		NS
D1959	Pepper Shaker		NS
D1960	Salt Shaker		NS
D1961	Santa Claus Mug	2¾H	NS
D1962	Side Plate		NS
D1963	Soup Bowl		NS
D1964	Soup Stand		NS
D1965	Sugar		NS
D1966	Tea Cup	2⅜H	NS
D1967	Tea Saucer	6D	NS

KILKENNY COLLECTION

(Designs from the Kilkenny Design Centre)

Degenhardt No.	Item	Measurement in Inches	Page
D1968	Bud Vase	6H	NS
D1969	Creamer	2¾H	113
D1970	Dinner Plate	10D	113
D1971	Oval Candlestick		168
D1972	Round Candlestick	4¾H	160
D1973	Serving Plate	11D	113
D1974	Side Plate	7D	113
D1975	Spill		121
D1976	Sugar	2¼H	113
D1977	Tea Cup	2⅝H	113
D1978	Tea Saucer	6D	113

KILLARNEY COLLECTION

(Painted, embossed pattern features rose, thistle and shamrocks.)

Degenhardt No.	Item	Measurement in Inches	Page
D1980	Bell	4H	122
D1981	Biscuit Jar	6½H	122
D1982	Candlestick	5¼H	122
D1983	Creamer	3½H	122
D1984	Flower Bowl	5H	122
D1985	Sugar	3½H	122
D1986	Spill	7¼H	122
D1987	Vase	8H	122

RING HANDLE IVORY WARE (BELLEEK SHAPE)

(Beginning with the 1928 catalogue this pattern was referred to by the pottery as "Belleek Shape".)

Degenhardt No.	Item	Measurement in Inches	Page
D1990	Covered Sugar, Low Shape, large size		NS
D1991	Milk Jug	6½H	NS
D1992	Plate	8¼D	NS

SET #36

(This exceedingly rare pattern was never given a name by the pottery. It was simply referred to as Set #36.)

Degenhardt No.	Item	Measurement in Inches	Page
D1995	Creamer		97
D1996	Sugar		NS
D1997	Teapot		NS

SHAMROCK WARE

Degenhardt No.	Item	Measurement in Inches	Page
D2000	Beer Stein		118
D2001	Bell		118
D2002	Cake Knife		165
D2003	Candy Jar	5¼H	NS
D2004	Covered Sugar, large size	3H	NS
D2005	Dresser Tray	5W, 10¼L	NS
D2006	Flower Pot, Pierced	4⅝H	114
D2007	Gaelic Coffee Cup	4H	NS
D2008	Gaelic Coffee Saucer	6⅛D	114
D2009	Honey Pot	4½H	114
D2010	Hurricane Lamp	6½H	NS
D2011	Letter Opener		165
D2012	Mustard	2⅝H	NS
D2013	Parlor Lamp	7½H	NS
D2014	Pie Server		165
D2015	Soup Bowl		NS
D2016	Thimble		NS
D2017	TV Set		114
D2018	Two Tier Cake Plate		NS

SPIRAL SHELL COLLECTION

(Diagonal swirls radiate from the base to the top of each piece.)

Degenhardt No.	Item	Measurement in Inches	Page
D2025	Biscuit Jar		117
D2026	Butter Dish		117
D2027	Candlestick		117
D2028	Creamer		117
D2029	Preserve Jar		117
D2030	Sugar		NS
D2031	Trinket Box		NS
D2032	Vase, low		NS
D2033	Vase, tall		NS

INDEX

Page references in *italic* type refer to photographs.